EDUCATION AND COMMUNICATION TECHNOLOGY

Education And Communication Technology

Dr. G.P. Pathak
(M.A., M.Ed., Ph.D.)

Reference Press

4831/24, Ansari Road
Darya Ganj
New Delhi-110 002
Phone: 51563444
Fax: 51563334
E-mail: info@essessreference.com
url: http://www.essessreference.com

First Published 2005

ISBN: 81-88583-97-9

Rs.700/-

Published by:
Reference Press
4831/24, Ansari Road, Darya Ganj,
New Delhi-110 002.
Phone: 51563444
Fax: 51563334
E-mail: info@essessreference.com
url: http://www.essessreference.com

Printed in India at:
Mehra Offset Press, New Delhi

CONTENTS

PREFACE

Modern Education sports a new look, as new technology in education and communication marks its impact on our education system. Concept of education, till now, is centred around books, classrooms, students and teachers. Library and book-stalls are the only sources for reference books and for books out of syllabus. Now somehow, education has come out of this gloom. Sweeping changes in the modern communication system has made the world a shrinking walnut. With the emergence of new avatars in the educational world, the concept of education itself has changed. Now, audio-visual media is playing a pivotal role in our academic life. Video-conferencing is not merely a luxury for the modern students.

At the click of the mouse, one gets information .which, he or she needs. The websites provide the capsuled form of information for a clear understanding. Science and medicine students are equipped with modern gadgets, which help them make their studies easier and enable them to comprehend the complicated matters.

No doubt, several books on education and communication have recently been produced, but in this work, the author has incorporated additional details from several sources. So, understandably, this book would prove to be worth reading and good for reference.

G.P. Pathak

1

INTRODUCTION

History suggests that science and technology, though wedded today, went through a long, indifferent courtship. They grew up independently, almost oblivious of each other's existence. Each made a point of ignoring the other's presence. Upon reaching the age of puberty, the Scientific Revolution in the case of Science and the Industrial Revolution in the case of technology, a mild flirtation started. There were tentative meetings of the hands, shy glances, and a few reluctant embraces.

The marriage, when it came at last, was a marriage of convenience, and the couple, predictably, have not lived happily ever after. Each partner has retained a good deal of independence, though lately, both have been having identity problems. There are constant bickerings about who is contributing most to the marriage. Frequently they are not on speaking terms. They quarrel over mutual responsibilities, the education of their offspring, and as might be expected, the household budget. Science and technology live independently, yet coordinately.

Metaphors apart, science and technology, though independent, are wedded and the advancement of one has resulted in the advancement of the other. The man's curiosity to learn nature and the natural phenomena around him depended upon the development of instrumentation in technology. The older generation of scientists required compasses, clocks, telescopes, barometers', thermometers, microscopes, micrometers, telemetry devices and a host of other instruments to observe and measure the phenomena of nature. Today the scientist is concerned with spectroscope, chromatography, acceleration and detection of particles, nuclear magnetic resonance, electron microscopy, micro wave and acoustic probes and computers.

Both science and technology are very old, and so is instrumentation, but not as a link between the two. Galileo who lived in the 16th and 17th centuries, is still regarded as the first scientist in the modern science. He was the first to emphasize the relations of theory to experiments in science, and the first to describe experiments in a way others could attempt to perform, yet technology can also claim him, since he built one of the first telescope, a microscope, a hydrostatic the balance, a thermoscope, and the like. Certainly he was the first to raise the question why pumps did not raise water on fertile Italian bills for more than about 32 ft. It was his disciple, Torricelli (1608-1647), who invented the barometer, concluded that air has weight and causes water to rise only 32 ft. in the suction pumps. Robert Boyle (1627-1691) ultimately laid the foundations for the law of gases now known as Boyle's law of gases.

Thus, a technological device, the suction pump, led to a scientific investigation and the conclusion that air had weight, which led in turn to the invention of an instrument the barometer, and still more scientific conclusion, Boyle's law. Thus, a technological device led to both a scientific advance and a new technological device. It may be generalised that the association of technology and science is a chain reaction of scientific discoveries and technological inventions.

With the advancing years of the 20th century, technology and science have come closer and closer. In the newest and the most sophisticated fields of research such as nuclear energy, space, systems, design, materials, structures, computer and engineering sciences they are indissoluble bound and the results have been explosive.

The Socratic way of teaching in the west and the guru-chela system in this country were based on a free dialogue between the teacher and the pupil or between the students themselves. In this manner even now the attention of the pupil is engaged, the mind is entertained, and the scholar is animated in the pursuit of knowledge.

A good teaching seems always to elude those who chase to capture and pin it on the dissecting table. This is not surprising. There are many kinds of good teaching for many kinds of teaching situation at many different levels. Attempts to reduce it to a formula are doomed to failure. There always are teachers who break all the rules and yet are profoundly successful. In other words, it is the good teacher, not teaching in the abstract, that counts. A successful teacher is known by the mark he leaves on his students.

When Leuis Agessiz was asked his greatest achievement, he replied that he had taught men to observe, Socrates taught men to question. Each great teacher has his own way. More often than not the two particular attributes found in a Successful teacher are : (i) the ability to awaken and stimulate delight in the use of the mind, and (ii) the ability to do work. Certainly such teachers have engendered in their students a pleasure, a joy, and a raised awareness in intellectual activity.

Marked changes in the teaching material and methods are today seen not only in sciences, social sciences, but also in humanities. The citizen of tomorrow must master the ways of analysis, must search deeply, if he is to cope with the uncertainties and changes of the decades ahead.

The problems of education, what to speak of Science education, in this country are enormous. As per the 1981 census the total literacy in this country is only 36.17 per cent. This includes even those who can only read, but not write. If this enormous number (63.83%) of illiterates of this country are to be made literate the problem is so gigantic that it can not be done by simply opening the primary schools, as there will always remain the dearth of suitable qualified teachers.

The picture which looks so gloomy, does not seem to be so, thanks to the recent introduction of new technologies of mass communication like television, video tapes, computers etc. The problem of illiteracy in this country can be overcome over a short span of time provided the population has a desire to learn and the Govt. has a well to educate its masses. In this process of teaching and learning the technology is only an aid, the role of the teacher still remains the same which it used to be in the days of Socrates or the Indian guru. For teaching of science at all the levels, primary, secondary, college and University, the pupil must be allowed to play with the tools, and that will be the real learning.

2

EDUCATIONAL TECHNOLOGY

The use of Educational Technology has been emphasised in both the National Policy of Education, 1986 and revised NPE, 1992, to improve both the quality and quantity of education for the first time in the history of Indian Education. No earlier document of national significance had pointed out the importance of educational technology so clearly and so strongly as it has been done by the NPE, 1986. Spelling out its deployment, the NPE, 1986 (p. 22) has observed, "Educational Technology will be employed in the spread of useful information, the training and retraining of teachers, to improve the quality, sharpen awareness of art and culture, inculcate abiding values etc., both in the formal and non-formal sections."

According to Eric Asbhy (1967), mankind is now in the midst of the Fourth Revolution in Education - the Age of Electronic Media which comprises radio, television, audio/video recorder, computer, and so on. The NPE '86 has therefore added (p. 22): "In the villages without electricity batteries or solar packs will be utilised to run the programme." It has also suggested that in order to avoid structural dualism, modern educational technology must reach out to the most distant areas and the most deprived sections of beneficiaries simultaneously with the areas of comparative affluence and availability.

The Programme of Action (POA), 1986 (p. 180) has rightly pointed out that several efforts have been made in the past to use technological aids for improving the quality of education. Audio visual units and film libraries were set up at the Centre and in States for promoting the use of educational films and projection aids. Educational Technology Centres and Cells were established at the national and state levels respectively for facilitating the use of various media, particularly radio and television. Although School Broadcast programme has been in vogue for more than four decades, it has not yet been accepted whole-heartedly and in massive scale throughout the country. Educational Television Programme, in spite of its glamour and potentiality, has not yet been popular in the educational institutions.

In many States and Union territories, State Institutes of Educational Technology (SIETs) and at the national level the Central Institute of Educational Technology have been producing, utilising, monitoring and following up the television and radio programmes for improving the quantity and quality of education. Under the project "INSAT for EDUCATION" launched in 1982, the SIETs have been generating educational software for children. The Audio Visual Research Centres (AVRCs) and Educational Media Research Centres (EMRCs) have been producing Educational TV Programmes for college/university students. Some Technical Teacher Training Institutions (TTTIs) have also been developing facilities for production of TV as well as other media programmes.

Video Technology has made a headway in the field of education. The Electronic Trade and Technology Development Corporation (ET & TDC) has formulated a TELETEACH Project to prepare software on videotape. A good number of secondary schools have been selected by the Ministry of Education for equipping them with VCRs and viewing equipment to work as viewing centres.

Computer Education has been popular in the country at various stages of education. The Computer Literacy and Studies in Schools (CLASS) Project has been implemented in hundreds of Schools and with availability of microcomputers there, the students have been familiarised with the application and potentiality of computer as learning medium. Computer education courses are now available in many universities besides Ph.D., M.Tech., and B.Tech Programmes conducted by the IITs and other technological institutions. Diploma level courses are being offered by a few dozens of polytechnics.

Although educational broadcasting has the inherent advantages of greater reach, management, convenience and cost effectiveness, the non-broadcast/non-project media and materials are more oriented to individual learning and more appropriate to the indigenous clientele and developing economy.

These media would also help in enriching the learning process. Large scale use of audio and video programmes in broadcast and non-broadcast modes would generate enormous demand for qualified manpower to work in educational media set-ups. It would be necessary to develop maintenance structure and train "technician entrepreneurs" for taking up such responsibilities.

As enunciated in the POA (1986) "Education requires media support which is related to the curriculum as well as enrichment. Curriculum-based education also requires materials which the teacher can draw upon in the course of this teaching. This could be provided in the form of charts, slides, transparencies, etc. Video technology offers considerable potential for improving the quality of education especially at higher levels."

Similarly computer technology is likely to influence education enormously and can play an important role in enhancing the efficiency of the teaching-learning process, making children more creative and providing them with an individualised learning environment. Computer literacy would be crucial in preparing children to cope with microcomputer explosion which has the same potential for social change as the Industrial Revolution. It is essential to integrate the same progressively with the school curriculum.

Nature and Scope

The modern world is confronting two general problems which are not only affecting the pattern of human life, but also inflicting their full impact on education. These two problems are called "information explosion" and the "population explosion." They are like two horns of dilemma in education-more things to learn and more people to be taught.

The term "information explosion" really means an explosion of knowledge. We all know, new frontiers of knowledge are opening day by day and the horizon of human knowledge and understanding is expanding very fast. In most of the subjects, moreover, knowledge is cumulative, so that every now and then, there is more to be learnt. Especially in arts subjects, new facts and figures take their place along with the old. In sciences although new knowledge or information often supersedes the old, the students and scientists have to learn both. Besides, closer relations among countries of the world resulting from wide international communications make information explosion more acute and complicated.

The second problem is "Population Explosion" which is immensely affecting traditional pattern of education. The problem of population explosion is more serious in the developing countries than the developed ones. For example, in India population has been increasing in geometrical progression. India now has more than 1000 million people.

Michael J. Apter (1968 p. 10) has rightly observed, "The increase in population has of course tended to occur fastest in the developing countries. For this reason the problem it poses for education is the greatest in these countries. Conversely, the information explosion has the greatest immediate effect on the technologically advanced countries. Fortunately, no country has experienced the full effects of both at the same time. Nevertheless, there is a fair degree of overlap between the effects of the two." The developing countries like India, however, are facing serious difficulties both from population as well as information explosion. Because they have to provide education for a larger population year by year and cover more and more technical and scientific ground for making up the deficiency. Since most of the countries are confronted more or less with the problem of more persons to be taught and more information to be learnt, this general problem is called "Education Explosion."

Importance in Education

The problem of "Education Explosion" has both positive and negative aspects. On the positive side the problem has unprecedented record to its credit. The bright features are -

1. Most countries of the world have spent more on education during the last fifty five years than we have in recorded history.
2. More enrolment of pupils than any time in the past has been made during the last three decades. It has more than doubled in most countries since 1950.
3. The educational systems of the world have produced 90% of all the writers, artists, scientists and technologists who have even lived during this time.
4. The products of our educational systems are so creative that they are making the quantum of knowledge double in scientific and technological fields.
5. The youths educated by the modern educational system during the last five decades have published more books and magazines both regards the number of copies as well as that of titles.

Seth Spaulding (1970 p. 9) Director of UNESCO's Department of School and H. E. has thus aptly remarked, "The record is, then impressive. We are, in essence, providing more education than ever before in history and the products of our systems are apparently more creative than all our forefathers put together."

The other side of the coin is however as follows:

1. Although in most of the countries educational expenditure has been enormous, it is estimated that as many as one third of the children of school-going age have not yet seen the inside of a school. If at all they enter the schools, less

than one third of them are able to complete lower elementary education. As many as 50% of the pupils' are only repeaters. The wastage and stagnation in many educational systems thus make cost of schooling spectacular and increase the number of illiterates and semiliterates.

2. In spite of the phenomenal quantitative expansion of education the world has still an army of illiterate adults.
3. Almost all governments of the world now recognise education more as an investment rather than as a social expenditure. Accordingly the so-called "investment" has been expanded enormously. But many countries are still finding it difficult to reach the quantitative targets like physical facilities and material resources suggested by various international conferences on education.
4. Grave doubts are expressed as to the relevance and effectiveness of education in the modern society not only in India, but also in most of the developed and developing countries of the world. Education cannot serve its purpose unless it is relevant to contemporary and future problems of the community and of the world. For example, education should deal with the pollution problems, population problems, agricultural problems, technological problems and war and peace. If succeeding generations are not able to tackle these problems successfully, education will be deemed to be a failure.
5. Although education has promoted the growth and development of science and technology, education itself has not yet been able to utilise their traits for being more effective and relevant. Seth Spaulding has rightly said, "The way we manage and administer our educational enterprises would probably bankrupt any other kind of business. Although education has shared in the creation of technological age, education itself has not learnt how to use the fruits of technology to improve the efficiency and the quality of its own institutions. In attempts to 'catch up' quantitatively education has usually attempted to multiply what has gone in a pre-technology system of schooling."

In essence, Mr. Spaulding (1970 p. 10) has said that we have provided more and more money to more and more of that we may be doing poorly. We hope that we could do it better. Educationists of international distinction have suggested that it will be possible only by developing suitable curriculum and applying educational technologies to make the curriculum more effective and the school more efficient.

Wider Perception

Educational technology, in its global sense, includes the entire process of the setting of goals, the continuous reforms of curriculum, the tryout of new methods and materials, the evaluation of the system as an integrated whole and resetting of goals on the basis of the findings of evaluation and innovations. But it is often identified as pointed out by Spaulding, with various devices and processes which make possible the recording, storage, manipulation, retrieval, transmission and display of data, information and printed and photographed materials with an efficiency and speed unheard of, even 20 years ago. If these capabilities are considered as part of a broad curriculum for research and development design, they have tremendous potential in education.

Technological materials and methods useful in the teaching-learning process range from chalkboards to television sets. Technology of education involves books and blackboards, paper and pencils, models and maps, charts and globes, tapes and slides, radios and televisions, projectors and computers. It comprises both "hardware" and "software" and both audio and visual materials. It also includes decisions about the educational objectives to be achieved and decisions about the size of the learning group, the learning sequence, teaching methods and selection of media.

In its wider perspective, therefore, educational technology deals with the systematic application of the resources of scientific knowledge to the process that each individual has to pass through in order to acquire and use knowledge. "Educational Technology" writes Geoffrey Hubbard (1974), Director of the National Council for Educational Technology, England "is the complement of curriculum reform concerned with the Method where curriculum reform is concerned with the content... Given an acceptance of the concept of educational technology as the process of improving learning method, we are faced with the problems of encouraging innovation in an educational system whose greatest strength is in decentralisation and autonomy. Certainly nothing will be achieved by elaborating authoritarian solutions. What is needed is more discussion of the contribution the different elements of the system can make to the problems facing education. Widespread dissemination of experience (both successful and unsuccessful) of innovations and supporting services, including training, consultancy and information activities are necessary to assist the teacher in the selection and introduction of the new methods appropriate to his own particular situation."

According to GOM Leith "Educational Technology is the application of scientific knowledge about learning and the conditions of learning to improve the effectiveness and efficiency of teaching and training. In the absence of scientifically established principles, educational technology implements techniques of empirical testing to improve learning situations." Hence educational technology seeks to apply scientific knowledge about learning and the conditions of learning for improving its effectiveness.

The Differentiation

We find that a large number of new methods and media constitute educational technology. But there is no proper coordination and articulation in their use. That is why, no satisfactory results are achieved by such a wide range of materials due to lack of a systematic planning and organisation. Henri Dieuzeide (1970), Director of UNESCO's Division of Methods, Materials and Techniques has aptly remarked, "The new techniques do in fact offer a vast range of possibilities, but their field of application often seems to be a wasteland scattered with spare parts which no one knows how to put together to form an efficient system. Here it is useful to discuss the difference between technology in education and technology of education. We have to move from one to the other, i.e. from the former to the latter. Technology in education is concerned with equipment, preparation of adhoc messages and integration with traditional teacher-centered activities. But as discussed earlier, technology of education deals with the active use of mass media and computer science for the individual pupils learning process under the teacher's supervision. Hence the latter one i.e. educational technology is more scientific, more psychological and more pedagogical than the former one i.e. technology in education."

With the advance of science and technology there are new learning aids which have revolutionized the learning process, in particular and education as a whole. In modern society with its emphasis on mass education and successful citizenship training, the requirement is for efficient learning. Education has now become an assembly-line like mass production factories. A nation can prosper if its education can be made effective. Education can be made efficient, if it uses modern technology. Technology in education will be useful, if it is properly planned and organised on psychological and pedagogical principles. Henri Dieuzeide has rightly observed, "The transition from technology in education to the technology of education involves a thorough appraisal of the existing educational system, of its objectives and of the means used to attain them, before any decision is reached to employ these new techniques for specific teaching purposes. The teacher-turned technologist can then gradually assume the functions of an 'educational engineer' whose job is to increase the output of the entire scholastic machine."

Although educational technology can be interpreted in a rather narrow sense as the use of sophisticated hardware in teaching or in a broad sense as the use of any new educational technique, in fact the concept means more than the sum total of all the media and methods, materials and techniques used for better teaching and learning. It involves or should involve greater psychological and pedagogical preparedness, a scientific attitude and a coordinated approach to the educational process as a whole. It should reflect one's professional interest and zeal for making experiments and innovations for development and success of education.

Educational Technology implies the use of all educational resources—men and materials, methods and techniques, means and media in an integrated and systematic manner for optimizing learning. According to the modern educationists, learning not teaching is the crucial task of the entire educational process and emphasis of teachers is regarded as a system which facilitates learning and makes learning effective as well as efficient. Efficient in the sense that the learning with the use of Educational Technology becomes easy and interesting, durable and comprehensive. Efficient in the sense that it is economical and financially viable. In fact, effective communication of educational messages in an economic way is the main objective of educational technology.

Hardware and Software Techniques

Educational Technology is not a new-comer, although the concept as such is comparatively new in the field of education. The educational process was teacher-centered, the method of rote-learning was important, a few textbooks were the main resource and chalkboard was the only aid. Subsequently, a number of audiovisual materials were introduced and used in the teaching-learning process. It was usually thought that teaching machines, film-projectors, slide-projectors, language laboratories, tape-recorders, cassettes, radio, television, video-tape recorders, computers, and so on, are educational technology. In brief, all the audio-visual equipments are regarded as the Educational Technology. But this is only one aspect of educational technology and is called hardware component. Another aspect is new-methods of teaching, tested principles and practices, innovation, e.g., programmed learning, micro-teaching, team-teaching etc., are called software component of educational technology. Both software and hardware constitute the concept of educational technology and both of them go hand in hand to maximise the effects of teaching-learning process. Thus, increased efficiency of the process is the keynote of the Educational Technology.

Important Factors

(i) increasing influence of science and scientific knowledge and skills of education.

(ii) appearance of a number of audio-visual aids which needed to be put together in order to avoid confusion and wastage of resources i.e. multimedia approach to education.

(iii) development of programmed learning approach.

(iv) explosion of numbers and knowledge, facts and figures.

(v) teaching revolution and recent development in pedagogy.

(vi) emergence of a systems theory.

(vii) expansion of educational broadcasting and computers.

3

PROCESS OF COMMUNICATION

In this age of revolution of information technology there has been explosion of knowledge in almost all fields, but man is still discovering, classifying and recording new information at a phenomenal rate starting from the minutest particle of the atom to the farthest body of the universe. Application of this new knowledge in various disciplines has minimised the problems of time and space and facilitated the discovery of still newer knowledge in an endless cycle. Therefore it has been felt imperative on the part of teachers, to keep themselves abreast with the latest developments in their subjects and develop skills in applying criteria to assess the accuracy and validity. The development of new knowledge has resulted in the constant expansion of the school curriculum. As the curriculum expands, not only teachers fail to do justice to teach, but students too get very few opportunities and too little time to learn all objects in depth.

On the other hand, student population is amazingly increasing year by year due to population growth and democratisation of education. Students come from varying experience, backgrounds and differing facilities. Their levels of motivation and aspiration are quite different from one group to another. Even in the developing countries like India a large percentage of students are first generation learners who are deficient in background as well as motivation. Such heterogeneity and diversity among the pupils pose great problems in teaching as well as learning. In view of such problems and developments, special attempts are to be made for two types of instructional media, methods and materials: (i) those which are likely to prove effective for use with groups consisting of individuals of widely varying backgrounds and abilities and (ii) those which can be used advantageously for individualised instruction with only a minimum of teacher assistance.

Fortunately, educational technology has come to our rescue with wide a range of hardware as well as software for tackling these problems. It is the development, application and evaluation of systems, techniques and aids in the field of human learning. The main objective of its use is to optimise learning processes and experience. Technology of education is intended to make learning effective as well as efficient. It facilitates learning through the systematic identification, development, organisation and utilization of a full range of learning resources, and through management of these processes. In brief, students are to be enabled to "learn more in less time" meaningfully and to remember longer what they learn without "watering down" or sacrificing quality.

Meaning and Various Process

According to Wilbur Schramm (1954, p. I) the world famous expert in mass media and communication, there are at least four elements of communication (1) the source (2) the message (3) the channel and (4) the destination. This applies to both human and mechanical communication. But education is mainly concerned with personal or human communication. In this context either an organisation or a person can transmit a message which may be received by an individual or many. The message may be conveyed by verbal expressions, gestures, spoken or written symbols or by hand drawn or photographed pictures. The source is also called an encoder, the message a signal and destination a decoder. These terms indicate the need for common understanding of language and word-meanings based on similar experience background for making communication a success.

Mere presentation of a message or a lesson by the teacher may be a communication, but cannot be effective unless it leads to true learning. For example, a teacher teaches a new word. The child can repeat the spelling of the word correctly, but he should be able to use the word rightly on subsequent occasions. True learning has not taken place unless the teaching as an act of communication has succeeded in making a permanent and meaningful addition to the student's own communication skills. Brown (1964, p. 9) and others have therefore observed that classroom communication involves far more than the unilateral presentation by the teacher of new words or new facts or new ideas; it requires intercommunication between students and teachers, a mutual sharing of experiences and a continual feedback process.

Theories of Communication

Learning means modification of behaviour. Change in response or behaviour is caused partly or wholly by experience. Munn (1954) has rightly defined learning as "the process of being modified, more or less permanently, by what happens in the world around us, by what we do, or by what we observe." Geoch instead of giving a rigid definition of the learning process has made a general statement as following, "Learning, as we measure, is a change in performance which occurs under the conditions of practice." Thus learning depends on the following:

i. Experience of the learner.
ii. Capacity and motivation of the learner.
iii. Methods in which the learning materials are presented to the learner.
iv. Meaningful or difficulty of learning task; and
v. Interaction between the above variables.

Sunitee Dutt (1960, pp11-12) has enunciated the characteristics of learning as follows:

1. Learning is purposive or goal-oriented. Human beings always learn to achieve something. Purposeless learning may not be effective. But when the goal is fixed and clear, the learning becomes more meaningful and effective.

2. Learning is an active process. There is no learning without self-activity. That is why, it is said, "whether or not you learn and what you learn depends upon what you yourself do, for learning an activity."
3. Learning is individual. Each learner has his own needs and interests, abilities and attitudes, hopes and aspirations. Some may learn quickly and some slowly. Thus the pace and depth of learning depends on that individual.
4. Learning is socially conditioned. It is not only individual but also social. It occurs in relation to social environment of the learner and a teacher has to take this into account.
5. Learning is the response of the whole individual to the total situation. It is unitary as man learns as a whole being. So for effective teaching and learning, the physical, mental, social and emotional aspects of his whole being are to be taken note of and setting up the environment is very important.
6. Learning is creative. It is not just an addition to the previous knowledge and experience of the learner. It is a creative synthesis of all the new and old knowledge and experience. True human learning aims at creative and critical thinking.
7. Learning is transferable. It is transferred to new tasks and the learner establishes relationship of the previous learning experiences with the new ones. Of course it is possible when there is identity of context, procedures and ideals and such transfer is necessary for economy as well as efficiency of learning.

Learning Through Communication

There are different principles of learning like readiness, exercise, effect and insight which are useful for success of communication. Again there are various approaches to learning. The association theories of learning lay stress on the responses of the learner and bonds with stimuli and the behavioural changes of the learner. The field theories emphasize the learner's perception of the whole field of events. Skinner, Thorndike, Guthrie and Hall are the proponents of association theories. Lewin, Tolman and the gestalt psychologists are the advocates of the field theories. The association theories put emphasis on the stimulus - response, environment and previous experiences and part elements in learning. On the contrary, field theories emphasise on perception and cognition of the learner, the whole rather than the parts and the relationship between parts.

Again, learning processes are classified into three: (i) inactive or learning by doing (ii) iconic learning by organisation of perception and (iii) symbolic, learning through symbols and language representations.

All these learning theories, principles and processes are of vital importance for successful communication which is equivalent to active learning. Participation, interaction, cooperation and different skills promote such lively learning experiences. Various media, materials and methods capitalise such principles and approaches for providing better learning experiences. That is why, educational technology consisting of all means, media and materials based on the psychological principles and precepts helps promoting learning as well as teaching.

The Report of the Meeting of Chief Technical Advisers, National Directors and UNESCO specialists in Methods and Techniques, Paris, December, 1979 has said that, Educational Technology is a communication process resulting from the adaptation of the scientific method to the behavioural science of teaching/learning. It is a communication process which may or may not require the use of extending media (i.e., radio, television, film and other audio-visual media). The process contains essentially the following components.

1. Specification of goals and behavioural objectives.
2. Analysis of the characteristics of the learners.
3. Selection and organisation of the content or subject matter to be learned.
4. Presentation of the content.
5. Evaluation of the results.
6. Feedback. Feedback must be continuously interacting among all of the preceding five components. It is not just a final component, but it provides essential linkages among all the components.

All these components are also essential elements in learning. Unless all these points are taken into consideration, learning cannot be made effective. These are the basic needs for organisation of suitable media and materials in order to optimise learning outcomes. Modern communication methods, visual arts, classroom organisation and teaching techniques are to be made use of and geared to achieve the instructional objectives. Communication processes supported by technology of education intend to bring about effective and efficient learning.

Pedagogy, the science of teachers' behaviour, has now given place to mathetics, the science of learners' behaviour, that is there has been a shift in focus from the teacher to the pupil and learners' behaviour has been given more emphasis than teachers' behaviour. In other words, the learning process is replacing the teaching process. Learning to learn is essential and learning is more important than teaching.

Learning is also a continuous process. It is lifelong. It is apt to be equivalent with education. Through education students learn how to learn, learn how to keep on learning, learn how to be creative and innovative, and learn how to contribute meaningfully and significantly to solving the new problems that are encountered in day to day world.

If learning is so important, what is the role of a teacher? Faure and others (1982 pp 77-78) have rightly replied, "the teachers' duty is less and less to inculcate knowledge and more and more to encourage thinking; his formal functions apart, he will have to become more and more an adviser; a partner to talk to, someone who helps seek out conflicting arguments rather than reading out readymade truths. He will have to devote more time and energy to productive and creative activities such as interaction, discussion, stimulation, understanding and encouragement."

The teacher is no longer the monopolistic purveyor of information and authoritative transmitter of knowledge. He is to inspire, motivate, guide and stimulate. His role is not merely to communicate the new knowledge, understanding and skills but to identify the pupils needs and provide facilities for their all-around development.

Different Principles

Communication and its advancement is vital to modern civilization. It has affected the entire world immensely as well as wonderfully. The whole world has been reduced to a close neighbourhood. The distance of time and space has been almost removed and all barriers of castes, communities, creeds and colours have given place to mutual fellow-feeling, interrelationships and cooperative ventures. Robert M-Hutchines, a distinguished educationist has named it "a communication revolution." In fact, today it has exerted inevitable influence on millions and billions of people all over the globe through various means and media. It is informing, entertaining and inspiring individuals in many ways.

The term "Communication" has been derived from the Latin word "Communis" meaning "Common." It implies common experiences, mutual sharing or give and take. It gives different meanings to different people.

Communication is defined as the sharing of ideas and feelings in a mood of mutuality. It involves interaction which encourages give and take. This provides feedback to individuals involved in the exchange of ideas. Effective communication is, therefore, a two-way process.

Communication assumes a democratic philosophy of life which implies the dignity and respect of all persons who enter into communication. It also assumes freedom to learn and criticize. John Dewey, an exponent of democracy has emphasized shared experience as a key element in communication and pointed out, "communication is a process of sharing experience till it becomes a common possession. It modifies the disposition of both the parties who partake of it."

Wilbur Schramm, an outstanding communication expert has said that it "is concerned with all the ways in which information and ideas are exchanged and shared. Thus we are talking about both mass and interpersonal communication. We are talking about the spoken word, signal, gesture, picture, visual display, print, broadcast, film-all the signs and symbols by which humans try to convey meaning and value to another."

The Constituents

There are mainly four components of communication. They are (i) source or sender which is technically called "encoder", (ii) message or signal, (iii) channel or medium, and (iv) destination or receiver which is technically known as "decoder."

In the communication process, the source or the sender has the correct information and transmits the same as accurately, clearly and speedily as possible. The content of transmission is called the message. It should be conveyed through the medium of words both written and verbal, gestures, pictures, and so on. Thus the medium or channel may be either audio or visual or both. Every medium has its peculiar influence on the message to a great extent. That is why, it becomes, in a sense, an integral part of the message and it is aptly called "medium is the message." The sender encodes the ideas or information as the message and channelises the same upto the receiver through medium or media. The receiver decodes or understands the message or interprets the information according to his background.

Since communication involves at least two or more persons, interaction is a "must" in order to make it effective. This ensures the mutual sharing or give and take of ideas and experiences. Such communication must also have a desired reaction called "feedback". Thus in any effective communication, in addition to the original four components, two more (i) interaction and (ii) feedback are also essential. Thus the process of communication can be represented by the following diagram:

But interaction is so much inter-mingled with feedback that many communication experts like Harold D. Lasswell take both as one-feedback. The five essential elements of communication are: "who, says what, in which channel, to whom, with what effect?"

Different Modes

There are mainly three modes of communication. They are (i) Speaking ⟷ Listening, (ii) Visualising ⟷ Observing (iii) Writing ⟷ Reading. They may briefly be discussed as follows:

(i) Speaking ⟷ Listening

In this type of communication one speaks and another listens. This is mainly face-to-face as in the case of conversation or listening to a speech. In some cases, there may be gap or distance in between the sender and the receiver or the source and the destination like in radio broadcasting. But both the sender and the receiver of messages share the feelings and may interact with each other if they are in eye to eye contact.

(ii) Visualising ⟷ Observing

In this type of communication one visualises and another observes. There is usually a physical separation between the producer of the message and the audience to whom the message is conveyed as in the case of a television programme or a film. Dramatisation may also be included under this category in which facial expression and gestures produce an effective communication.

(iii) Writing ⟷ Reading

In this model of communication, the sender and the receiver are physically separated all the time, but both are able to share the experiences and feelings. An example of this model is the writing of a book by an author and reading of the same by a reader or a group of readers who can enjoy and appreciate the feelings and ideas of the writer properly.

The arrows moving both ways indicate that in all three kinds of communication, interaction and feedback are essential features in effective communication.

The basic communication theory indicates that there must be four elements - source, message, channel and destination, in the communication process. Any communicator sends message through a channel to the audience. In the technical jargon, the communicator is known as the encoder, the message whether words, pictures or signs is called symbol, the channel may be one of the media or means and the audience is called decoder. The diagram of this basic theory is as simple as this:

In this process, an adept communicator knows what he wants to communicate as message, understands the characteristics of the channel and the social as well as psychological background of individuals constituting the audience.

Then it was found that feedback is essential for making communication effective. The communicator should know the reaction or response of the audience, so that it will be possible on his part to modify his message as well as the channel. There must be interaction between both the communicator and the audience. Thus the second model may be represented like this:

Everybody has his own background physical, social, psychological and sociological. He sends or understands a message from his own background. The physical and emotional conditions like health, mood, attitude and ego involvement influence his understanding or reception of the message. The audience provide their reaction to the message and the communicator modifies or revises his message and media according to such feedback effects. This classic model is again modified by some communication specialists like Wilbur Schramm who advocated a circular diagram to represent the communication process. According to them both the parties - communicator as well as audience - should play the ideal roles as senders and receivers. This diagram is as follows:

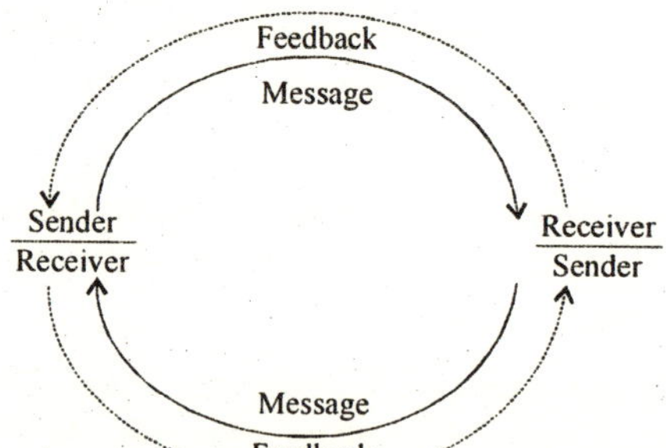

This is a kind of communication that occurs normally in conversation between two persons. But in order to ensure effectiveness in communication, it is felt imperative that there must be interaction and feedback continuously and mutual sharing or give and take of experiences and ideas.

Another theory or model of communication is known as SMCR developed by David K. Berlo. This model emphasizes the psychological nature of communication and provides an analysis of messages and of sensory channels of communication. In this model, source is considered along with communication skills, attitudes, knowledge and socio-cultural context; message includes content, treatment and code; channel consists of eyes, ears, taste, nose and touch and receiver comprises communication skills, attitudes, knowledge and socio-cultural context. The model is represented in the following diagram

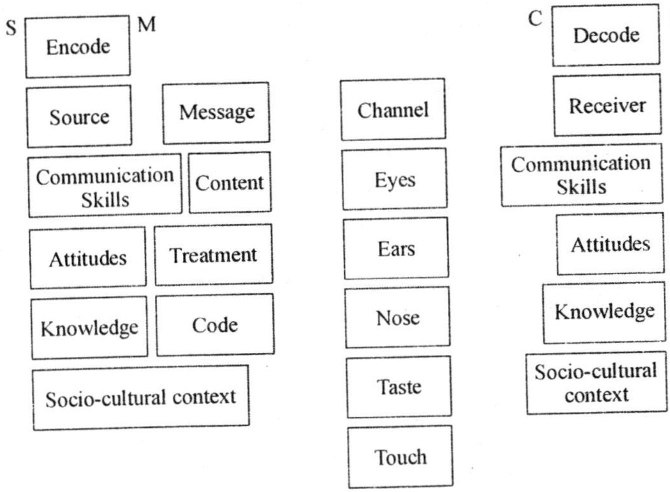

SMCR Model of Communication by David Berlo

Berlo has rightly made it clear that encoding or decoding a message successfully will depend heavily on the communication skills. But the sender's as well as the receiver's attitude is of immense significance. For example, if the attitude of the recipient is favourable towards the source, reception of the message will be different, if it is otherwise. Similarly, knowledge and socio-cultural background of the source as well as of the receiver are equally significant for successful transmission and reception of the message. It is a fact that the message actually does not convey the meaning.

The meaning is grasped according to the psychological, emotional and sociological background of the receiver. Berlo has aptly said, "Communication does not consist of the transmission of meaning. Meanings are not transmittable, not transferable, only messages are transmittable, and meanings are not in the message, they are in message - users."

Significant Features

It is said that beauty lies in the eyes of receiver. Similarly, meaning lies with the listener. Edgar Dale has corroborated Berlo's statement very strongly and clearly, when he observed that you can present stimuli to an individual, but his needs and background determine whether it will be accurately interpreted, and create the intended meanings. Furthermore, messages are also distorted by the receiver. They see what they want to see, hear what they want to hear, and distort messages unintentionally. Even there is selective perception; for example, heavy cigarette smokers do not quit smoking when they read about the harmful effects noted in research, rather they quit reading about cancer studies.

Even today the experience of Galileo about refusal of persons to see the truth holds good to a very great extent. Galileo wrote to his friend Kepler, "Here at Padua is the principal professor of philosophy, whom I have repeatedly and urgently requested to look at the moon and planets through my glass, which he perniciously refused to do... what glorious folly!". In this context what can the communicator do? He may take the horse to the water, how can he make it drink? If the meaning lies with the receiver, neither with the message nor with the channel, what can the sender do to make the communication effective? The next chapter looks to answer these questions.

Social Change Tools

Change in the human society is continuous, perennial and pervading. Change takes place always, everywhere and in all aspects of the society. It may, therefore, be said that the only 'changeless' element in the society is the 'change' itself. That is why *Democritus*, the Greek philosopher has said that you cannot live in the same society a second time.

It is only through change that progress in the society is brought about. More are the changes, greater is the progress. Human civilisation has reached the present stage only due to social changes. The primitive society was comparatively less prone to change than the modern one and the lethargic, dull and backward people are more averse to changes than the energetic, ebullient and advanced persons. Thus the social change is the key to social progress.

Types of Social Change

Social changes are mainly of two kinds. One is structural and the other is functional. When the entire structure of the society is changed by means of a political movement or national struggle, it is a structural social change and when a change take place in man's behaviour, ways of living, dress and food habits through education and culture, it is functional. The American War of Independence, the French Revolution, the Russian Revolution and the Struggle of Indian Independence come under the first category and change over from wearing the untailored dhoti to putting on a pair of suit, from using the bullock-drawn plough to a power driven tractor, from squatting on a mat for eating to dining at a table are the examples of the latter. Both structural and functional changes have almost the same degree of difference as between the major and minor operations. Thus in the struggle parlance 'operation' and in the social science "social change" have both the broad and narrow connotations and have immense significance for physiological and sociological life.

Social Change Dynamism

According to Ottaway (1962) social change is the result of interaction of both techniques and values. It is of little use to desire social change either in terms of technical progress or in terms of a change in values when one is considered independently of the other. The state of society depends on both and they are inseparable. It is also not easy to say which influence is dominant or takes the lead in any particular social change.

It is said by some social scientists that new inventions and discoveries are a primary cause of social change. But any invention or discovery alone is not adequate to explain the social change. Its use depends on the prevailing set of values in the society. The aims and objectives, life-styles and philosophy of a community determine how its techniques will be used. The same technical invention can be used differently in different societies or its use may be delayed if the existing conditions of the society are not favourable or it may be accelerated if the society is amply prepared for the same.

On the other hand, some sociologists believe that the value-systems, ideas and aspirations play a dominant part in changing the society. We must, of course, recognize the force of technology, which brings about changes in our habits of work, thought and belief. Thus we have to deal with the problems of social change by considering a number of variables, each influencing the other.

Maciver and Page (1950) in their important work "Society" have distinguished between the technological factors and the cultural factors in bringing about social change. These two factors may be compared with techniques and values given by Ottaway. All these three authors also equally believe in interaction between the two sets of factors and reject all theories which place the technical and cultural factors in opposition to each other and stress the dominance of the one or the other in determining social change.

Ogburn (1947) has also used the terms material culture and non-material culture and described the "cultural lag". When the former comes first, it is more rapid and more effective in determining the social change. That is, non-material factors likes values lag behind the material factors or conditions like techniques. Marx and Engels had earlier put forth their extreme views of economic or material determinism in the change. Recently, Thorstein Veblin has developed a thesis that the kind of work and leisure which men do determine the social structure. Here he has stressed the importance of adjustment to changing techniques.

It may thus be concluded that both material and non-material aspects of culture are simultaneously involved in any social change and that neither is necessarily dominant. The relative significance of these factors will be different on different occasions. The cultural lag or social leeway however often comes into being when a man's values cannot keep pace with his technical development and a cycle of interaction always revolves involving both techniques and values simultaneously, but not equally.

Social Change Communication

Communication is the powerful means of bringing about social change. Mac Luhan has developed a thesis of technological determinism which says that changes in the technology of communication brings about social changes. The revolution in the media of communication has helped accelerate the pace of social change during these few decades. Radio, television, newspapers and other mass-media have not only made this world "shrunk" but also have revolutionised the values, attitudes, interests and social milieus.

An important task of communication is to promote development and without its support no project can be made successful. Balcomb (1975) has aptly mentioned that many ambitions projects have failed because of poor all round communications. From his own experience he has clearly pointed out that the UNICEF and other agencies had supplied a considerable amount of audio-visual equipment to various projects but much of this equipment was being poorly used. The hardware was there, but the software had very often been left to take care of itself.

That is, proper dovetailing and adequate coordination as well as integration of the technical equipments used for communication purposes and the messages or information that are to be transmitted through these mechanisms are essential for effective communication. Thus for implementing projects in every field whether health or agriculture or education, the building of such overall communication systems is technically called the "Project Support Communication."

It may be mentioned in this connection that at least four elements are required for communication: (I) a source (II) message (III) channel and (IV) destination, (Schramm, 1954). These involve both human and mechanical segments of communication. There must be person (s) to initiate at one end and receive at the other end and a message to be conveyed by expressions, gestures, spoken or written symbols or by drama or photographed pictures. This process emphasizes the need for common understanding of language and word meaning based on similarity of experience background for effective communication.

The source must have the correct message to be transmitted clearly to the receiver. It is also to be ensured that the receiver is understanding the message accurately and producing a desired response. Thus the communication must be a two way process resulting in intercommunication and based on mutual sharing of experiences and a continual feedback.

Communication Effective Steps

With a view to making communication effective, motivation of the persons concerned is to be generated. The people should think for themselves and on their own initiative. They must do whatever they think right and desirable for them, not as they are told to do. They are to function as project participants, not merely as project's beneficiaries.

Without the needs being felt by the beneficiaries themselves the project howsoever need based and useful, cannot be implemented successfully. A small example may be cited here. In a tribal village women had to go to distant hilltops to fetch drinking water. Under the Community Development Project in that village a well was sunk and sweet water was also available. But alas! the tribal women were so much used to bringing water from a high altitude and not oriented to draw water from a well nearby that the well turned to be a big dustbin!

Another interesting incident of this nature has been narrated by Matheson (1975). Many years back a big project was started in the vicinity of Rome to clear the Pontine Marshes for eliminating mosquitoes and the diseases from the city and at the same time to create more arable land for cultivation of vegetables and fruits. But fishermen living in the swampy places and earning their livelihood from fishing grew irate at the prospect of swamps being drained. As a matter of fact they broke the walls of the water tanks that had been created to lead off the water and soon the ambitious drainage project was completely wrecked.

These phenomena clearly indicate the communication gap as the tribals and fishermen were not explained about these projects which were meant for a better and happier life. Matheson has therefore remarked that unfortunately although the tools of technology are available today to help improve the lives of people throughout the developing world, too many projects are failing to achieve their goals because communication experts and development planners often do not communicate effectively with each other or with the people they are trying to help. Unless the people themselves are made ready for the changes and feel the needs, no project can be a success.

We may use various kinds of mass media and audio-visual aids but our message must be clear at first and communicated as effectively as possible. In order to facilitate this, audience have to be motivated through various means, most important of which is felt to be interpersonal communication. Matheson has again hammered this point when he says that finding the right message for the right medium for a specific audience is a constant challenge to communication experts and development planners and workers. Much has been claimed for the power of the mass media and it has certainly achieved wonders in bringing people instant information and in shaping life-styles and beliefs. But when it comes to rural societies especially where literacy levels are low and traditions deep-rooted, the effectiveness of mass media in bringing about change is very limited. Experience has shown that probably the single most effective means of communication is the interpersonal one - dialogue between two or more people.

Every medium of communication has its own limitations. So it has to be selected according to the socio-cultural conditions of the clientele and be used in appropriate time and place with much caution. Nevertheless communication elements should be built into a project in the initial planning stage. They must be integrated with the whole system and not just tagged on as an after thought. Moreover adequate awareness of the target population should be generated, their needs felt by themselves, their motivations created and attitude changed so that communication is made effective to achieve the desired kind of social change.

4

SIGNIFICANCE OF INFORMATION

Information is one of those misunderstood concepts. Yet it is at the same time one of the most used. We go to the bus station to seek information from timetables. We obtain information from government offices such as the DSS and the DVLC. Banks, supermarkets, leisure centres, libraries and even the police ply us with more. Newspapers, television and the radio present us with their own ideas of what information should be. In many instances, however, we may not agree with their conclusions. McLeod termed its subjectivity as being one person's junk and another's treasure.

We all understand and deal with this accordingly when extracting news from the media, for example. Yet many of our Organisations consider information to be something more.

They see it as a vital resource, to be managed like any other valuable resource. How it is used and disseminated through the available technology can determine how efficient, and indeed effective, an Organisation is. Peter Drucker sees information acquired in a systematic and purposeful way as enhancing an Organisation's productivity.

Information is important, we cannot operate without it. But more than this, we are discovering that our ability to process it by increasingly sophisticated technological means is fundamentally changing the way that employees perceive their Organisational environment. The consequences of this could be either to break down established functional controls or indeed to enhance them by becoming super-efficient. Much will depend upon the characteristics of the Organisation before implementation.

As firms become increasingly 'information dependent' we need to identify the perceptual relationship between ourselves and the information we use. How, for instance, can we possibly design an adequate information system if we do not understand the nature of information? The answer to this lies, in part, with the conventional wisdom of the day. Managers, like everybody else, develop their views through exposure to established ideas. Thus, the way in which they understand information will influence the way in which they treat it. Such conventional wisdom is coloured by the technicians, on the one hand, and the user's own experience on the other.

Anecdotal prescriptions abound as guidelines to the way presented for all who care to listen. These arise from a blanket of professional and academic thinking which surrounds the business environment and provides remedies for action. We could categorize all these ideas into two bodies of thought, two paradigms. The first could be termed the resource-driven paradigm. This is because its central theme in understanding information is the continuity and consistency of the information itself. It is very much in vogue at present.

The second body of thought is the perception-driven paradigm. Information is seen as an abstract concept, the product of individual perception. It is a temporary phenomenon and as such belongs only to the receiver. The difference is not merely one of academic debate. Managements adopting one or the other can affect the design of their Organisations. If information is considered to be a resource then resulting systems are usually more centrally controlled, the assumption being that all information is corporate property. Whereas information considered to be personally owned is seen as being outside the formal structure.

Within the framework of this paradigm the view of information is coloured by its use as a resource. Like any other resource it can be tapped at any time with the certainty of achieving a predictable value from it. Information is regarded as unchanging, and therefore can be easily accommodated into a firm's formal procedure. There are a range of propositions available which seeks to explain information. Each proposition has a consequence for Organisational design. Listed below are those major themes and what their implications might be on business.

Herbert A. Simon took the view that information, along with energy, constitute the two basic currencies of our society. We need energy to breathe, to move, to think, to live. But this alone is not enough. We need to know when to breathe, when to move and how to think. Information provides us with that knowledge. To adopt this perspective is to interpret information as an independent entity. It is all about us waiting to be picked up and used. There may be minor variations in its interpretation by different individuals, but consistency can be easily achieved through better training.

Specific sets of information, such as finance information, are given a unique value by Organisations which are usually based upon departmental rather than individual needs. Particular information is thus attached to particular departments. This allows information to be generally accessible because perceptions of it are bound by the formal departmental framework. Information is then tied into that framework and cannot be used legitimately within any other context, thus guarding its consistency. What is excluded, therefore, is an important role for the individual receiver. This is not to suggest that information cannot be perceived by individuals. Psychologists such as Anderson and Bower have long been aware of the importance of information reception in determining an individual's behaviour.

However, information can be received automatically without an individual having to understand it. For example, through training an employee could process production statistics without knowing what they mean. In this case it is the functional process (through its formal procedure) that is acting as the receiver rather than the individual. An accounting process, for instance, responds to specific inputs without anyone having to understand them. A motor car responds to certain information transmitted through mechanisms such as the throttle, steering wheel or brake. Both of these examples are designed to act as receivers to specific information.

By implication, information can be transmitted to any receiver that logs into the particular transmission. In the same way as a radio picks up a station when it is switched on, the right form will pick up the right information. And like radio waves, information is omnipresent, only needing the correct tuning. Such a view allows information the continuity and consistency required to be regarded as a resource. It also allows a further proposition.

The design of any formal information system must assume that information does not change during transmission. It can, however, be transformed from data or other information sets before transmission. Within such a framework it is the transmitting functions (departments, processes, etc.) which are considered to be the main determinants. The information receiving functions (also departments, processes, etc.) are designed to link into the operational needs of the transmitter functions.

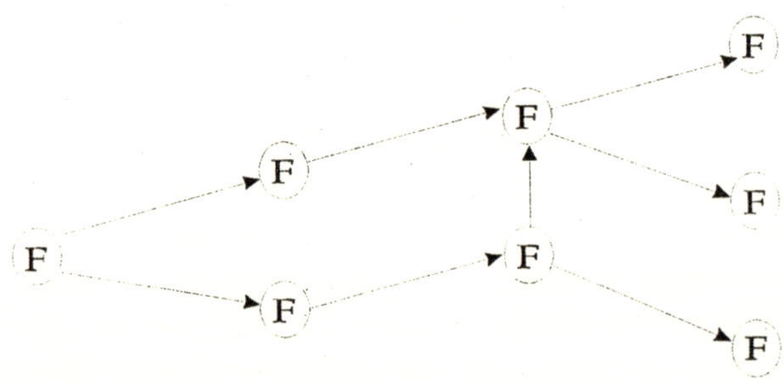

F = functions

Fig. : An information network between functions

Each function, however, can be both transmitter and receiver of information, and together with other functions will form part of an integrated network (Figure). The functions are tied by their simultaneous roles as information receivers and transmitters, thereby being prevented as much as possible from deviancy in their information usage.

Consequently, business Organisations are driven by those functions which transmit information. The higher the value that a particular set of information is given, the more important will be its relating transmitter function. For example, the finance department could both transmit and receive information. Indeed, each job function within that department could also do the same. A cost clerk, for instance, receives information from the factory floor which he then processes into other information and transmits to some other source, perhaps management. The value of the information he processes will depend upon the utility his Organisation has placed upon it. If the utility is high, then the prestige attached to the transmitting function will also be high irrespective of job complexity. In the same way, if a department has a great number of important information transmitters within its control, then it too will be prestigious and possess influence. Why certain sets of information are prestigious and others are not will depend, amongst other things, upon the Organisation's political processes.

Concept and Nature

The perception-driven paradigm does not consider information to be a resource. Individuals or groups are seen to own their information. What belongs to the Organisation are the data sets, the facts and figures specific to certain functions. For instance, data on how an Organisation is performing in its market quite obviously belong to that firm. How well that data is used is dependent upon the individual's own competence in interpreting it. Management can control this indirectly through training, but they cannot directly control the thought processes which turns data into information. Once again, there is a collection of propositions or ideas about information which formulate a general approach.

Adherence to this paradigm, as in the previous paradigm, may not necessarily be by conviction but rather by default because people not treating information as a resource automatically form part of this group. However, there are others who are members by conviction. Information is said to be receiver-dependent, in that, any set of information can be considered to be information only if it is recognised as having value by a particular individual. Thus, a river flooding may be information to someone who lives on its banks but of no consequence to someone living several miles away.

It would be difficult, therefore, to understand information as a group or Organisations property since its determination is subjective. Management teams have implemented computer technology and in so doing also developed their information sets into a resource. They experience problems, usually some time after a successful launch, and then abandon using their technology in an integrative manner, returning to the 'islands' approach (that is, a computer system, perhaps physically integrated through networks, etc., but perceptually segregated into different functional areas). Information is no longer seen as a resource; indeed its treatment as such is often seen as the culprit and not the technology itself.

Both paradigms recognize a difference between data and information. Computer personnel, for example, have long known of the distinction. Information is seen by them as processed data. The two are interrelated, data being the input to a process, and information the output. In the same way that an output of one system can form the input of another, information from one system can form the data of another. This is consistent with treating information as a resource. Perceptually-conceived information on the other hand is not the consequence of a formalized process. Data are a factor, but then so are other aspects such as individual traits, culture, structure and political processes.

The relationship between data and information is, therefore, not so strong. This contradicts the objectives implied by the creation of management information systems and data processing. The former allows the individual access to established information, whilst the latter converts data into information. Since the production of information cannot be formalized there is no point in trying to achieve it. Systems should, therefore, be designed to produce the most accurate and readable data in order to enhance easy conversion into information.

When Ligomenides describes information as a fundamental force, he should be referring to data. Levitan, on the other hand, is correct in claiming information to be dynamic and continuously evolving. The logic of these two views can be seen when data and information are differentiated. It is only data which is time-independent, and therefore unchanging and static— a fundamental force. By this we mean that data retains a constant empirical value: a fact is a fact and cannot be altered. Information, on the other hand, can be altered and changed. It is time-dependent and thus its value can alter from one moment to the next. It is dynamic and evolving because it is determined by an individual's perception.

It is, indeed, time and utility which transform data into information. If at a particular time a set of data is useful to an individual then it can be described as information. Equally, at another time the same set of data may not have utility and therefore not be information. The data themselves have not changed in any way, remaining always constant. What has changed is the individual's perception of those data. Information is in reality the consequence of a complex psychological process which transforms perceived data, into usable thought inputs.

It is, therefore, data which the individual receives from the environment, the brain which transforms these data into information. No formal system can directly pre-empt this stage; thus no formal system can transform data into information.

Data can be transformed into different data, transmitted and received. For example, production data submitted to the cost department and processed into second generation costed production data, which are in turn submitted to the financial director. Information is transformed, in part, from data; it can only be received and never transmitted. The financial director may attach value to costed production data and thus receive it as information. If he/she passes it on, it will once again be as data, perhaps refined into third generation data. There cannot be information systems because information is so transient.

The individual's subjectivity, which can be developed by training and formal procedure, determines what is information. At another time that perception may be different. Information systems cannot work in this way. Their assumption must be that information is not transient but consistent.

Quite obviously information systems do exist in one form or another. They may not be what they claim to be but they are nevertheless working. Is it worth arguing the difference? The answer to that lies within ourselves. Our actions and behaviour, and consequently our Organisations, are governed by our perceptions. If, therefore, we understand information to be permanent rather than transient then how we organize ourselves will be coloured by that. We will design systems which use information as a resource and expect it to be totally consistent.

Problems in Initial Phase

The difference between these two paradigms may seem subtle, and in terms of information usage it may well be. However, NBS research indicates that the effects upon Organisational design can be major. Structural characteristics consequent upon individually-owned information, for instance, can adopt two extremes. On the one hand they can be organic and informal (adhocracies) whereby all members are seen as contributing equally, each possessing a particular range of techniques to interpret data, whilst at the other extreme there are formal and mechanistic Organisations (bureaucracies). The rigidities of structure stifle any use of information as a resource, so by default such processes are left to the individual. These contrast with the resource-driven paradigm in which the structural characteristics of Organisations are seen to be centrally orientated, with spheres of influence at the periphery, their importance dependent upon the perceived value of particular sets of information.

Various Difficulties

The development of an Organisation oriented toward the resource-driven concept of information is well known, and many large firms are aligned in that direction. A sophisticated network is established, more than likely computerized, accessing and distributing information. Particular attention is paid to ensuring standardization of information sets. For example, a piece of costing information is so devised that it can be used by accounts, marketing and production. These Organisations treat all information as their property, attaching to it a value like any other asset. This denies the employee any sense of ownership and tends to detach them from the work process with consequential inefficiencies evolving. It is asserted, that a motivated staff is a contented and efficient staff.

One important way to motivate is to give the individual responsibility within their job. Such responsibility is manifest in how much ability a person will be given to determine the information need of their particular function. To standardize information in the way that many corporate systems do, takes away that fundamental element of responsibility. Levitan, on the other hand, would claim this to be an inevitable consequence of increasingly sophisticated corporate structures. In addition, Karen Levitan and others imply that information which is not used as a resource is inferior. On the contrary, one could argue that giving the individual ownership could result in a greater entrepreneurial drive.

Standardization is the killer of innovation. It is difficult to conceive of any substantial Organisation, however, where such a degree of individuality could be tolerated. Their size demands a need for cohesion through standardized practice. Therefore it is only in the smaller establishments where such freedom would work. Large Organisations which do not treat their information as a resource still exist.

Their mechanisms of control, however, are not informal or organic. Indeed, the realities are the converse. Individuality is stifled by greater control, rather than less. No-one is trusted to use information for the Organisation's good without formal control procedures. Classic examples of such Organisations are to be found within the civil service or large quasi-government institutions such as the post office.

It has been suggested that there is a relationship between the way in which a firm uses its information and its structure. A matrix can be established differentiating Organisations in terms of how they treat their information and the consequential structural characteristics. If, for example, information is plotted against size (another important contingent of Organisation) four major structural types could be identified. Each is the outcome of the way a particular firm uses its information.

On the vertical axis of the matrix are the two extremes of information. On the horizontal axis are the two extremes of Organisational size (Figure). Both information and size are considered to be contingents, that is variables which affect the characteristics of an Organisation. The four possible combinations of these two variables determine four Organisational structures. Thus, each structure is an ideal for each of the four combinations. For example, a managerial structure is the appropriate structure for a large firm using information as a resource.

Resource	Managerial	Technical/ Professional
Treatment of information	Bureaucratic	Entrepreneurial
Perception	Large	Small

Structure parameters

Managerial	: larger in size with central/top control but with more departmental integration
Bureaucratic	: larger in size with formal structure and a diversified control
Technical/professional	: smaller in size with a professional body and formal structure
Entrepreneurial	: centrally controlled but with less formal structure and smaller in size

Figure : Information/structure matrix

Research into the validity of such a matrix is by no means complete. There is evidence from the NBS regional survey, for example, that such a correlation does indeed exist. In general, the more successful managerial-style firms tend to treat their information as a resource, whilst the more successful entrepreneurial Organisations tend to treat their information as a perceptual phenomenon, and so on. It is not yet certain whether the matrix is predictive, that is implying combinations which are not successful. There is sufficient evidence, however, to support the claim that information usage affects Organisational structure.

The issue of information is much more than whether or not it is a resource. Information is indeed the essence of an Organisation, shaping and determining its structure.

For example, bureaucratic Organisations could hot effectively treat information as a resource because their mechanisms could not control it that way. A technical/ professional Organisation, on the other hand, is better able to handle its information as a resource because of its structural characteristics.

The implication is that there should be a natural balance between the design of an Organisation and its information structure. Where this has not been achieved it is because managers are not matching the structure of their Organisations with an appropriate usage of information. NBS research has also shown that the implementation of computer technology can worsen any potential for imbalance. This is perhaps because of two factors.

Firstly, the characteristics of the technology itself do tend to enhance resource-driven rather than perception-driven information. Secondly, the greater volume of information generated makes the problem more apparent.

If the matrix in Figure is valid then there is neither a right nor a wrong way to control information: much depends upon the individual circumstances. Resource-driven information and perception-driven information are opposite extremes of one continuum.

Management teams were grasping eagerly at the new computer technology as a solution to their efficiency problems. There were at that time forces in the environment—market, political, social or economic—with which the traditional methods of Organisation could not cope; it was believed that the computer would provide all the answers. In the space of that time many colleagues began to discover that the impact of computer technology seemed to be contradictory. On the one hand, it did tend to improve efficiency, whilst on the other it was not always so certain that an improvement in effectiveness followed. It seemed that underlying, and as yet not understood, forces were at work.

Departments employing the same technology were more or

less successful than others. Business Organisations with all the ingredients of success and implementing computers to further fuel their growth quite often experienced failure a few years later. Since those early days there has been considerable discussion and research on the impact of information technology. It seemed that the perceptual aspects of Organisation were not merely misunderstood but often ignored, and thus we were not able to understand fully the implications of introducing information technology. We now realize that not only does it have an impact on the way we run Organisations, it also has an impact on our behaviour. There is a readily understood physical aspect of any firm and a more abstract, perceptual aspect which arises from the way that people behave as a collective. Information technology is not the only agent in this process, but because of its particular characteristics it can have an extraordinarily powerful effect on both these aspects. One of the two main objectives of this book, therefore, is to underline the importance of the relationship between, information technology (and to a lesser extent general technology) and its Organisational structure.

The two are inseparable. Models that seek to understand either technology or Organisation must do so within the framework created by this relationship. Otherwise an essential factor leading to an appropriate analysis will be missed. The other main objective is to produce a model which can do this. Unlike many of its predecessors, the model will not concentrate on the functional or hierarchical nature of Organisations but rather on the dichotomy between the physical and perceptual aspects. This exists whether or not there is information technology present, but in many cases the implementation of such technology can exacerbate potential dysfunctional forces existing between the two. In effect there are two Organisations—a physical Organisation and a perceptual or virtual Organisation.

The impact that information technology can have on the sometimes tenuous relationship existing between the two can be quite profound. The model explores thoroughly this relationship. It proposes virtual Organisation as the antithesis of physical Organisation. That is abstract, unseeing and existing within the minds of those who form a particular Organisation. The point being that because the framework of virtual Organisation is often subjective and open to many different perceptual interpretations, it is difficult for anyone to establish an appropriate response to it. This makes it no less real; nor does it reduce the need to respond to it. Left unattended the effects of virtual Organisation can be quite catastrophic, especially if stimulated by the impact of information technology. This has considerable significance for the practitioner, especially those who have introduced, or are thinking of introducing, information technology. The model suggests that for a firm to survive there would ideally exist a dynamic equilibrium between the two Organisations which has been termed the Organisational balance. Anything which upsets this balance, such as the introduction of information technology, has to be compensated for by proactive action of management. If managers do not understand, nor indeed perceive the existence of virtual Organisation, then they will not be able to take the appropriate measures. Long-term structural weaknesses or even total failure of the business can result.

Demonstrating the existence of virtual Organisation can be problematic. By definition it cannot be observed directly since it exists only in the mind. At best one could ask a selection of staff for their impressions and make certain deductions, but these are likely to be dubious and tainted with the researcher's own perceptions. As such there has deliberately been no direct empirical research to establish the foundations of this model. Support for its validity has been sought in three other areas. Firstly, there is indirect empirical data gained from several research projects conducted at the Newcastle Business School. This comprises a study over two years by Stuart Maguire and myself into eighty-five small to large firms in all sectors of the North East. We examined particularly the strategy that firms employed to implement and control their information technology.

The data were gathered through a series of observations, interviews and involvement in the process. Other data were obtained from one or two firm studies on the impact of information technology by a group within the Newcastle Business School called AMBIS (Advanced Manufacturing and Business Information Systems). The argument for using these data rather than dedicated data is that they should be less contrived. Secondly, there is support to be gained from relevant personal experience. Although many would find this approach invalid because it does not comply with traditional or conventional ideas about research data, there is an increasing acceptance that such data can prove useful. In the social sciences, for example, Duke argued that such an approach (amongst others) would make a valuable contribution to the understanding of social experience. It is accepted that it cannot provide the only data, but the data that it does provide should be considered no less valid than any other.

We return to a more traditional style in support of the main arguments. That is, rather than gathering empirical evidence first and then developing a model, we should develop the model first from experiential instincts and then support it with data. This is put forward in the belief that to pursue the traditional methods of data-first research would not produce the generic model necessary to achieve the objectives set above. We have become unimaginative in our ideas about Organisation because we have been blinkered by too many sets of data.

How the book is structured in terms of presenting a logical argument takes on a greater significance than if it were based merely upon direct empirical data. It requires presentation of basic argument, counter-argument and a compromise position which leads the reader forward to the logical conclusion. This is the dialectic which involves thesis, antithesis and synthesis.

This overview, therefore, should not only cover the background to the book's major arguments and supportive material, but also provide the reader with a basic chapter plan.

To explain the impact of information technology we must look beyond the functional aspects of business Organisations. The importance of information is reflected in its ability, through the appropriate technology, to corrupt departmental boundaries. This chapter, therefore, proposes that it is better to understand an Organisation as a network of information flows, which is itself set within other network flows of region, market, industry, and so on. Such a perspective is underlined by many firms accessing information beyond their established functional boundaries. Within the Organisation, this could involve different departments accessing a common pool of information from the company database.

Externally, employees can gain entrance to public databases such as Prestel, which are run by autonomous bodies. The drive is towards centralization and hence better management control. Paradoxically, the opposite is being encouraged, whereby every user has the potential to access information which enables them to operate more efficiently, and also to do so outside the control of their manager. Under these conditions it is difficult for managers to control not only who reads and writes what but also, and perhaps more importantly, who knows what.

Large amounts of information can be processed and communicated via a network without managers ever being able to determine whether it runs contrary to their own policy. Security has, as a consequence, become an extremely important issue. The more the dissemination of information is allowed, the more likely control mechanisms will become corrupted.

In simple terms, data are facts, whilst information is the consequence of interpretation. What is information to some is not to others, and it is the subjective interpretation of what is and is not valuable which has caused managements considerable problems. The control parameters on the Organisation's database are based upon managers' own perceptions of its value as information which may not coincide with that of a potential intruder or misuser. But more than this, individual employees' perception of their information stock widens because of their greater accessibility to the information network. As a consequence, their perception of their own job parameters also widens beyond what management might think desirable.

Fundamental Approach

While mankind has developed myriad ways of applying and controlling power to dominate and shape our environment, through the use of — tools, weapons, machines, fuels, vehicles, instruments, clothing, buildings and roads, metals, plastics and drugs, agriculture, and electricity — the handling of information has lagged considerably, perhaps because the human brain is itself so remarkably powerful.

Until recently, there have been only three major developments in this area: the invention of written (or painted or carved) language, some five or six thousand years ago; that of simple arithmetic operations, using what would now be called a digital representation of numbers, about a thousand years later; and that of printing, about five hundred years ago. With written language, we get the capacity to make a permanent record of information and also to convey messages across space and time: storage, retrieval, and communication.

With digital arithmetic, we get the ability to perform accurate, repeatable manipulations of quantitative data. With printing, we can make many identical copies of the same record and so broadcast a single message to a wide and continuing audience.

Beyond these outstanding advances, until the last hundred years or so, the only progress has been in the engineering department with increasingly plentiful production of more powerful and reliable and efficient, faster and cheaper devices to implement these concepts. In the last hundred years, we have seen the rapidly accelerating advent of a technology so powerful, novel, widespread, and influential that we may indeed call it the Second Industrial Revolution. Its basis is electromagnetic, in many interconnected forms: photography, photocopying, cinematography, and holography; telegraphy, telephony, radio communication, radar, sonar, and telemetry; sound and video recording and reproduction; vacuum tubes, transistors, printed circuits, masers, lasers, fiber optics, and (in rapid succession) integrated circuits (IC), large-scale integration (LSI), and very large-scale integration (VLSI) of circuitry on a tiny semi-conducting 'chip'; and, finally, the bewildering variety of electronic digital computers.

Computer Revolution

The progress has been truly amazing. In only about 40 years, electronic communications and news media have become commonplace and indispensable. Computers have proliferated, becoming increasingly fast, powerful, small, and cheap, so that now there is scarcely a human activity in which they are not to be found, bearing an increasing share of the burden of repetitive information processing, just as the machines of the First Industrial Revolution have taken over the majority of heavy and unpleasant physical labour. Now, information can not only be stored, retrieved, communicated, and broadcast in enormous quantities and at phenomenal speeds; but it can also be rearranged, selected, marshalled, and transformed.

Until recently, these activities were the sole domain of the human brain. While creative, judicious, moral, and aesthetic choices are still best left to people, all the tedious and mechanical mental processes can now be relegated to the accurate, fast, and tireless machines. Any sequence of operations on information that can be precisely specified can be carried out without further human intervention or supervision.

At first, computers were the experimental toys of university researchers; then they became the tools of government establishments and giant corporations, huge, expensive, individually designed and manufactured, and beyond the reach of any but the wealthiest Organisations.

People thought of the future in terms of machines of ever-greater speed and capacity; centralized behemoths would hold all the world's information in gigantic data banks, whence major decisions would issue to be imposed upon the populations at their mercy.

With the emergence of powerful, cheap, mass-produced computers-on-a-chip, the picture has changed radically. Now we see tiny computers everywhere: in wrist-watches, microwave ovens, electronic games, pocket calculators, cameras, typewriters, musical instruments, etc.

What used to be done, with few options, by intricate mechanical devices is now performed, with great flexibility and convenience and at much less expense, by the ubiquitous preprogrammed microcomputer.

The probable future has become one of millions of small yet powerful computers, controlling virtually every machine and appliance. These are distributed in every home, on every desk, in every workshop; many of them connected in a maze of small and large networks, much like the present telephone network. This enables individual computers to communicate, sharing information in a gigantic distributed database, and gaining, through distributed processing, computational power whose extent is yet difficult to gauge; all this following the individual requirements and choices of the owner or operator of each machine. Increasingly, we are confronted, not only with the results of the use of computers throughout industry, commerce, banking, advertising, science, the communications industry, newspapers, airlines, and hospitals; but with the realistic possibility of purchasing computer power for our own small enterprises, offices, and homes. This may be done in a variety of ways; but in all of them, the real cost of computation is constantly diminishing.

It is probably fair to say that the question of computerization is not "whether," but "when" and "how." We must choose whether to lease equipment or to buy it; whether to install terminals, connected to a computerized "service bureau," or a complete local computer system; whether to get a package of standard programs directed towards our kind of work, to commission new programs tailored to our special needs, or to learn programming and write our own; whether to go it alone or to share a system with a number of similar users (especially if they are in the same building); how far to take our first efforts at computerization; what to include and what to continue doing by hand. Computer programming is likely to become the literacy medium of the third millennium AD.

Elementary schools may well be teaching it before long, and we might be well advised to gain at least a smattering of knowledge of computers and of programming competence, especially since computer languages and programming environments are becoming increasingly helpful and friendly to the uninitiated user.

A computer is a machine for the automatic processing of information. Historically, this information was numerical, and computers were machines for doing arithmetic.

Unlike the simpler calculating machines, which can perform only one elementary arithmetic operation at a time, they need to be told what to do next (usually by suitable button-pushes); computers can be given a list of operations to perform (often with branching and repetitions, depending on tests of sign or value included among the operations), which they will then execute in proper sequence without further intervention. This sequence of instructions is called a *program.*

A digital computer stores its information in the form of words, finite ordered sets of digits, each of which can have only one of a finite set of values.

Considerations of simplicity, reliability and economy dictate that electrical engineers should design computers to consist of a great number of similar pieces of circuitry, each of which can only be in one of two states, usually denoted by 0 and 1.

Such *binary digits* (or bits) are the elements of which computer digital representation is built. A row of eight bits is called a *byte,* and the majority of computers have their storage of information organized in words of one, two, four, or eight bytes (8, 16, 32, or 64 bits).

The number of bits in a word is termed its *length;* if this is *k,* then the number of possible distinct pieces of information that can be stored in such a word is 2. In particular, four bits together can have 16 different contents, and these are standard binary representations of the numbers 0-15:

0000 = 0 0001 = 1 0010 = 2 0011 = 3

0100 = 4 0101 = 5 0110 = 6 0111 = 7

1000 = 8 1001 = 9 1010 = A 1011 = B

1100 = C 1101 = D 1110 = E 1111 = F

with A = 10, B = 11, C = 12, D = 13, E = 14, and F = 15. These may now be viewed as the 16 possible digits of a representation (the hexadecimal, or hex), which is much more compact and humanly intelligible than a long string of zeroes and ones. For example, the byte 10110010 becomes "132," and the four-byte computer word 01001100011100101101000110001110 becomes the eight-digit hex word "4C72D18E."

The following are various parts of which any computer is composed. These are, essentially,

1. a *central processing unit* (CPU), which is the controlling and computing centre of the machine;
2. a *memory,* possibly of different levels, in which both *data* and *instructions* are stored;
3. a variety of *input* and *output (I/O) devices,* through which the machine communicates with the world outside it.

The CPU consists of an operation control unit (OCU), an arithmetic/logical unit (ALU), and a relatively small, very-fast accessible local memory (LM). The OCU keeps track of the memory location of the next instruction to be executed, and analyzes the current instruction, so as to activate the proper operation of a memory transfer, nonsequential jump (by appropriately changing the address of the next instruction), input or output of information, or computation (performed by the ALU), as is indicated by the instruction code.

The ALU actually carries out the elementary arithmetic operations (addition, subtraction or negation, multiplication, division or reciprocation) and logical operations (these being bit-by-bit operations, without carry' such as not, and, x or; eg., not 1010= 0010, 1100 and 0101 =0100, 0110 xor 1010 = 1100) on the data given to it by the OCU. The LM receives the operands called for by the OCU and also the results of the ALU'S operations upon them. For example, the OCU may retrieve the factors of a multiplication from the main memory into a pair Of LM registers and instruct the ALU to multiply them and place their product in another LM register. Such registers are usually called accumulators, and they are normally double-length (since the product of two k-bit numbers is a 2k-bit number). Other LM registers are used for counting (eg. repetitions) and are called index registers; others hold intermediate values and are called buffers; and, finally, there are one-bit or two-bit registers which reflect the information on which tests are made by the OCU (for example, the occurrence of a carry, the vanishing or positivity of an answer, or the occurrence of an arithmetic overflow): these are termed flags.

Originally, the CPU was a sizable piece of electronics, hand-assembled and highly complex. With the advent of micro-miniaturization of circuitry, printing, and photographic techniques, and the mass production of components only the largest computers (mainframes) are built in the old way. Smaller systems generally have the entire CPU on a single chip. Among these, the name microcomputer is now applied to those with less than a million words of memory and a word length of one or two bytes; the name minicomputer applies to the larger machines, with two to four-byte words and one to a hundred million words of memory. (The smallest micro is probably more powerful than the big computers used by universities and industry in the 1950s.)

The *main memory* (mm) consists of magnetic or electronic components which store the information (both data and instructions) needed by the computer. The individual words are directly addressable from the CPU by number (rather like houses in a street), and their contents are retrievable in very short times, of the order of the operation time of the CPU (ranging from fractions of a *nanosecond,* 10^{-9} or one billionth of a second, for the fastest mainframes to several *microseconds,* 10^{-6} or millionths of a second, for the slower micros). This is often referred to as high-speed storage or random-access memory (RAM). While most of the mm is erasable and may be changed at will, some memory is used to store constants and often-used utility programs and is not erasable by the CPU: such memory is called *read-only memory* (ROM). Sometimes this is optional and can be plugged into the computer : this is called *firmware.*

Note that a computer with one-byte-long addresses can have at most 28= 256 words of mm; a two-byte address can reach 256^2 = 65536 words; a three-byte address can select any of 16777216 words of mm; and so on. In practice, most micros and minis have mm ranging in size from 2 14= 16384 to 218= 262144 words. It should be noted that 10^3= 1000 and 2^{10}= 1024. Because computers are so heavily slanted towards base-2 representation, it has become almost universal computer parlance to use the prefix *kilo* or K (which usually denotes a thousand units) to denote 1024 and the prefix *mega* or M (which usually denotes a million units) to denote

$2^{20} = 1024^2 = 1048576$. Thus, we write 16K for 2^{U} and V4M for 2^{18}. Perhaps the commonest size of MM consists of 64K = 65536 words.

Almost all computer instructions comprise an operation code (usually one byte long, allowing 256 possible operations to be specified), followed by an operand reference (number, index, or address) of variable length (since some operations require more data than others; for instance, the STOP instruction needs no operand, so it is one byte long).

The *extended memory* (EM) is sometimes considered under I/O devices, both because it is often physically located outside the computer (while the CPU and the mm are usually in the same enclosure), and because its speed of access is much slower than the speed of operation of the CPU and is comparable with the range of speeds of I/O devices. Most read/write memory is magnetic (optical memory is read-only, and fast RAM is either magnetic or electronic), either in the form of tape, drum, or disk, coated with magnetic material, much like sound recording equipment; it is similarly erased, read, and recorded upon by "heads" which contain electromagnetic sensors/ polarizers. The cheapest (and most limited, in both speed and capacity) device is a common portable cassette recorder, with 1/4" tape cassettes. From this, one moves to specially engineered cassettes and recorders, and thence to high-speed 1/2" or I" reel-to-reel drives carrying thousands of feet of tape at very high speeds. Access times can be quite good for sequential access, along the tape, but random access time is poor at best, running to seconds or even minutes. Economy and a virtually unlimited total storage capacity (on numerous cassettes or reels; but only as many units as one has on-line tape-drives are actually accessible without human intervention) are the only advantages.

When we wish for practically useful EM, combining large capacity with relative economy and speed of random access, we must turn to drum or disk memory; and, nowadays, the former have been practically replaced by the latter. Disk memory is of two types: floppy disk and hard disk, the first being the cheaper, slower, smaller-capacity option. Floppy disks are flexible, have diameters of 51/4" or 8", generally, and are removable from the disk-drive, so allowing one to build up an unlimited library of stored data. The information is stored on concentric circular tracks (not on a single spiral track, as on a sound record), on one or both sides of the disk. The number of tracks and the number of bytes per track vary (the density increasing with precision of engineering, and so with cost of the drive), but the total capacity of a floppy disk is in the range of 50KB to 1MB. The disks rotate at, typically, 300 rpm, and access time is governed by the time required to place the movable head on the right track, a fraction of a second, plus the fifth of a second taken by the head to traverse the circumference of the track, in search of a record; thereafter, consecutive bytes are accessed at some thousands per second.

Hard disks are rigid and have larger diameters. There are drives which range from anything from one to a dozen disks, rotating at about ten times the speed of floppy-disk drives (and so diminishing the access time of records in a track) with one or several heads.

Fixed-head drives naturally must have a head for each track (which costs more), but save head-movement time in random access. Winchester disks are movable-head drives with sealed-in disks, where the heads ride very close to the disk, cushioned by the layer of air between. In floppy-disk drives, the head actually rides on the disk, eventually wearing it out.

The capacity of hard-disk drive ranges from 10 MB to 100 MB in a single drive. Some movable-head hard-disk drives have removable disks or disk-packs, allowing for greater library storage.

The I/O devices are the computer's link with the outside world. In large mainframe computers, we see *paper card* (as in Hollerith or "IBM" cards) and paper tape readers and punches: the perforations in the paper carry the information. Increasingly in large computers, and almost universally in small ones, the main input is from the keyboard of a terminal. This is much like a typewriter keyboard, and depressing any key sends an 8-bit code to the computer.

When the computer is waiting for input from this terminal, it reads the code and interprets it as a datum; when it is busy, either the message is lost or it is held in a "buffer" for subsequent input (this depends on how the connection is made and what the computer is made to do). It is quite common for the computer to be connected to several terminals, all competing for its attention. This is called time-sharing. The computer cycles around the terminals, look for their several inputs while dividing its CPU time among them. The main output of the computer is to the display devices of the terminals; these are either video displays (cathode ray tubes, CRT, just like the screens of black-and-white or color TV sets; indeed, simple micros sometimes use ordinary television sets as display devices) or printers (in so-called hard-copy terminals). Of course, the computer may be connected to additional video displays and printers, of different qualities, as well as to plotters, a kind of printer for drawing graphs and diagrams. Many types and speeds of printers exist. Other input devices, such as audio amplifiers (receiving signals from radio tuners, record players, etc.), video receivers and recorders, laser disk drives and a variety of scientific instruments, can all be classified as transducers (devices that transform physical quantities, such as position, conductivity, pressure, temperature, vibration frequency, or amplitude, into electromagnetic impulses) linked to digitizers (which convert such impulses into sequences of zero/one pulses). Output from the computer can similarly follow the reverse process, yielding visible or audible results, or the control of mechanical or electrical equipment. Thus, computers can draw pictures (often, moving pictures), make music and other sounds, and can control appliances, machinery, and whole manufacturing processes.

In order to connect remote terminals to a computer, use is often made of telephone lines; and, for this purpose one employs a device called a modem (for "Modulator/DeModulator"), which converts the computer's digital signals to and from telephone audio signals. This has a cradle shaped to hold the ear and mouth pieces of a telephone's handset. It is also possible to connect several computers in this way. This is called the formation of a computer network. Of course, computers may also be connected by cable, fibre-optics, or microwave link. It should be noted that terminals usually, and other I/O devices often, themselves contain computers of varying degrees of power and complexity; so that even a multi-user computer with a central CPU may still be seen as a kind of computer network in its own right. The computers in I/O devices such as terminals or printers are often referred to as peripheral processors (PP).

Many networks do not have a central computer at all; but are simply a collection of independent computers linked for the sharing of information and, sometimes, computing capabilities. Often, they permit the exchange of messages *(computer mail)* and the pooling of data *(distributed database).* They may also share a common bank of memory, accessible to all.

Finally, since the invention of computer networks, designers have been investigating the possibilities of computers made up of an array of CPUs *(multicomputer, parallel processors, distributed processing).* These new ideas are very powerful and far-reaching: they will probably revolutionize our ideas of computers, and of their applications, in the next few years.

The various peripheral devices are connected to the CPU without examining how. In fact, this may be done in several ways. We can simply have a separate connection (or port) for each device, but this limits rather severely the number of devices that may be connected to the CPU. Another way is to have a single bus (or connection) to which any number of devices may be attached.

The information signal must then carry an appropriate address. The bus receives all signals, and individual devices (including the CPU) seek out and decode only those addressed to them. It is also possible to have a switching device, which receives addressed data and directs them to the appropriate recipient device, rather like a central post office.

The decision on what communication arrangements to adopt is made on the basis of considerations of cost, capacity, and speed. It is often the case that the several devices forming a computer or a computer network have their data coded in different ways.

It is then the job of the CPU(s) and PPs to share the work of interpreting signals into appropriate codes for each machine.

This is broadly termed the problem of interfacing devices. Sometimes, the solution is to have a standard code or structure for the communications device (one meets the s-100 bus, the rs-232 serial port, the ASCII character-code, and so on).

Another interfacing problem arises from the difference in the rate at which different devices can send and receive information (this is measured by the baud rate, named after Baudot, the inventor of the first five-hole paper-tape code; one baud is one bit transferred per second; hence kilobaud (kb), and megabaud (mb) typical rates range from 200 baud to 200 kb). One solution is to send each piece of information (usually one character at a time, which takes 8 to 10 bits) only when the last has been acknowledged (this is referred to as a handshake); this is sure, but slow. Another way is to use a storage buffer in which a large batch of information is accumulated for fast transmission, thus not wasting the time of the faster device.

One last kind of choice must be mentioned: some channels of communication are serial (they transmit one bit at a time), while others are parallel (they can transmit a byte or a whole word at a time); the latter are obviously faster, more complex, and more expensive. When devices are connected by cable, the degree of parallel communication is exhibited in the width of a flat ribbon cable, carrying several wires, side by side, and in the number of pins in the plugs and sockets by which they are connected to the machines. Parallel transmission is a variation on multiplexing. What we have described is generally referred to as the hardware of a computer. By contrast, the programs that make the computer work, the "soul" of the machine, as opposed to the hardware "body," are collectively called its software. Inevitably, there came to be programs that were hard-wired (in the now outdated phrase) into the computer, in the form of ROM. These are termed firmware.

A computer without software is a helpless set-of circuits, and the expertise required to create the basic software that will bring the machine to useful life is comparable to that required to design the machine itself. Indeed, these days, computers are designed in cooperation between computer architects, who design what the computer will do, hardware engineers, who design how it will be constructed to be able to do it, and software engineers, who design and program the operating system that will run the machine. Beyond this, the computer will also need application software of many kinds, to enable it to do a variety of jobs, such as file-handling, accounting, statistics, payrolls, inventories, complex graphic displays, games, and so on. Typically, the application software is written (i.e. programmed) by the endusers (if they are sophisticated enough) or firms of consultants and programmers and system analysts, often called software houses. Sometimes, a software house will produce part or all of an alternative operating system, or an addition to an operating system, to make a computer more flexible or more efficient than the manufacturer's own software system allows it to be.

The CPU of any computer is designed to accept and execute a specific set of *operation codes (op-codes),* ranging in number from a dozen or so to several hundred. Different makes and models of computers and microprocessors may have entirely dissimilar op-codes; but the operations that they represent are much more alike than different, both through functional necessity and historical development.

The interpretation of the op-codes is built into the hardware of the OCU (though sometimes the details of interpretation may be modified by the user through what is called *microcoding),* and it is part of this interpretation that the complete instruction being decoded contains a certain amount of further information (such as parameters, indices, and one or more memory addresses).

The "length" of a computer instruction (the number of consecutive memory words, or of bytes, occupied by it) may vary, but the OCU automatically adjusts to this. An executable program (sometimes called "object code") consists of a sequence of machine instructions, consecutively stored in the computer's memory and (with the exception of "jump" instructions) executed in the order in which they are stored.

The aggregate of possible machine instructions is called the machine language. In the computer, a program consists of a long string of binary digits (bits), usually written as 0's and 1's; and, of course, the same program would be interpreted quite differently (usually as nonsense) by any computer for which it is not designed. Indeed, the slightest error in a program almost always leads to an error in its output (usually a fatal error!). This state of affairs is sometimes expressed by the computer adage, "Garbage in; garbage out," or just "GIGO." Errors in programs are called bugs; and the tedious, odious process of finding and correcting such errors is termed debugging. It is estimated that, in the production of a working program, the debugging time may be two to four times as long as the time it takes to plan and write the program initially.

To give the reader a feeling for the nature of machine language, we present a simplified, fictitious, but typical, machine language specification. Our computer has two 16-bit accumulator registers (acc), X and Y, which may be coupled into a single 32-bit ace XY, with X holding the more and Y the less significant digits; these are attached to the ALU; and a program control register (pc) Z, also of 16 bits, attached to the OCU, which contains the address of the next instruction to be executed. Instructions will contain a 2-bit acc code a, with a = 0 referring to X, a = 1 to Y, a = 2 to XY, and a = 3 to Z. The memory consists of 216 = 65536 16-bit words, directly addressable with a 16-bit address, n.

There are four addressing modes, denoted by a 2-bit mode code d, with d = 0 referring to absolute address (address *n*\0 refers to the actual number *"n"), d* = I to direct address (address *n*\1 refers to word n in the memory), *d = 2* to indirect address *(n*\2 refers to the memory address which is the content of the memory word with address *n),* and *d* = 3 to relative address (n\3 refers to the memory address that is the sum of *n* and the content of the pc register Z, with any carry to the seventeenth bit ignored). We will write {{*a*}} for the acc denoted by a, *(n\d)* for the memory word with address *n* in mode *d,* and C[*x*] for the content of word or acc *x* (so, e.g., C[{n]2}]=C[C[n]], while C[{n\3}]=C(n+C[Z]). *A port code p* selects one of 8 *output ports (p=0,* 1, . . ., 7) and 8 *input ports (p = 8,* 9, . . . , 15), these ports transmitting 16 bits at once and having to be reactivated before each function (i.e., each output instruction sends out one 16-bit number, and the machine must wait for the output to be acknowledged before making another output; while each input instruction reads one 16-bit number, if an input is available, and the machine must wait for a new input each time). Finally, a bit code b refers to each of the 16 bits in a word (bit 0 being the least significant-rightmost and bit 15 the most significant-leftmost). In some cases, the codes a, d, p, and b are interpreted somewhat differently, depending on the particular op-code c.

As an example of a very simple computer program, we consider the solution to the following computer problem. Our computer is to be fed a sequence of one thousand 16-bit numbers at input port #9 (these may be keyed in by hand or fed in by a digitizer connected to some experiment). They are to be stored in memory words with addresses 5000, 5001, 5002, . . . , 5999. Their sum is to be computed and stored in address 6000 and output to a printer through output port #2. The program is to be stored beginning at address 0 in the memory.

Again, what is important about this example is not its detailed form, but the difficulty of its interpretation, and therefore also the difficulty of verification and debugging.

The programmer must deal with a mass of details that are of a purely mechanical nature and have no relevance to the problem being solved. "Higher-level languages" are attempts at making the computer understand the programmer's way of thinking, rather than forcing the programmer to think like a machine.

After some introductory description of an imaginary computer, and especially of its CPU, and the establishment of some essential notation. Presented with a set of arithmetic and other transformations required by potential users of a proposed new computer, the electronic and logical design engineers seek the simplest circuitry that will execute operations sufficient to generate all the required transformations. Circuits must be simple to be fast, efficient, reliable, and cheap. However, when an instruction has 16 or more bits, most of which should for the sake of efficiency, have some significant effect; the exact and complete specification or the action induced by it may well be somewhat forbiddingly intricate! And indeed, simplicity of circuitry does not usually lead to simplicity of use.

An ample of a program in this machine language, which takes 16 instructions and 28 16-bit words of memory storage, to read in one thousand numbers, store them in consecutive memory locations, sum them, and print out the sum. However, please note that the English description of what the program does (though much easier to say and comprehend) itself requires 103 characters, each equivalent to 8 bits; so that it is almost twice as long as the machine-language program. Indeed, the difficulty of the latter lies not in its length, but in its alien and opaque form of expression of what it does. The first improvement on machine language was assembly language. This is not very different from machine language, but removes the most glaring and trivial irritations. First, instructions may be labelled, so that one no longer needs to count lines to address jump instructions; one jumps to the label. This is also a great help when one wishes to insert additional instructions, either to correct or modify a program (every jump need not be changed). Second, memory may be labelled, so that numbers may be stored in symbolic addresses and retrieved therefrom, leaving it to a computer program to assign actual storage. Third, the entire program becomes relocatable anywhere in the computer memory. Finally, and perhaps more trivially, the op-codes may be replaced by abbreviated mnemonics, and the instruction layout may be relaxed, using punctuation marks. Of course, a program written in assembly language is no longer directly intelligible to the computer or executable by it. It becomes a piece of textual input, to a "translator program" called the assembler. Naturally, the program may be stored in the computer's memory, like any other piece of text; but, before it can be executed, it must be "assembled." The assembler finds appropriate space for the object code (i.e. the machine language equivalent of the input program) and for its needed storage space (often called variables). The assembly language instructions correspond, one-to-one, to machine-language instructions.

For example, we may denote memory locations by one, two, or three lowercase letters (both for labelling instructions and naming variables). A numerical address will still be allowed. Absolute addresses (i.e. actual numbers; d=O) will correspond to quoted numbers (e.g. "6000"); direct addresses (d=l) to variables named as stated; indirect addresses (d=2) to variable names placed in parentheses; and relative addresses will not be used. With relocatable programs and symbolic addresses, they are no longer useful). Accumulators (X, Y, XY, or Z) will not be referred to symbolically, but only by these names. Instruction labels will precede the instruction and will be terminated by a colon (:). Spaces will be ignored. Op-codes will be denoted by strings of capital letters and terminated by a comma (,), which will also separate multiple arguments.

A sample specification of assembly language op-codes is shown in Figure. In the assembly language notation, A denotes X (a=0), Y (a= 1), XY (a=2), or Z (a=3). Italic letters (p, x, or b) denote numbers (possibly in quotes, to denote absolutes) or variables names (possibly in parentheses, to denote indirect addressing), and are interpreted according to the op-code (e.g. A cannot be XY in IN and OUT instructions; if A is XY in instructions with c = 1, 2, and 4 (with p > 5), the operand must be 32 bits long-either a double-length number, or an address referring to the first of two consecutive 16-bit memory words. Again, the reader must remember that it is not the particular details of our specifications that are important or memorable but the kind and degree of detail occurring.

Assembly language mnemonic	*Machine language instruction*
IN A, (p-8)	*c* = 0, *a* ** 2, *p* >8
OUT A, *p*	*c* = 0, *a* ** 2, p < 7
TO A, x	*c*= 1
FROM A, x	*c* = 2, *d* > 1
FROM A, B	*c* = 2, *d* = 0
CL, A	*c* = 3, *d* = 0
NEG A	*c* = 3, *d* = 1
NOT A	*c* = 3, d = 2
RNDx	c = 3, *d* = 3, a = 2
ADD A, x	c = 4, p = 0
SUB A, x	c = 4, p = 1
AND A, x	*c* = 4, p = 2
OR A, x	c = 4, p = 3

Contd...

Assembly language mnemonic	*Machine language instruction*
XOR A, x	c = 4, *p* = 4
LADD, x	c = 4, p = 5
LSUB, x	c = 4, p = 6
LAND, x	c = 4, p = 7
LOR, x	c = 4, p = 8
LXOR, x	c = 4, p = 9
CSHL A, P	c = 5, *d* = 0
CSHR A, P	c = 5, *d* = 1
ASHL A, P	*c* = *5, d* = *2*
ASHR A, P	*c* = 5, *d* = 3
JMP, x	c = 6, *p* = 0
JPCZ A, x	c = 6, p = 1
JPCNN A, x	c = 6, p = 2
JPCNZ A, x	*c* = 6, p = 3
JPCP A, x	c = 6, p = 4
JPCB A, 0, *b*, x	c = 6, p = 5
BIT A, 0, *b*	c = *6, p* = 6
BIT A, 1, *b*	c = *7, d* = 1
BITNOT A, *b*	*c* = 7, d = 2
STOP	c = 8
INTER	c = 9

Figure : Typical assembly language mnemonics

Consider Figure. Here, numbers are given in decimal notation. Note the tremendous improvement in direct legibility of the program in comparison with the binary strings. The assembler is left to figure out where to store the sum (the variable "sum" which the machine language program put into address 6000) and the current address of the listed numbers (the variable "w," which the machine language program puts at location 28 if the program begins at location 0, necessitating counting the words occupied by the program; if the program were to be modified or relocated, this would have to be changed, and would be an unnecessary source of programming errors); and similarly, there is no need to count words to determine the addresses of "ret" and "out" (placed by the machine language program at 5 and 24 ' as it happens). As an exercise, the readers may wish to try to modify the program so as to allow for the possibility that the sum of the 1000 numbers might occupy more than 16 bits. In machine language this requires no less than 12 changes and seven shifts of memory location.

```
        CL X; FROM X, SUM; TOX, '5000'
ret:    FROM X, W; SUB X '6000'; JPCZX, out
        INX, 1; FROM X, (W); ADD X, sum
        FROM X, sum
        TO X, W; ADD X, T; JP, ret
out:    TO X, sum; OUT X, 2; STOP
```

Figure : The summation program in assembly language

In assembly language only the substantive changes (from the programmer's point of view) need be made. The amended program is given in Figure. Here we note that only seven changes are needed; but observe that "sum" becomes a double-length address-just another piece of bookkeeping handled automatically by the assembler.

```
        CL XY; FROM XY, SUM; TOX, '5000'
ret:    FROM X, W; SUB X '6000'; JPCZX,
        out IN X, 1; FROM X, (W);
        TO XY. sum ADD XY. (w);
        FROM XY, sum TO X,W; ADD X, T; JMP, ret
out:    TO XY. sum; OUT X, 2; OUT Y. 2: STOP
```

(Underlined material represents changes from previous program). Alternative version would have third line replaced by:

```
        CLX: IN Y 1, FROM Y (W); LADD, sum FROM XY sum
```

Figure : The summation program modified for long sums

Of course, a program in assembly language still represents, instruction-by-instruction, a program in machine language, and therefore still has the defects of "walking the road in extremely short steps," as we put it earlier.

All that shuffling of numbers in and out of the accumulators, counting and restricted testing, is not natural to us, and its mechanical nature suggests that an improvement is still possible. Thus it was not long before programmers devised much more humanly natural languages, which are generically called *higher-level* (or *algebraic) languages.* Some of the more common ones are ADA, ALGOL, APL, BASIC, C, COBOL, FORTRAN, LISP, PASCAL, PL/I, RPG-II, SNOBOL, SPITBOL, WATFOR, and WATFIV. There are more; and all come with a variety of versions and dialects.

The characteristic that puts a language into this class is that one higher-level instruction translates into several assembly or machine language instructions. Beyond this, the languages differ according to the kind of program they are intended for.

While most languages will perform most tasks, FORTRAN was clearly intended to do scientific and engineering computations, COBOL to perform business data-processing, LISP to manipulate lists, and SNOBOL, strings of text. As a final illustration of the power and intelligibility of such languages, we present higher-level versions of our summation program in BASIC, WATFIV, and PASCAL. Once more, note that the details of the individual languages do not matter to us at this point (though, if the reader ever intends to program, then some language will have to be thoroughly understood; but assume that many of my readers have no such intention); it is their general flavor and appearance that is noteworthy; and the casual readability of the samples presented is their salient characteristic.

Of all the hundreds of programming languages devised, it is safe to say that more lines of program have been written in FORTRAN or COBOL than in all others combined, though this reflects their age rather than their desirability. The fast-gaining runner-up must surely be BASIC, which comes with every micro and most minicomputers; though some would say that BASIC, which perpetuates the style of FORTRAN, spoils any chances of producing really good programs and should be replaced by PASCAL. Fashions come and go in programming languages, not always fully based on rational arguments, and personal preferences vigorously touted.

Given a higher-level language, it is necessary to have a translator program to turn it into machine (or more frequently assembly) language. Such translators are of two kinds.

An interpreter operates at execution time: beginning with the first instruction of the stored higher-level program, it translates it into one or more machine language instructions, which it proceeds to execute; then it reads and translates the next higher-level instruction and executes that; and so on. If a jump is encountered in the source program (as the higher-level language program is often called), the interpreter goes to the next instruction in accordance with the jump and proceeds to read, translate, and execute it, without taking into account whether it has already encountered it. Thus, the same source instructions will have to be passed and translated a thousand times (a very time-consuming and wasteful procedure). But the (usually much longer) object program need not be stored, and interpreters themselves tend to be shorter and simpler programs. This is why a BASIC interpreter is a natural adjunct to a microcomputer, which tends to be a little cramped for space; especially since many microcomputer users are riot interested in extremely lengthy computations.

By contrast, a *compiler* is a program that translates a source program into an object program, the former being in higher-level language and the latter in machine or assembly language.

The program is translated as it sits in memory, not during execution; so that the problem of repeated translation is avoided. Indeed, there are many so-called "optimizing compilers" which pass through the compiled object code several times, eliminating redundancies and inefficiencies to produce faster object programs (something that would be impossible for an interpreter to do). Speed is greatly increased, in general, at the expense of space in the computer memory. Of course, once a program has been compiled and proven to be free of bugs (debugging is far easier in source code than in object code), the source program may be stored for future use and only the object program kept in main memory. Compilers are available for almost all higher-level languages on almost all machines, and are essential for extensive applications.

The programs, or software, available for computers fall into two classes, *system software* and *application software*. The system software comprises those programs that are considered indispensable to the general operation of a given computer system, forming what is often termed the operating system of the computer, and generally are supplied by the manufacturer, though alternative operating systems are sometimes available from software houses. The applications software includes all those programs that are needed by one computer user but not by another, even if such programs are widely required, and while some manufacturers will sell applications software (as optional additions to their systems), more often this is obtained from software specialists.

We begin with the *operating system.* This may be divided into a kernel of absolutely indispensable programs and a shell of almost indispensable, so-called utility programs. The kernel (or nucleus) is also sometimes termed the monitor. To understand why this kernel program is needed, we consider what happens when we type a character (say an "A") on our keyboard, as part of a message to the computer. Because our timescale recognizes perhaps 1/20 second, while the computer may deal in units of 1/1,000,000 second, if we want to type an "A" we may find ourselves actually transmitting some 50,000 A's to the computer, before our finger leaves the key! If the keyboard mechanism were to transmit the A for only one microsecond, on the other hand, the computer might will be busy elsewhere and miss it altogether. Therefore, it is necessary to establish a protocol (in the usual diplomatic sense, a formal structure for the orderly passage of information) or "handshaking" procedure. This is often done by sending the A on one line (or lines) and simultaneously sending a pulse along an auxiliary line, which sets a "flag" bit in the CPU. When the computer is ready to receive a new character, it checks the appropriate flag bit over and over, until it detects that it has been set. Then it reads the character, resets the flag to its "null" state, and sends a signal pulse back to the keyboard (or its controlling circuitry), telling it that the character has been received. The flag is always open, so the transmit pulse need only be sent once by the keyboard; but the character continues to be sent until it is acknowledged by the computer. Thus a keyboard character will neither be missed nor read repeatedly. In addition, either the CPU or the keyboard controller should send the "A" to whatever device displays the typed characters.

If the particular keyboard were to be the only input device ever to be connected to the CPU, it would be best to incorporate all this in the circuitry of the CPU; but since there may be several different inputs to the CPU, and several types of terminals may be used, coming from different manufacturers, it is found preferable to have the I/O procedures made part of the operating system. In addition to the keyboard input already described, there will be short machine language programs for input from any other devices attached to the computer and corresponding programs for output to display screens, printers, and so on.

The orderly operation of a computer is subject to interruptions (or *interrupts,* as they are known in Computer jargon), either because a program contains an instruction that at some point, is not executable (such as a division by zero or a reference to a nonexistent memory location), or because someone needs to terminate execution for some overriding reason (such as the decision that a program is in error and is generating garbage or is in an infinite loop). Handling errors and interrupts is another function of the kernel of the operating system, as is the start-up (or "bootstrap") procedure which initializes operation. If, as is often the case, several users are connected to the computer, then the operating system must handle the tasks of Job-scheduling (and Job accounting and billing, if this is appropriate), and the allocation of storage, in main and extended memory, and of other resources (such as printers or communication lines), and the management of *time-sharing* (as between several terminals). Another task that is handled by the operating system is the management of *user files,* and their transfer between main memory and extended memory (such as disk). Indeed, one sees frequent reference to *disk operating systems,* such is the importance of this function of the operating system.

Another function of the kernel is to provide protection and security to users and to itself, both from authorized users encroaching on forbidden territory and from unauthorized users attempting to use the computer.

Ideally, each user should, on giving the correct access code (such as a "password")—this feature did not exist on the first computers, and is still absent in personal microcomputers with only one user/owner-who has access strictly limited to the parts of the computer allocated to him or her by the operating system, but in such a way that the impression is maintained that he or she is the only user present.

Another very congenial aspect of this concept is that some operating systems conduct their memory management function in such a way that the user need make no distinction between main and extended memory; this is referred to as a virtual memory system. The kernel program has to be able to display, move, modify, and search, at least the main memory, and to initiate execution at any given address, or activate any of the peripheral devices. Using these functions, by means of appropriate commands in the "operating system language," together with its file-handling capabilities, the system can load, compile, or execute any program stored in its memory (main or extended) written in machine, assembly, or higher-level language, provided that a suitable compiler or other translator is available to it.

We now turn to the utilities provided by most operating systems. First, we have an assembler (and perhaps also a *disassembler,* which translates a program written in machine language into the more intelligible assembly language; as well as a *macro-assembler,* which allows the user to define his own macroinstructions in machine or assembly language), together with a selection of translation programs, either interpreters or compilers, for the higher-level languages that the user wishes to employ.

The smaller microcomputers will provide an interpreter for

some dialect of BASIC, since this a relatively simple language to learn and to interpret into machine or assembly language; beyond this, one must pay for additional languages. There may also be a variety of TRACING and DEBUGGING utilities, according to the cost, size, and sophistication of the computer and its operating system.

There will be facilities for linking or chaining programs together. While the kernel will contain the rudiments of a file-handling system (to create, destroy, list, locate, and transfer files), there will also be utilities for further management of these. Such programs will sort, find (among other files), search (in a given file, for information specified), transform, edit, and combine files. Indeed, a good program editor can enormously facilitate the rapid and painless creation and modification of files, which include both text and programs.

The line separating the kernel from the shell of utilities is purely conceptual and far from sharp. Similarly, the boundary of the entire operating system is far from definite. What is available beyond the essentials mentioned above will be called part of any decent system by some, part of a compiled language by others, and just applications software by still others, depending on their point of view. The ability to handle a variety of data structures (such as arrays, lists, strings of characters, trees, queues, and stacks) may come from the use of a suitable higher-level language or from an extended "system development" utility package.

Similarly, languages intended for scientific and engineering applications usually handle floating-point and multiple-precision arithmetic, though this may be provided even in computer hardware. The same applies to routines for computing, for example, sines, cosines, logarithms, etc., and pseudorandom numbers (the last beloved of, computer games inventors!).

A *database management system* (DBMS) may be just a glorified file-handling utility; or may be an elaborate program, cross-indexed and relational, with its own language of special commands, for answering any conceivable question about a large amount of intricately structured data.

As is often the case, you get what you pay for, both in money and in memory space; and vendors' claims have to be carefully scrutinized and verified. It is advisable not to overbuy one's capabilities beyond one's needs.

Similarly, a graphics package may simply allow one to produce passable graphs, histograms (i.e. bar-graphs), pie-charts, and perhaps games, with a resolution of some 200 by 300 delightfully named pixels; or it may allow you to resolve perhaps 2000 by 3000 pixels, in a variety of colors, with the ability to draw complex three-dimensional shapes, properly shaded, illuminated, and textured, and move them by commands in a special language. The latter systems are a lot of fun to operate, and can be most helpful to draughtsmen, animators, film designers, and simulator-trainer designers; but they cost a bundle, and they require quite powerful computers to hold and run them.

Another offshoot of the file handier is a cluster of programs for generating reports, journal ledgers, and accounts of all kinds, as well as forms and mailing' lists (the latter leading to a kind of DBMS in which mailing lists are matched to interests and characteristics of the individuals itemized).

Again, there are statistical packages of various degrees of sophistication, from a mean-variance-covariance calculator, to systems able to analyse very complex sets of data by elaborate techniques, using a whole statistical computer language. What has been described as "the most popular program ever written" is usually given the generic name of an *electronic worksheet,* though the trade name of the first such program, Visi-Calc, like Kleenex and Vaseline, has become almost generic.

A table is presented on the video screen and each entry is allocated either a numerical value or a formula relating it to other entries. When the data are sufficient, the resulting numbers are displayed. When an entry is changed, it and all entries depending on it are altered accordingly at once. This provides a representation of a given situation surpassed only by a graph in its impact, and a first-class planning aid. Finally, among the borderline system/applications software utilities, will put what is usually called a word-processing package (though would prefer either character or text processor). This is an extension of an editing utility, in which the text may by "scrolled" up and down on the screen, edited in the usual ways, but also more specifically for producing letters, articles, reports, and other written copy.

Margins may be set and the text right, left, or double justified, or set up in multi-column pages, with page numbering, indexing, and even the use of different sizes and styles of typeface, in the most sophisticated systems. Here again, cost rises steeply, and one should buy only what one will need.

Beyond these programs, there lies an endless variety of unquestionable applications programs. There are programs for ballistics, boat design, analysis of molecular structure from x-ray diffraction data, tabulation of Bessel functions, simulation of naval battles and economic cycles, etc.

Most of these are not in the market and only work on one machine; but there are very many programs available in the open market, produced or distributed by software houses, with various levels of efficiency, and sophistication. *Programming* is a fascinating, intricate, rewarding, but unforgiving and at times infuriating occupation. We will encourage all of you who have the time to try it. If you have a computer at your disposal, it would be a shame not to learn a simple language, such as BASIC or PASCAL and try your hand at writing a simple program or two. The sense of achievement when you have a working program is great; perhaps because the process is addictive and consumes much more time than you would believe possible.

The Format

The explanation of Organisational structure was left to two mainstream approaches. The first was the economic model whereby the business Organisation was subsumed into the market. Structure was thus defined as an extension to the market. The second was through the Taylorist and management science movements, where Organisations were seen as no more than vehicles for management control. In neither case was sufficient analytical sensitivity provided to appreciate the close-relationship between structure and its technology.

Today, different ideas about Organisation are prolific. The traditional views are still around but there are many others which have greater sophistication and which span a range of academic disciplines. They can be condensed into three major perspectives or metaphors. Scott, for example, identified these as follows. Firstly, Organisations are rational systems, based upon some collective rationale such as profit maximization or growth. This perspective also embraces the two approaches already mentioned above. Secondly, Organisations are natural systems; arising from the behaviourist movement of Elton Mayo whose perspective views Organisations as a living organism. Thirdly, Organisations are open systems which are seen as processes being open to the environment.

Watson, on the other hand, identified 'waves' of Organisation theory. The first sees Organisations as machines, portraying the view that, like machines, they are predictable. The second wave sees Organisations as organisms to demonstrate that they are as complex and unpredictable as a living organism. The final wave sees Organisations as processes, thus highlighting their dependence upon interactive behaviour. Others, such as Gareth Morgan, have gone further in identifying metaphors of Organisation (brain, machine, psychological prison, etc.) that we use to aid our understanding of them. Whichever perspective is supported, they all agree that Organisation structure provides some form of framework.

Mintzberg's book places considerable emphasis on structure and his definition proposes it as the summation of the ways in which a firm's labour is directed and coordinated into tasks. Although this definition's simplicity is appealing, it leads us to view an Organisation in terms of a division of labour and the co-ordination of management control to maintain that. It is an outlook typically portrayed by the firm's Organisation/ management chart, which identifies quite precisely who is responsible for what and to whom. This merely lists a functional relationship, which although important, reveals only part of the Organisation structure. Handy hints that there may be more when he talks 6f linking mechanisms between roles and co-ordinating structures. Although the elements of line control and co-ordination are still present, Handy extends his definition to cover the perceptual domains of an Organisation. This can lead to a more open definition. The concept of linkages increases our awareness of both interdependence and independence between factions; of how resource groupings can either contradict or complement other resource groupings. Linkaging is, therefore, necessary to cement the otherwise contradictory elements to prevent dispersal, or to reaffirm the complementary to prevent them becoming contradictory.

Linkaging, therefore, provides the Organisation with its completeness, establishes a boundary (perceptual or physical) which can be identified as being the domain of a particular Organisation. The idea of a boundary is an important aspect of structure since it enables us to determine how integrated the structure is with both its internal and external environments. For managers also, the boundary is useful since it enables them to identify their area of control. However, with the increasing implementation of information technology the issue has taken on greater significance. Boundaries can no longer be so easily identified. Modern technological systems directly link Organisations into other Organisations, thus merging in part their established boundaries. For example, a major retail outlet requires all its suppliers to link into their own stock control network. Those firms have thus become tied into their customer. In this situation it is difficult to determine where the supplier's boundary ends and the customer's begins.

Robbins proposes a traditional view of the relationship between a structure and its boundary. He determines the structure being defined by its boundary in the same way that a human skeleton defines a person. However, by equating boundary with human skeletons he has missed an important point. The body of a person is a finite concept in that it is spatially bounded within the physical domain.

On the other hand, an Organisational structure, although providing a framework, is as much perceptual as physical. That is, it exists because its members perceive it to do so. To someone who does not understand the concept of an Organisation, the distribution of its physical resources has no significance and thus they will not see an Organisation. This problem is not as remote as it may appear. It is common, for example, for small business Organisations to share resources such as office space, equipment and even staff, therefore possessing the same physical structure. There is no suggestion, however, that they are the same Organisation. Their differentiation is thus established by the perception of the actors (employees, suppliers, customers, etc.) and not the physical aspects. Organisations are not like people even though they comprise them. They are not necessarily spatially bounded; their buildings, for example, do not represent their outer edges. Indeed, some Organisations have no formality about them or physical structure, such as some political or religious institutions, but they are just as real as a small business enterprise. Organisations are not bounded by a temporal framework in the same way that people are. Individuals have their historicities which influence their behaviour, but they are creatures of the here and now. Their socialization has made them believe that all there exists is the physical domain which is governed by the present. The operational levels of Organisations are also bounded by time and the physical domain. However, the structure is not. It exists in the minds of its members and therefore is in the present, but it is also equally valid in the past because its existence is just as dependent upon past interaction.

For example, a firm's production process, which forms part of its structure, is physically bounded by time. It can produce only so many items within an hour or a day. This is its operational level—the dimension of doing. But the same process is time independent because how it can produce is and will be determined by decisions taken in the past, the present and the future. Structure, therefore, has to be more than a static framework, of functional and co-ordinative hierarchy, because Organisations themselves are fluid, perceptual entities and as such could not be supported by a rigid framework. Robbins' model of complexity, formalization and centralization does suggest a certain fluidity in structure, but only to the extent of differentiation between particular Organisations and not within the unit itself. In other words, Robbins recognizes an infinite variety of structures befitting the mode of operation, but once set they provide a rigid framework in the short term which can be changed only in the longer term.

Watson's ideas about an Organisation's structure provide a better match for a considerably more complex form of structure than so far developed. He does not see structure as a given framework but rather as a fluid, abstract entity which is the outcome of ever-changing employee interaction. Such a view can present no definitive solution to the quest for perfection, because the outcome is dependent upon so many variables.

With such a cost comes also a benefit. There is a freeing of structure from the constraints of 'conventional wisdom', by allowing greater flexibility in Organisation design and therefore enabling a more appropriate framework to be established for the analysis of the impact of other forces such as technology. Watson's words reflect a school of thought which considers the only reality of an Organisation is to be found within our minds. The structure we put on that Organisation is also within our minds. It will change as people's actions and perceptions change, and can never be completely controlled. Innovating forces like information technology, for example, can have the greatest impact upon an Organisation's structure through the minds of its participants. Structural change could occur through differing actions/perceptions of the employees, which may be beyond the control of management.

Structure must be seen to be more than a rigid framework. It may well be that some Organisational structures have become increasingly flexible in the past few years as a consequence of their information technology systems. However, it would also seem likely that structures have never been as rigid as many would suggest. Some are more stable than others within a given period. Others are more responsive to certain situations such as crisis or particular market conditions. They may all have areas of rigidity within them which can subsequently cause problems. Whatever their apparent characteristics they are manifest not because of the way we organize our physical resources but rather as a consequence of the way we relate to those resources. Structure is indeed in our minds. As such any boundaries which are obvious to us are there only because we perceive them to be. If we then introduce a technology with a strong perceptual impact, such as information technology, it is not surprising that a change occurs in the way we view our Organisation. Such changed perception may lead to a changed structure.

The idea that Organisations are perceptual maps has implications for their analysis and design. How we view them, and hence how they manifest themselves, will depend upon the particular Organisational model we use. Thus, in a self-determining way we align our particular Organisation's characteristics, as far as possible, to those found within the model which matches our own opinions. For example, if we believe along with our colleagues that the most realistic metaphor for an Organisation is a machine in terms of formality and controllability, then our behaviour would be governed by that belief. The Organisational structure would then be affected and to a limited extent changed by such perceptions if there is not a match. Problems can occur, of course, if these perceptions are not fully disseminated throughout the Organisation. The models of Organisation we have, therefore, are themselves affecting the environment which they are attempting to analyse. From this aspect alone it is worthwhile determining what these models are. However, we need to also consider them in terms of their suitability for the impact analysis of information technology.

The mechanistic view of Organisation is the first wave of theory, which comprises the metaphor of Organisation as a machine. Like a machine, its characteristics are determinable and controllable. The degree of its formality is not considered because all actions and behaviour within it are considered to be purposeful and co-ordinated. In other words, Organisations are rational processes. Therefore the underlying assumption is one of an Organisation as a formalization of a need to meet certain objectives. Such objectives are seen as rational in that they are based upon an obvious range of criteria suitable for the type of Organisation. Thus, a business Organisation's objectives could be to maximize profits, to grow or to dominate a particular market or industry.

The emphasis is on goal attainment and its management. The profound question presented by this metaphor is, why are some managements better at achieving their objectives than others? This metaphor evolved from the economic model in which Organisations are perceived to be unitary entities pursuing the same collective objective, controlled and driven by market forces. As such, Organisations do not have any analytical value other than as a unit of the market. From this, however, four softer perspectives developed, each a response to the demand of business managements at the time for better understanding.

The first is Taylor's scientific management. The second is administrative principles proposed by people such as Henri Fayol. The third is Weber's theory of bureaucracy, and lastly Simon's discussion on administrative behaviour. There are many books which cover these areas quite adequately. Apart from an introduction below, these will not be dealt with in detail. The emphasis will be placed on examining their approaches to technology.

The founding father of the scientific movement is claimed to be Frederick Taylor and subsequently developed by others such as Lillian Gilbreth. Their perspective is an extension of the economic model by recognizing that Organisations are not determined solely by market forces but can be moulded by management activity. They prescribed a methodology for action through a scientific analysis of tasks in a firm so that formal procedures could be established for optimum efficiency. The approach, in short, is prescriptive in that it presents patterns for management behaviour. Although lacking in fundamental academic support the traditions of scientific management are still reflected in many of our management training programmes.

The 'modern' view is more developed in its recognition of greater uncertainty but nevertheless still portrays a controllable environment. The elements of that environment are also controllable, Thus, the notion of technology is coloured by the certainty of its predictability. Technology in all its forms is a management tool. The original exponents of scientific management thought this, as do their followers. There is no relationship between a structure and its technology because neither is seen as a social process but rather as building blocks for management use. Thus, the impact of innovations such as information technology is not seen to affect the Organisational structure as such, but rather the relationship between management and workers: any impact is regarded as an input to be controlled.

Innovation, therefore, changes only the way in which management operates (although this might have an indirect effect upon the Organisation itself). Impact assessment of information technology is in terms of functional analysis or efficiency criteria (how good or bad its contribution is to management objectives), the assumption being that the technology will always fit into existing Organisational structures with the appropriate implementation strategy. The emphasis, therefore, is on performance measures and the ability of information technology to meet them. There is a range of literature which explores the scientific management viewpoint of information technology. Its presentation is prescriptive and consultative.

The remaining three perspectives within this metaphor are dealt with under the one heading. They are the models initiated by Fayol, Weber and Simon. Their collation is not because the themes they support are necessarily in agreement, although they do cover broadly the same principles, but rather because their implications for the analysis of technology are similar. The major difference between these and the previous approaches is that scientific management sought to establish the Organisation as a management phenomenon whereas Fayol, Weber and Simon sought to establish the Organisation as an administrative process.

The immediate implication of this is that, as an administrative process, the Organisation is less controllable and less predictable. It is no longer a tool but a set of administrative interactions. The objective of this group, therefore, was to identify such interactions and then to determine their appropriate control. Fayol was perhaps the first to recognize the importance of the administrative process in understanding Organisation. However, his work was not translated until the late 1940s and thus not widely known.

A sociologist, Max Weber, was also developing an ideological set of administrative principles. He identified bureaucracy as being the ideal form of Organisation. The formal and impersonal structural characteristics allowed for the most appropriate administrative processes and for an efficient achievement of objectives coupled with a certain humanity. Although advances were being made in other areas, it was not until the late 1950s, with the appearance of Herbert Simon's ideas, that advances in this area were made. He sought to portray a more open administrative process in which the actors are not machine-like in their rationality but more human in pursuing their own interests and in many ways ignorant of their total environment. He saw their rationality bounded by the complexity of the environment and thus their decision-making was not perfect or indeed predictable. Simon, along with others such as Cyert and March, perhaps provided the link between this metaphor and the second wave. They viewed people as being less predictable than did their forebears, but still nevertheless determined the Organisation itself to be of machine-like stature.

Perhaps by default, technology is, therefore, more integrated into the administrative mechanisms of the Organisation. There is concern about technological fit, thus the approach is directed away from one of expert handling to one of greater integration. This is particularly evident in this view's handling of information technology. The literature which reflects it concentrates upon the user end: it is here that a controllable interface exists between the administrative process and the machine. A classic example of this view is to be found in a book by Whisler, although it is becoming outdated. In the 1980s, with the increasing power of computer technology, many other books found their way onto the market. They all sought to merge the computer with the work processes of the Organisation rather than to allow it to dominate them, but stopped short of seeing it as a social process.

Peter Blau determined that it is irrational to view an Organisation as rational in the way that the machine metaphor does because it does not take account of the non-rational behaviour of people. Such a perspective summarizes the natural or organismic metaphor, in that Organisations are seen as complex, living entities which do not have machine-like qualities. They are no longer refilled, cohesive units which act in harmony and with total rationality towards a common set of goals. In the same way that a living organism is a collection of competing and interacting forces, some living and some not, so too the Organisation comprises individuals and social forces which compete with and contradict each other.

The consequence is that the Organisation cannot be so easily prescribed for management action, being at best a rather fuzzy area for common agreement. Technology, therefore, as an element of Organisation, cannot be so predictable in terms of a resource. Neither is there agreement on how to model the metaphor. With some justification it is claimed that Elton Mayo provided a foundation with his Hawthorne experiments. As social psychologists, their contribution was in recognizing the importance of behaviour in Organisational design. Their work initiated the behaviourist school for the explanation of firms.

The offshoots are many and are still very much in vogue today. Since Weber's work the sociologists have also been major contributors to this metaphor, particularly through the work of Selznick and Parsons. Rather than placing the emphasis upon the people element of an Organisation as the behaviourists did, these and other theorists who followed were interested in the complete entity and how it worked. In true functionalist tradition they identified various component parts and studied interaction between them. Selznick highlighted the relationship between these and the Organisation's employees, whilst Parsons developed a dynamic model in which people were an integrated part. The technological tradition which grew from this metaphorical approach is less prescriptive and more analytical than that of the machine metaphor.

The earlier ideas are typically represented by the works of Gouldner or Wedderburn and Crompton. Theirs is mainly an examination of production technology and its relationship with the workforce. The structure of an Organisation was a consequence of the way its workforce produced, in particular of the relationship existing between workforce and technology. However, a more formalized development of this took place in the late 1950s and early 1960s which was influenced in part by Elton Mayo and also by considerable empirical research. Although not labelled until much later, the approach became known as contingency theory. In contrast to the classical approach (whether the machine or natural metaphor) which sought to achieve a universally best structure for a business Organisation, the contingency theory proposes that there is no one best solution.

Different situations demand different Organisational structures, which are governed by forces of change known as contingencies. Thus, the prevailing contingent would shape the corresponding Organisational structure. For Woodward, after extensive research of over a hundred firms in Essex, the most important contingent is technology. If, for instance, a firm has a mass production technology, then its structure would develop in terms of the other contingents, such as size and culture, which would best suit that. So mass production technology, for example, by its very nature determines that firms generally be large with formal cultures. Quite apparently, therefore, technology is seen by Woodward as a determinant of Organisation. Although others, such as Pugh and the Aston Group, do not agree with her upon the extent of the power of technology to determine structure, there is a general consensus on the nature of technology itself. It is no longer a resource as such, but as much an element of Organisations as structure, people and their culture.

Information technology is perhaps not addressed as positively as it is in the previous metaphor. This is because there is no formal distinction made between general technology and information technology. Both are social processes and therefore to be treated as such. That is not to say there are not writers on the subject. Miles *et al.,* Anderson and Mumford and Zuboff are typical of the works produced. Information technology is analysed in terms of its ability to integrate into society or business. In general, the conclusions seem to be doom-laden, predicting dire consequences if we do not get it right.

This metaphor describes the Organisation as a complex conglomerate of interaction which does not necessarily produce a clearly identifiable form. An Organisation exists because people are told it does by management teams, corporate identity, and so on; although, in reality, apart from resource allocation, members/ employees act very much for themselves as individuals or within groups, occasionally forming alliances to get things done. It is the process of doing (production, administration, etc.) which is the major input to Organisation structure, so that the Organisation is a series of different or interlocking processes. Its structure is shaped by those processes because it is the arena in which they are actioned. As with the other two waves there are disagreements, in particular over the identity of the process. Some put forward the decision process as a dynamic which determines the Organisational structure. Others view the Organisation as a political arena in which structural adjustments are made through political mechanisms such as ownership of power. Yet others, such as Johnson *et al.*, regard these processes in terms of their relationships with one another and how open they are to external influence. Contingency theorists Lawrence and Lorsch, on the other hand, determined a particular relationship between the Organisation and its environment as being the important process, whilst Weick highlighted the processes between the individual and their social formation.

In general, Organisations are no longer seen as hierarchical and solid (albeit at times fuzzy) frameworks. Structure is considered not to be as important as the processes themselves because it is a transient thing, created and remoulded by the whim of changing interactions. Watson described this Organisation as being formed in the minds of the employees through their perception of its interactions. The process or open systems metaphor, therefore, shifts the emphasis of analysis from the design of the Organisation to the functioning of its elements. It allows these elements (e.g. technology, politics, decisions) a far greater impact than the previous two metaphors. For technology in particular the approach is significant. In the machine metaphor, technology is not part of the Organisation, whilst in the organismic metaphor technology is part of an Organisation's social process and a determinant of structure. In the process metaphor, technology can be a process in its own right, determining the perceptions of individuals and affecting their behaviour. Its ability to affect the characteristics of an Organisation are thus considerably increased because the mechanisms involved (i.e. employee perception) form the essence of an Organisation. These ideas have been most prevalent in the analysis of information technology. The relationship between the behaviour of people and the technology they use is portrayed by the socio-technical systems theory. This applies a systems methodology to the analysis of information technology and how it affects the way we organize. Its roots can be traced back to Mayo and his Hawthorne experiments in terms of the paradigm's behavioural aspirations. It was Mayo who first formally stated the link between our behaviour and Organisational design. But it was Trist and Bamforth who galvanized those ideas into understanding the impact of technological innovation.

With the growth of computer technology as the dominant innovative technology it was, therefore, not surprising that Trist and Bamforth's methodology was quickly taken up by others to analyse its impact. Burns and Stalker produced an impressive model based upon empirical research describing a close behavioural relationship between our technology and the way we organized. If the structure of the firm did not suit the technology employed then pathological responses evolved on the part of management.

Just as firms are not merely a collection of resources, human or otherwise, nor are they merely a collection of processes. As with all social entities, they are a combination of physical and perceptual: but it is how the relationship between the two is understood which is important. Quite obviously many Organisations do have buildings which figure strongly in the image they project but also quite obviously the influence of the Organisation does not end at a brick wall. They do comprise physical beings constrained by their physical environment but beyond such environments they have resources which can be both physical (machinery, etc.) and perceptual (knowledge). Any complete model of Organisation must accommodate both domains. Organisations, however, must be more than the summation of individuals, resources and perceptions within them. Unfortunately the metaphors discussed describe no more than this. Yet Organisations tend to develop some sense of being in their own right. This is not in terms of a conscious, spatial positioning, as any individual would have, but is rather a consequence of history.

Continuity of an Organisation, for example, cannot be solely explained as the perception of individuals or the particular allocation of resourcing. There is a logic within it which outlives any temporary input an individual may care to make. It is indeed a process, but one which is at the same time both independent and dependent. For example, previous decisions made by management can constrain and develop the Organisation's structure in future years.

Both the physical and perceptual aspects of the decision as real as each other. One could be seen in the production line whilst the other, although not seen, is ingrained within the management culture. Together they form ail inheritance passed onto subsequent management which constrains their action. It is in this sense that an Organisation can be said to be existing independently. Decisions and actions are taken all the time which can then exist beyond their initiators and add to a bank of knowledge within the firm. To a certain extent we are referring to the Organisational culture, but culture's form relates only to the rules for action and does not express the logic of the actions themselves, as does structure. Structure can thus be determined by neither domain alone. More probably, it arises as a consequence of a relationship between the two domains continually interacting with one another through a historical process which in turn feeds the logic of the Organisation. In the same vein, information technology (or technology in general) cannot be treated as either a physical or perceptual phenomenon.

The way in which each of the three metaphors provides analytical tools for the assessment of its impact restricts our being able to see the whole framework. Information technology does have a strong physical impact: it can, for example, turn an inefficient firm into an efficient one. The criteria used to assess such a change are based in the physical domain in that there can be more information output in terms of management reports or invoices billed, and so on. It can also change user behaviour, as we see in socio-technical systems, so that, employee perceptions of their tasks or indeed their firm change. In many models the two domains sit either separately or uncomfortably side by side.

However, it is not so much the consideration of the individual domains that is important (although obviously for line managers it cannot be ignored), it is the relationship between them which must be analysed and the subsequent effects such interaction has upon Organisation design.

Information is the life-blood of a community information service and the information file is at its heart. Unless the heart is sound and continually pumping a supply of regularly renewed and fresh information into the system, it will not function at its best. Therefore, it is important to give extra care and attention to planning the resources needed to set up a sound information base and a workable system for keeping it up to date.

Some basic things you will need to consider are as follows:

— How is the information to be collected?

— What method is to be used for processing and storing information?

— How is the information to be retrieved?

— What size is the file likely to be?

— What areas, geographical and subject, is the file to cover?

In addition, you will need to consider how the information is going to be disseminated, if it is not just for internal use; but that is the subject of the next chapter. The kind of system you choose and the degree of its sophistication will depend on the nature of your information service, the size and complexity of the information you need to store, the staff, and the financial resources available. When designing a system, make sure it is readily understandable to all those using it-volunteers and public included-and not just to professionals.

In identifying the need for your community information service, you should have reached a decision already on the community to be served. This may be either a geographical community or a community of interest or both. Either way, you will still need to make a decision about the extent of your information base. For example, a neighbourhood information service must decide what information to collect on the wider area-town, county, region, nation-outside its local community. An information service aimed at a fairly wide area may need to limit its interests to a particular sector of the community or to a particular range of subjects, e.g. the low paid, those receiving income support, or those with debt problems. Even an information service in support of a local campaign may benefit from collecting information on similar campaigns or problems country-wide.

The information base of your service is most likely to include the following types of information:

Soft Information : Details of clubs, societies, Organisations and services; individuals; events, etc. Usually this information will not be available in a published form, or at least not in sufficient detail, and it will be necessary to make a conscious effort to collect it. This information may comprise the major part of the resources file.

Hard Information : Factual information on a specific subject e.g. benefit rates for single-parent families, how to get legal aid, how to change your name. This information will be available in a variety of Banns, some ephemeral such as leaflets, pamphlets, booklets, broadsheets, posters, periodical articles, etc. Such items are usually kept in a vertical file, in storage boxes or similar receptacles and accessed via some form of index or classification scheme. Other hard information may be in the form of books, multi-volumed reference works, law books, or even audiovisual forms. If there are many items of this type, they will need to be classified and shelved.

Supplementary Information : Information already produced in a particular format-directories, handbooks, diaries, annual reports, constitutions, newsletters-of Organisations appearing in your information file.

'Soft' Information

It is highly unlikely and undesirable that an information service should need to 'go it alone' in the collection of information. Such is the volume, complexity and variety of sources of information in present-day society that, unless your service has very narrow terms of reference, it will be virtually impossible for it to collect and keep up to date all the information that is required.

Therefore, it is important that you first of all identify the information providers, support services and 'gatekeepers' in your community and establish effective contacts with them. These links may already have been forged in the process of conducting a community profile. They now need to be fostered and strengthened, so that there can be a mutual exchange of information. These contacts will also be able to provide you with useful feedback from the community as to the success or otherwise of your service. The network of contacts can be maintained on a fairly casual basis as the need arises, or you might want to formalize the arrangement. Some ways of doing this include irregular 'get togethers', informal luncheon clubs, regular meetings with agendas and minutes, or the circulation of a newsletter or bulletin. Other activities that could develop out of such meetings are joint collection of information, shared publicity, compilation and publication of directories, information handbooks and leaflets, training, and general discussion of common problems. Collecting information is a time-consuming process and there is no one method of going about it. You will probably have to use a combination of several techniques to build up a satisfactory information base. One thing definitely to be avoided is duplicating work that has already been done. So first of all identify the following:

Existing Information Files : Contact all the other community information services, council departments and Organisations who are likely to maintain information files and ask if they would be willing to share this information. Try to offer something in return, either an exchange of information or some other help you can provide.

Local Directories : There are several types of directories that may be available in your area and which are useful sources of soft information: (a) local government authorities often produce directories or town guides of their area which contain a certain amount of local information or they may produce a guide to council services; (b) telephone directories, especially Yellow pages which have an alphabetical subject arrangement; (c) area directories, such as those produced by Thompson's Newspapers, which are similar to Yellow pages but also contain a section of community information-your local newspaper may produce a directory of local services, sometimes in conjunction with local information groups; (d) citizen's guides may also be produced by the local newspaper as a supplement to an existing newspaper; (e) CVSs or RCCs sometimes produce directories of voluntary Organisations in their area or you may find these listed in your local CVS/RCC annual report; (f) directories covering a special subject, such as accommodation, halls for hire, etc.; (g) directories aimed at a particular interest group or groups e.g. people with disabilities or senior citizens.

National directories are useful not only for the wider network of services but also for identifying local offices of a national Organisation.

Other methods to use in building up your information base and maintaining its currency include:

Looking and Listening : A lot of information can be gathered by simply walking around your community, looking at notice-boards, picking up leaflets, or attending open meetings, fairs, fetes and other community events. This method of collecting information is unpredictable and requires more than a 9-to-5, five-day week.

Contact with Individuals : People are a major source of information in any community and there are always those to whom others naturally go for information. Try to identify such people and enlist their help, possibly by offering something in return-bartering is a time-honoured system! Direct contact with individuals in other information services and Organisations is often a better way of eliciting information than impersonal methods and also paves the way for further cooperation. Pay regular visits to such centres.

Scanning newspapers, magazines, newsletters, etc., can turn up details of new Organisations; changes of personnel, premises or hours of opening; new services introduced; and may highlight problem areas where information may be needed.

Other documents, including council minutes and agendas,. planning regulations, annual reports (ask to be put on mailing lists for these), leaflets and manifestos.

Media publicity Local press, radio and cable television stations may be prepared without charge to put out a call for Organisations to contact your service. If not, then consider inserting an advert or, where there is, a local directory produced, have a tear-out slip included for Organisations to fill in and return to you. As a result of these various methods, an amount of raw material will have been obtained which may be of use to your information service. How accurate, up to date and complete the data is will depend very much on the reliability of the source. In most cases, unless you have every confidence in the source, the information will have to be checked before it is entered in a more permanent form in your resource file. So, at this stage, simply record it onto say a scrap 5in x 3in card and put it into a temporary file.

The information you have obtained will be of several different kinds but the most common will probably be that relating to Organisations, clubs and societies. This is the most difficult type of information to collect since it is ever changing and therefore unrelenting effort will be required to achieve even reasonable completeness or accuracy-100% will be impossible. However, with a good system for collecting and updating the information, you should be able to build up and maintain an acceptable file.

A lot of staff time will be needed to carry out this work, so first of all investigate whether there are other local information services that need this type of information and would be willing to help in its collection. It may be possible to collect the information through an umbrella group, where the work can be framed out so that it is not too great a burden on any one Organisation. Alternatively, a joint approach can be made on behalf of a number of Organisations.

Ideally, the most effective way to collect information of this kind is to pay a personal visit to each Organisation or service, but rarely will that be possible without extensive staff resources or a very small community. The cheapest and quickest way to collect this information is by telephoning. Prepare a standard list of questions to ask so that entries in your information file follow the same format.

Telephoning is only practicable if you have a reasonably small number of Organisations to contact, say up to one hundred. If visits and telephoning are ruled out, then the information can be collected initially by postal questionnaire, with a request for up-to-date information sent at least once a year and also when it is known from other sources that changes have taken place. A covering letter should be sent with the questionnaire or update request, explaining "Why the information is needed and asking for cooperation. If the information is to be passed on to other Organisations or commercial bodies, either free or for payment, this should be drawn to the attention of the recipient of the questionnaire, so that they have an opportunity to decline to give the information or insist that it is not so disseminated. If the information is to be stored in a computer, then you will need to meet the requirements of the Data Protection Act.

If it can be afforded, include with your questionnaire some means of returning it free of charge, as this will significantly improve the response rate. Separate forms may be required to collect different kinds of information. The following is a suggested list of headings which you might need to include on forms for collecting information from two of the most common types of Organisations.

Clubs and Societies

— Name: the name by which the club is best known, plus the full name if different. Indicate relationship to larger body, i.e. branch, regiment, lodge, etc.

— Secretary's name, address and telephone number or those of a similar person if the Organisation has no secretary.

— Place, day and time of meetings.

— Purpose of Organisation if not self-evident from the name.

— Eligibility: any restrictions by age, sex, ethnic group, occupation, status (single, divorced, widowed) etc.

— Subscription: any charge to become a member or to attend meetings.

— Annual general meeting: the date of an Organisation's AGM can be a useful indication of when to send out update forms as this is when officers or policies are likely to change.

— Other officers: names, addresses, telephone numbers of treasurer, president, chairman, publicity officer, membership secretary, etc.

— History of the Organisation including special events or persons associated with it.

— Publications: newsletter, diary, commemorative brochures, annual report, etc.

— Date the information was obtained and/or last updated or checked.

Agencies and Organisations providing a service

- Name: popular name and full name, e.g. CHAT (Come Here and Talk), SHAC (Shelter Housing Action Centre), plus relationship to parent body where necessary.
- Address: street address and postal address, Post Office, box number if used.
- Telephone and fax number, including-service number, administration number, after-hours or hotline numbers.
- Contact person: personal name, title and address, if different from above.
- Hours of opening: days and times; note if seasonal, e.g. holiday period, term time.
- Services provided: advice, counselling, practical help, etc.; types of enquiry the service would like to have referred to them.
- Eligibility: age, income, sex, residency, status.
- Application procedures: walk-in, appointment or waiting list; what papers or documents need to be brought.
- Cost: free, fees, means-tested, donations; any facilities for payments to be spread over a period; help available from local or central government, charities, etc.
- Geographical area served: neighbourhood, city, county, region, adhoc area; no geographical restrictions.
- Branch offices: extension bureaux, mobiles, surgeries, etc.; include hours of opening, routes and times of stops.
- Director, administrator or executive director of the service; name and telephone or extension.
- Volunteers: does the service use volunteers and for what purposes? Method of recruitment.
- Publications: directories, handbooks, leaflets, annual report, etc.
- Funding: local government grant-aided, donations, etc.
- Special facilities: foreign languages spoken, access and facilities for people with disabilities, photocopying or fax service, escort, advocacy, etc.

— Transportation: how to get to the service, e.g. bus route numbers, underground line and station, etc.

— Date information was obtained and/or last updated or checked.

These two lists represent most of the facts that a community information service might need to know about an Organisation or service. In practice, depending on the scope of your service, it may not be necessary to include all the fields in the questionnaire. It is a good idea to get the person filling in the questionnaire-to-sign it, thereby giving the information service some-protection against claims of giving out wrong information—a not uncommon occurrence, especially when the information is committed to print.

There are other types of 'soft' information that your service might need to collect, for example halls for hire, places of local worship, accommodation, 'What's-on' events, local industry. The procedure is much the same:

— Decide what information you need to know.

— Devise a standard format or list of questions to ask.

— Identify possible sources of information.

— Decide which method or methods to use to collect the information: telephone, personal visit, postal questionnaire, press advert, etc.

How to Store 'soft' Information?

There are various methods that can be used for storing information:

> A list is easy and quick to consult, can be photocopied for clients to take away and can be faxed, but has very little flexibility for inserting and updating information.

A strip index provides flexibility, can easily be photocopied, and is available in various forms: large binders holding many pages, smaller folders containing just a few pages, address books, wall-hung panels, rotunda units, etc. Strips are available in several colours, which allows for a simple categorization, and various widths. Even so, they are limited as to the amount of information that can be contained on them. It is also not quite as easy to insert new strips as the manufacturers claim.

Cards are still one of the most commonly used systems for storing information. They are infinitely flexible, easy to insert and update, can be sorted into any preferred order, and require very little technical know-how.

The most popular sizes are 5in x 3in, used mainly for indexes or temporary information waiting to be checked, 6in x 4in, and 8in x 5in, which are large enough to contain sufficient information about most Organisations or services and to be preprinted with a standard grid for recording the information.

There are more superior types of card files available, such as the Rondofile or Rotadex systems which use custom-designed stationery and therefore tend to be more expensive. With systems that use standard cards, you can-if you are hard-up or want to save trees-use the reverse of scrap cards. Card files have a number of disadvantages: they are not so easy to carry around, they arc not easily reproducible if someone wants a copy of a particular section, multiple access (e.g. by name, subject, area, service, etc.) requires duplication of cards, and the updating process can be tedious.

You may still find around edge-punched cards which offer a primitive type of multi-access to the information on the card-through the strategic use of knitting needles or rods. Personally speaking, I would save up and get a computer.

Loose-leaf binders with one sheet for each entry, sometimes called 'sheaf' binders, have a similar flexibility to cards. They are slightly slower to add to and amend but are more portable. They are suited best for alphabetical arrangements as they are difficult to guide.

Microcomputers now have the capacity to handle immense information files that can be accessed by any number of predetermined variables or even free-text searching by keyword, depending on the software used. With a printer attached, all the information or sections of it can be printed out on demand or to provide a master for printing by conventional methods. Personal computers now begin at prices that bring them within the range of most community information services. However, there is danger in automatically seeing the computer as the best solution for maintaining your information file, as this may not always be the case. A lot depends on the size of your file and its complexity, what you want to do with the file, and to what other uses you want to put the computer. The importance of the computer in, information and advice work is such that it merits a chapter to itself, and you will find these and other aspects.

Filing System

Whichever method is chosen for physically storing the information, except for that by microcomputer, it will be necessary to decide the best way of arranging entries so that the information can be retrieved swiftly and accurately. In order to ensure that the total resources of your information service are used to the full when answering an enquiry, it will help if the system used to organize the information file can be integrated with that for the vertical file and the book-stock. This point needs to be borne in mind now, although it will be dealt with more fully later.

The bulk of the information file is likely to comprise 'soft' information -which you have collected about Organisations, clubs, societies and services and, to a lesser extent, about individuals who are a valuable source of information or advice, plus items of 'hard' information not available or conveniently available in printed form. There are several ways in which you might want to retrieve this information-by the names of the Organisations, by subject (i.e. area of interest), by clientele, by the type of service (e.g. counselling), or by place. In practice, the 'clientele' and 'type of service' approaches are usually catered for through the subject file rather than, as separate files.

Organisations file: The master file for the whole system will usually be an alphabetically arranged sequence of entries by name of Organisation. It is generally recommended that the full, official name of the Organisation is used, with references from other forms of the name. In practice, it does not really matter as long as there are references from the alternatives to whichever form is chosen.

There is a good argument for putting the main entry for an Organisation under the form of name by which most people refer to it, even if this differs from or is an abbreviation of the official name. This is especially so where the file is to be used by the public.

In addition to details of Organisations, each entry in the master file may also contain certain 'housekeeping' details relating to the maintenance of all the information files, plus references to appropriate headings in the subject file, where relevant information can be found, and a classification number.

Subject file: Most enquiries received by a community information service are likely to be about the need for a service or activity or for help with solving a problem, rather than for information on a specific named Organisation. So the information you have collected about Organisations, services and individuals will also need to be accessible by the services and activities they provide. There are two ways this can be achieved, by either using a subject index or having a subject file of Organisations. In both, you will need to choose or adopt a set of subject headings which will adequately describe the information on file or elsewhere in the system and the interests of your clientele.

If you are compiling your own list of subject headings, choose terms that are in common use by your clientele, especially if they will be consulting the files directly, rather than the 'official' term, e.g. OUT OF WORK or ON THE DOLE instead of REDUNDANT. Always refer from alternatives not used to the chosen term.

A subject index is rather like the index to a book. It is an alphabetically arranged file of subject heading cards on which reference is made to where information on that subject can be found. The cards themselves do not contain information. The subject index can contain references to Organisations, individuals and other supplementary material such as pamphlets, periodical articles, audiovisual material, books, etc.

A subject file consists of an alphabetically arranged set of subject heading cards behind which are filed copies of the Organisation cards appropriate to that heading and possibly cards containing items of 'hard' information. An alternative is to arrange cards according to a classification system either devised by yourself or adopted from another service, such as the NACAB classification scheme.

Place file: Where an information service covers a number of distinct towns, villages or neighbourhoods, each having a similar range of Organisations, it may be helpful to have a file that can be accessed by place. There are a number of options. You could sort the Organisations file initially by place, especially if it contains few Organisations whose responsibilities extend to the whole area covered by your service. Alternatively, if most of the Organisations are prefixed with the name of the place (e.g. EXVILLE ATHLETIC CLUB, EXVILLE COUNCIL FOR THE DISABLED), the alphabetically arranged master file will automatically bring together those from the same location, provided inverted headings have not been used.

Some arrangements will have to be made for Organisations which do not conform to the pattern, either because the place-name does not feature at the beginning or because it is not contained in the name of the Organisation at all. In these cases, an additional card can be made out with either an inverted heading (e.g. EXVILLE, ROTARY CLUB OF) or the place-name can be prefixed.

The third option is to have a separate file of Organisation cards arranged initially by place and then alphabetically by name of Organisation or by subject.

Filing Alphabetically

Filing alphabetically is not quite as simple as ABC, as any librarian will tell you. There are two recognized methods, known as 'word by word' and 'letter by letter'. In word by word, entries are initially sorted by the first word in the heading, then headings that begin with the same word are sorted by the second word, and so on. Another way to describe this method, which may be more helpful, is to treat spaces between words in a heading as an imaginary letter coming before 'a' in the alphabet, then sort letter by letter.

In letter by letter, you simply ignore any spaces in the heading and sort one letter at a time from left to right. Here is how a small group of headings would look sorted by the two methods:

Word by word	*Letter by letter*
DO SOMETHING! BOYS CLUB	'DOG AND BONE' DARTS TEAM
'DOG AND BONE' DARTS TEAM	DOGSBURY RESIDENTS'
DOG SNIFFERS ANONYMOUS	ASSOCIATION
DOGS HOMES	DOGS HOMES
DOGSBURY RESIDENTS'	DOG SNIFFERS ANONYMOUS
ASSOCIATION	DO SOMETHING! BOYS CLUB

There are several other niceties to do with filing alphabetically but we only need mention here that hyphens are treated as spaces in word-by-word sorting and numerals are spelt out as said, so that 1900 (the year) is considered for sorting as Nineteen Hundred and 1,900 as One Thousand, Nine Hundred.

File 'housekeeping'

In addition to the information needed to answer enquiries, there are other items of information to do with the maintenance of the file which may usefully be included on each entry, such as the following:

- the date the information was obtained, last updated or last checked, which will indicate not only the degree of reliability to be placed on it but also when to update;
- the date a questionnaire or update letter was sent - a check for chasing up non-returned forms;
- additional contacts or other information which does not fit into the main part of the entry;
- subject headings used in the subject file;
- place headings used in the place file, if not obvious from the name of the Organisation;
- feedback-comments from users of the service;
- 'tracings', i.e. a list of other cards that refer to they can be traced and amended or withdrawn when necessary.

The amount of this 'housekeeping' information you need to include will depend on how sophisticated you need your file to be. The bigger the information service and the larger the file, then the more likely it is that you will need to introduce a systematic procedure for processing information. In such a case it is usual for the housekeeping information to go on the reverse of each entry, using a standard grid like the one illustrated here. It is arguable that if your information file requires this degree of sophistication, you ought seriously to consider keeping it on computer.

For a small community information service, it may be quite adequate just to note the date when the information was collected, checked or updated.

Updating

By their very nature the entries in your database will be changing continually. Hours of opening, meeting places, officers, membership fees, subscriptions, charges, etc., are all susceptible to frequent change. Therefore, it is important to have a system for regularly updating each entry in the database. There are several ways of achieving this but, whichever method you adopt, it must be regular and ongoing.

Interim Updating

All the entries for Organisations should be checked at least once a year to ensure they are still correct. In between times, however, new information will be brought to your attention by various means, including word of mouth, newspaper reports, Organisation newsletters, company reports and by direct contact with the Organisation itself. If the source of information is reliable, it can be substituted immediately for the out-of-date information in the database but, if not, it should be noted and a further check made to verify its accuracy. A simple way to add new information to an entry in a card file is to write it onto self-adhesive labels or slips (obtainable at most stationers) which can be stuck over the original information. Even though an entry has been updated in between times, it should still be checked formally once a year.

Annual Updating

Once a year is probably a reasonable time-span for updating

your database but a shorter interval may be necessary if the information content changes frequently. You will need to decide how the annual update is to be carried out. Some Organisations like to update the entire file at the same time, so that they can say the file was as accurate as possible at a particular date. However, this does create a tremendous amount of extra work for a period of several weeks and you may feel it necessary to get extra paid, work-experience or volunteer help. Another disadvantage of this method is that it captures a picture of Organisations at a set moment in time. Some Organisations may be just about to make changes, and your records for these would be out of date for almost a year.

Alternatively, you may decide to update on a continuous basis by using either the date the record was added to the database or the Organisation's annual general meeting (AGM) date as a trigger. This is easy to do if your database is kept on a computer, since a date field can be used to produce a subset of records and, by linking the database with a word processing package, a personalized standard letter can be printed out for sending to each Organisation. It is less easy with a card or any other kind of file. You can get little coloured metal tags to clip on to the top edge of cards, a different colour for each month, or you could use an appropriate symbol on the heading of the card, such as a coloured dot, a letter or number. Tags can make the file look a bit messy and are easily knocked off if it is in constant use; symbols require the whole file to be checked through.

It is better to update records shortly before or after each Organisation's AGM, since most Organisations, if they are going to change their officers or constitution, generally do it once a year at the AGM. This is so because many Organisations do not know their AGM date a year in advance, it is enough just to indicate the month in which the AGM is usually held. For those Organisations and services which do not have an AGM, you will need to use the date the information was added as the trigger.

When writing to Organisations to update their information, it is better to send them a copy of their record with a request to indicate any changes, rather than sending a blank questionnaire.

This saves the secretary unnecessary time in repeating information that has not altered.

An alternative to writing to each Organisation is to phone, but this is time-consuming and costly, and only feasible if the number of Organisations to contact is fairly small. Avoid sending out updates at times when people are likely to be away, such as during the summer. There are certain times when it is more appropriate to update other kinds of information, e.g. social security benefit rates (which usually change in April and September), adult education classes or school, college and university courses which change term-wise.

When an updated entry is returned it should be checked to see if the subject or place headings still apply. Minor changes can be recorded on the master card and any other cards in subject or place files; major changes may require a new set of cards to be produced. For those with computerized databases the process is simpler as just the one record has to be updated. Don't forget to change the date the information was last checked or updated.

'Hard' Information

As well as the database, most information services will need a certain amount of 'hard' information to answer enquiries. Short, unrecorded or inadequately recorded items of 'hard' information, as we have already seen, can be incorporated into the database. However, the majority of hard information will usually be found in one or more of the vast range of print forms, starting from locally produced free broadsheets to extremely expensive multi-volumed loose-leaf reference works.

Within the scope of this book, it is not possible to go into detail about the sources of this material, since they will vary considerably according to the type and subject range of the service you are operating. Community information changes rapidly so any printed sources should be treated with care. However, you might find useful a chapter on the sources of community information that I contributed to Printed reference material and related sources of information, 3rd edn, Library Association Publishing, 1990, which concentrated on Organisations and on those items which are regularly updated.

The following framework for collecting community information was originally devised by Grainne Morby, who at the time was working for the Community information Project, with some additions of my own:

Distinguish between Subject Areas

In other words, identify the main topics into which the subject scope of your information service naturally divides. Throughout this framework I will take as an example an information service for which the main area of interest is housing. It is sometimes useful to apply a consistent criterion when dividing up a subject, although obviously this would not be so easy for an information service whose scope covers as broad an area as, say, 'community information'.

However, taking housing as our example, you could decide to divide it by type of accommodation, e.g. owner-occupied, private-rented, council-rented, New Town, Housing Association, institutional accommodation, tied accommodation, mobile homes, etc. In most cases you would probably need an additional category for subjects that cut across all or more than one category. In the case of housing, this might be 'squatting' or 'homelessness'.

Since the material you want to collect will usually be written to meet a particular need or needs, it is advisable to collect information around those needs rather than for fitting into a theoretical framework. The kind of broad client groups that might be identified in the field of housing are landlords, tenants, owner-occupiers, squatters, transients, elderly people, people with disabilities, the homeless.

Then, one could identify client groups who share a common problem or need associated with their particular type of accommodation, such as eviction, dampness, house repair, renovation, harassment, mortgages, rent arrears, planning permission, redevelopment, etc. Once these subject areas and client needs have been identified, it should give you clearer guidelines when you come to select material from the various sources identified in the next part of the framework.

Print Sources

1. Official

(a) National

— *pre-legislation:* political party manifestos and policy documents, speeches by Ministers, the Queen's Speech at opening of Parliament, White Papers, Green Papers.

— *Legislation:* Bills, Hansard reports of debates in both Houses of Parliament, Acts, Statutory Instruments.

— *Guidance to local statutory bodies:* circulars and letters from Ministers, guidance notes, reports of Inspectors.

— *Reference books:* collections of legislation, e.g. Statutes in force, Legal aid handbook.

— *Periodicals:* from government departments and agencies, e.g. Department for Employment gazette.

— *Guidance to the public:* leaflets, posters, videos and other A/V material.

— *Ombudsmen.*

(b) Regional

— Health authorities, British Rail.

— Privatized utilities: gas, water, electricity, telephone.

— Consumer watchdog bodies: Post Office Users' National Council (POUNC), Office of Gas Supply (OFGAS), Office of Electricity Regulation (OFFER), Office of Telecommunications (OfTel), Office Of Water Services (OFWAT).

(c) Local

— *Local authority policies and decisions:* agendas, minutes, standing orders, bylaws and regulations.

— *Guidance to the public:* handbooks, leaflets, etc. from local authorities, area and district health authorities, Community Health Councils, local offices of government agencies.

2. Non-official

(a) National

— Reference books and handbooks from commercial publishers.

— Voluntary Organisations.

— Pressure groups, self-help groups.

— 'Umbrella' Organisations, e.g. National Council for Voluntary Organisations, Federation of Independent Advice Centres.

— Professional bodies, e.g. The Law Society.

— Trade associations, e.g. National Association of Retail Furnishers.

— Educational bodies, e.g. National Extension College, Open University.

— Trade unions.

— The media.

— Practitioners in the field who publish.

(b) Local

— Claimants' unions.

— Law centres, other specialist advice centres.

— Neighbourhood and generalist advice centres, resource centres.

— Local 'umbrella' groups.

— Pressure groups, campaigning groups, action centres. Voluntary Organisations..

— Local media: newspapers, community newspapers, radio, cable television.

(c) New technology

— Video-text systems: Prestel, teletext, private viewdata.

— Online computer databases, e.g. Volnet

— CD-ROM, videodiscs, etc.

This list is not intended to be exhaustive but will give you some idea of the range of sources in which to look for information. Howard Matthews, in his book *Community Information* has drawn up a set of criteria for selecting community information materials. It is aimed particularly at library community information services but may be generally helpful for anyone setting up such a service.

1. Selection should be done by those who know the community best.

2. Material should relate to specific, local, identified needs.
3. All material should be current.
4. All material should be written at a level appropriate to its intended use.
5. Material should be concerned with the practicalities of problem solving.
6. All new material should either fill a gap, offer a new viewpoint, or promise something better.
7. Material should take into account the level of use the client will make of it.

Obtaining Publications and Other Material

Once the material you require has been identified, you will need to obtain it. Some material will be priced, in which case- you will need to order it, and some will be free.

Priced Publications

The procedure for obtaining priced publications, particularly in the field of community information, is not as simple as you might suppose. Since a lot of the material may well be fairly cheap and the small or community publishers, booksellers and library suppliers are reluctant to obtain it as the profit margin is likely to be too low for the amount of effort involved. The alternative is to order direct but this also has its difficulties as many small publishers now insist on money with order, and this can cause problems for some Organisations through the need to raise a cheque or limitations on the amount that can be spent from petty cash.

A few national voluntary Organisations, e.g. Age Concern England, operate a standing-order system for their publications-this is one solution, although you may need to accept blanket coverage of the Organisation's output. In the larger cities, you may find a community or alternative bookseller who is prepared to supply this material to order. A directory of alternative bookshops is published annually by the magazine *Radical Bookseller.* Whatever the method of ordering, it is important to keep a record of what has been placed on order and from whom to avoid duplication of titles and as a check on supply. For each title make out an order or slip. This can be either a scrap 5in x 3in card or one specially printed with a standard grid. The following indicates the kinds of information that need to be recorded:

— title of publication-more important than author for this kind of material, since authorship is often unclear;

— author-might be an individual or an Organisation;

— price, date of publication and, if a periodical, frequency;

— supplier-this may be a bookseller, library supplier or the address of the producing body;

— date of order;

— source of information about the item;

— location, if you are ordering for more than one centre.

You may find it helpful to use the order cards later as the basis of a catalogue of the publications in your information centre; in which case., leave space at the top of the card for either a subject heading, classification number or filing code. After an order has been placed with a supplier, the order cards are filed, preferably by title, in one alphabetical sequence known as the 'order file'. When a publication is received, the order card is removed from the file and accompanies the publication·to the next stage if it is to be used later as the catalogue card. If not, you may find it useful to file the order card in a 'publications received' file, until such time as the publication is permanently recorded in the system, after which the card can be thrown away.

Periodicals

Publications which arrive at regular intervals—weekly, fortnightly, monthly, quarterly—will not require an order card but you will need to keep a record of each title taken. This should include the following items of information:

— title of periodical;

— frequency;

— supplier;

— when subscription is due for payment;

— a grid to record receipt of each issue;

— instructions for disposal of back copies.

For those using computers, there are software packages available for periodicals managèment but these are aimed at Organisations who take an extensive range of periodicals and such packages are not cheap. If you have a database management package on your computer, you would do better to devise your own periodicals database.

Free Material

This can vary from quite substantial loose-leaf binders plus updates to leaflets, posters and bookmarks and may be required in bulk for clients to take. Since this is likely to be a frequent type of request, it may be quicker and simpler to duplicate a standard letter to send to Organisations, with space left to fill in address, title of item, format (leaflet, booklet, poster, etc.) and number of copies required. It is advisable to keep a record of what is requested, if only as a check on whether it has been received or not.

A lot of the sweat has been taken out of identifying free materials, and addresses from where they can be obtained, through the setting-up of Camden Libraries' Free Leaflets Information Service (FLIS). For an annual fee (E120 in 1992) subscribers receive a copy of the Frills directory of free information leaflet suppliers, a monthly batch of new and updated leaflets and amendments to the Frills directory, and details of a model system for organizing leaflets. Details of this service can be obtained from Community Information Services, Camden Leisure Services Department, St. Pancras Library, 100 Euston Road, London NWI 2AJ. A similar, but not so extensive, service is provided by the NACAB as part of its Information Service, but you would need to have approval to subscribe to the full pack.

Organizing Hard Information

We have already seen that hard information can be found in a great variety of forms. For the benefit of organizing it, the following categories can be identified:

Material in book form for use by clientele or information workers will be best arranged on shelves in the broad subject groups identified when acquiring the material or according to a classification scheme.

Ephemeral material for use by information workers is best stored in a vertical file using the same subject headings as those in the subject sequence of the information file, though probably with more subdivisions, or using a classification scheme. Alternatively, the material could be kept in file boxes on shelves using broad subject headings.

Ephemeral material for use by clientele on the premises is best kept in file boxes, ring or display binders and ideally interfiled with books. Vertical files are not recommended for public use as they tend to be a deterrent. Another way of dealing with ephemeral materials is to gather them together in packs on particular topics and, for maximum impact, to display them face outwards on sloping shelves.

Ephemeral material for the public to take away can be displayed in special leaflet dispensers, on a sloping surface or on tables. Ideally, they should be displayed in broad subject groups or by originating Organisation, e.g. Benefits Agency, Department for Employment, but this is rarely possible because even within Organisations leaflets are produced in varying sizes.

Extra Information

Many Organisations produce printed material in the course of their work or activities. The most common types of material are directories or address lists of members (individuals or constituent groups), newsletters, events sheets or cards, annual reports, constitutions, posters, leaflets, funding appeals, campaigning literature, advertising brochures, balance sheets and commemorative booklets (anniversaries, etc.). All this material is potentially useful as back-up information to the database but there is no sure way of obtaining it. When sending out the original questionnaire to Organisations, you can ask to be put on their mailing list for this type of material, if one is maintained.

Some Organisations that operate on a shoe-string budget may make a small charge for their mailing list facility. Even when you are put on a mailing list, regular receipt of material may depend very much on the enthusiasm or efficiency of the secretary of an Organisation. Often the best solution to obtaining material is to maintain regular contact with Organisations and to pester them continually. When material arrives, it should be dated, so that you know roughly how old it is, and carefully filed for future use. The simplest method is to have an envelope or folder for each Organisation. Write on the outside of the envelope the name of the Organisation as used in your database and arrange envelopes alphabetically in boxes or a vertical file. You should also add to this file any cuttings from newspapers or magazines concerning those Organisations. The file should be checked regularly, at least once a year, to remove out-of-date material. When writing to Organisations for updated information for your database, ask them for any new literature.

Before throwing away the withdrawn material, check to see if it would be of use to some other Organisation or section of your service which collects material on local history.

Categorisation

It is not my intention to go into any great detail about the classification of community information materials. For most small information services, it will be quite adequate to arrange material by broad subject groups subdivided according to the form in which the clientele's needs and problems are presented. For ease of labelling vertical files, book spines and boxes, a simple notation can be used based on the initial letter or letters of subjects. For example, Cambridgeshire Libraries' community information service covers 21 categories:

Ben	Benefits	Gov	Government
Bus	Business	Hea	Health
Car	Careers	Hou	Housing
Corn	Community	Law	Legal rights
Con	Consumer	Mon	Money
CR	Community relations	SC	Senior citizens
Dis	Disability	Tra	Transport
Edu	Education	Ump	Unemployment
Emp	Employment	Worn	Women
Env	Environment	You	Youth
Fam	Family		

Some libraries also include as separate categories: Death, Equal opportunities, Fuel (or Energy), Gay rights, Leisure, and Trade union rights. These categories can then be broken down into smaller subcategories as necessary. Taking the earlier example of Housing, a possible range of subcategories with a mnemonic notation might be:

A	Agricultural accommodation	Re	Rented accommodation
H	Homelessness	ReC	Council housing
I	Institutional accommodation	ReH	Housing Association housing
M	Mobile homes	ReP	Private rented
O	Owner-occupied	S	Squatting

Numerals could be introduced for more detailed subdivisions, e.g. O1-Buying and selling a house; O2-Home insurance; O3-Planning applications; O4-Development; etc.

An effective method that can be used where you have only a small number of broad categories (no more than ten and preferably less) is colour coding. Allocate a colour to each subject and attach an appropriate coloured sticker or tape to the spine of each book or file box. Colour coding can be used in conjunction with notation to provide more detailed subdivision of a subject. When a community information service grows to a size where broad categories are not adequate to 'contain all the material and allow efficient retrieval, then it may be necessary to consider using a classification scheme.

Two choices are open to you, either using or adapting a ready-made scheme or constructing your own. There are a number of general classification schemes used in libraries, of which the most well known is the Dewey Decimal Classification. These schemes have been constructed to organize the whole of knowledge and subjects are usually arranged on philosophical or logical principles. Consequently, they may not be sufficiently detailed or treat subjects in the way your clientele express their information needs. Most schemes have a degree of flexibility and it might be possible to adapt them. The NACAB has its own scheme for arranging materials in the broad area of community information, but it hardly merits the description of a classification scheme. However, it is sufficiently detailed and client oriented to be worthy of consideration.

learning strategies, reinforcement techniques, reading readiness, school-based projects and content-based programmes for developing suitable video programmes for the different groups. The software approach is often referred to behaviour technology, aiming at modification of behaviour and enriching learning achievement. Maximisation of learning experiences can be possible through the judicious use of software inputs in man-machine systems.

Procurement of hardware, even production and transmission hence [illegible] activities, but software development is a continuous process and purely academic in nature. Software must be relevant to the curricular needs, specific to the courses. [illegible] teachers and students can interact and develop the material according to their capabilities and requirements. The entire process must be taken as integrated and interrelated. The objectives should be precisely identified and software has to be developed by professionals and academics. These useful material can be utilized in video production.

Software production for educational TV or video cassettes requires a combination of knowledge of subject matter, media production techniques and communication strategy to reach the target audience. Just recording a chapter of the book cannot make a good video tape. The video/TV productions are only tools for communication and some basic questions need answering and understanding before production. Some of these questions are:

i. Who is the target group?

ii. What is their socio-cultural background?

iii. What are their needs?

iv. What are their experiences?

v. Material to be produced by what means/medium

vi. For which age-group/occupation?

vii. What behavioural modification is needed?

viii. With what infrastructure?

ix. How [illegible] are [illegible] in terms of time and money to produce the material?

The production personnel [illegible] the [illegible] should

5

SOFTWARE DEVELOPMENT

Production forms an important part of the process of audio development. Planning production, distribution, utilisation and evaluation are five significant steps of educational broadcasting on play-back of cassettes/tapes. These steps are interrelated, and efficiency in all these stages results in good and suitable educational radio/audio programmes. Deficiency at any one or two stages spoils the entire radio/audio programmes. Although no stage is less important, production is found to be very significant and its success largely determines the effectiveness of these programmes.

In this unit we intend to discuss the software development's various features of production, importance of audience profile, script writing, tryout of the script as well as the radio/audio programmes in order to make these material effective and interesting.

Directional Objectives

After going through the unit, you will be able to :

- know the need and importance of software for radio/audio
- realise the importance of production of these programmes
- acquaint yourself with various features of production

- identify the need of audience profile for good production
- feel the significance of script writing
- know the need for editing the radio/audio programmes

Production of Audios

Among the stages of planning, production, distribution, utilisation and evaluation, production is most important step of audio/radio broadcasting. The curricular needs and objectives should be identified and planning has to be made for production of suitable audio/video programmes. Audience profile is found useful at this stage to know the needs and interests of the clientele group. After planning, suitable script is prepared by subject experts on a particular topic and then production takes place either in the studio or outside. Various steps are taken by the producer to see that the programme is recorded properly. Sound being the main strength of the radio/audio programme, the "clarity and the quality of what is heard is fundamental to the understanding of the listener" (John C. H. Ball 1974).

A figure of the production process is given here. All these aspects are taken care of more or less in order to ensure "quality" of production.

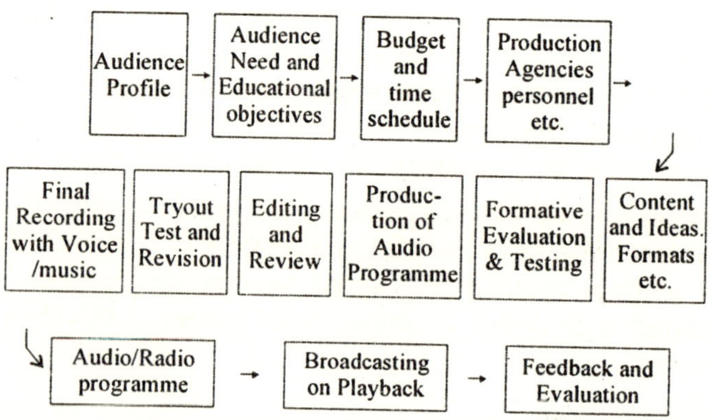

Hardware and software are like two wings of audio-production. All kinds of machines and equipment are essential, but the material therein on the academic input of the programme is called software. Both of them should go hand in hand to make the programme meaningful and effective. Hardware has its origin in physical and engineering sciences and software owes its origin to the social and behavioural sciences. Software is developed according to the principles of these science and is used for modification of behaviour known as learning.

Software development is closely related to psychology and pedagogy. It is very much associated with the principles of programme learning and is characterised by task analysis, identifying objectives, selecting suitable strategies, reinforcement etc. The software approach is often referred to behaviour technology aiming at modification of behaviour or enriching learning experiences.

Achievement of educational objectives is possible only through adequate use of software inputs and organisations. Procurement of hardware is one-short activity but software production is a time taking process which has to be continuous and academic by nature. Software had to be need-based, need-specific and relevant. Teachers and students can easily produce software and also programmes according to the curricular needs and provisions Agarwal (1981) has rightly observed, "One of the major lessons of SITE is that the planning for software rather hardware requires more time. Hence the planning for software aspects must start many years prior to the planning of hardware aspects."

Therefore, preplanning should be made for software development much before hardware planning and production. A systems approach to software planning and production is desirable and the entire teaching learning process should be viewed holistically with reference to the curricular needs and interests as well as abilities of the clientele group. Optimum achievement of the instructional objectives has to be emphasised for software development.

Software production for audio programmes requires a combination of content knowledge, production techniques and communication strategy to reach the target audience. It is rightly said that as merely copying a picture from a book into a large sheet of paper does not make a good illustration, similarly just recording a chapter or story of a book does not give an audio programme.

Some basic questions should be answered for understanding the production needs. Some of these questions are-

i. Software for whom?
ii. With what needs?
iii. With what objectives?
iv. With what background experience and knowledge?
v. With what means and medium?
vi. By which agencies?
vii. With what infrastructure?
viii. With what advance preparation?
ix. What targets are set in terms of time and money?

Answers to these questions are very relevant for properly planning and producing the audio programmes. Sometimes while answering these questions we see that change in one does not suit the needs of audio production. The stereotyped ways or outdated rules and regulation do not promote creativity and productivity. The objectives of software production may be one or more of the following.

i. To inform
ii. To entertain
iii. To impart skills
iv. To instruct
v. To solve problems
vi. To generate thinking and curiosity
vii. To stimulate imagination and creativity
viii. To change aptitude and interests
ix. To modify behaviour

Some of these objectives can be easily realised, but some are not so easy to be achieved. Some objectives are quite challenging and some are very stimulating. The production process is long drawn-out and adequate insight into the process is developed for ensuring effectiveness of the audio programme.

Before producing any programme, its medium of production,

its nature, its strength and weaknesses have to be properly understood by the personnel concerned including scriptwriter and producer. Otherwise due justice cannot be done to its potentialities, nor its deficiencies can be made up and limitations can be overcome, so that programmes can be meaningful and interesting. The strengths and weaknesses of radio and audio programmes have been discussed before. In spite of its potentialities, it suffers from a few limitations and steps are taken for effective audio production. The following points need be taken into account for production of suitable audio programmes. These are (i) Instructional Objectives, (ii) Audience Profile, (iii) Content, (iv) Format, (v) Sound/music Effects.

Instructional Objectives

In the curriculum, there are various provisions which are dealt with in the textbooks presented in radio and television or audio/ video programmes. Some topics are identified for radio programmes in view of their presentation facilities in the same medium. There are some specific objectives and teaching points which are dealt within the audio programme and attempts are made to realise those objectives. To the extent these objectives are realised, the programme is proved to be a success proportionately.

Audience Profile

Before production of an audio programme it is essential that the producer and scriptwriter should have a clear concept about the background knowledge, experience, attitude, interests etc. "Know your audience" is the basic motto of the electronic media production. Radio/audio programme can be planned and developed successfully with adequate knowledge about the audience. Broadcasting on audio programming without this prerequisite is a dull diction or a dry exercise. The psycho-socio-economic and political background of audience for whom the audio programmes are mainly meant, should be given prior attention, so that the programmes can be produced effectively.

As mentioned in the para (i) above, curricular content/ provision should constitute the backbone of the programme. The audio programme should be based on the subject matter or main highlights. It may be merely a syllabus-based or an enrichment programme.

Format

The styles of presentation called format of the audio programmes should be varied. Some of these are stories, talks, discussion, interviews, demonstrations, dramatisation and so on. Some topics are very good for dramatisation, but not for discussion or demonstration. Some are quite effective in interviews, but not suitable for other styles. The scriptwriter should have the necessary skills and competence in developing such formats. Any interesting audio programme should be produced in a suitable format.

Sound/Music Effects

Since sound is the most important strength of the audio programmes, it is essential to make use of various sound effects and musical effects at appropriate places.

Script is the backbone of the audio programme and the basic material for the audio programme. It is not the final product, but the basis for the audio programme. It is aptly said that if you have a good script, half of the battle is won in making a good audio/ radio programme.

A script is prepared to communicate a theme or an idea to listeners through radio or audio programme. The link between the scriptwriter and listeners is established through the producer who translates the script into sound. Necessary instructions should be given by the scriptwriter to use relevant and meaningful sound effects and musical sounds at appropriate places. For example, if the scriptwriter wants a boy to participate in a dialogue for a specific reason, this should be indicated in the script. If the scene on the deck of a ship is given in the script, sound of sea waves, singing of sea-gulls, etc., should be suggested.

Every radio programme is introduced by a compare or an announcer. If the scriptwriter is to tell specifically to the listeners, it can be mentioned by him in the beginning very clearly. It should be indicated in the script, whether it should form a part of the script or just an announcement. But such an introduction should be brief and catchy. After making an interesting beginning, occasional attention-catchers must be used for making the programme interesting.

Similarly, the end of the script should be natural and not abrupt. But climax should not be the end. Care should be taken for a smooth, but heart touching end. In the educational audio programmes, it is desirable to make some repetitions for reinforcement and recapitulation. Such repetition should not be made haphazardly, but in a planned manner repeating only the important highlights.

Some activities can be suggested for the listeners who should not be just passive participants. Appropriate support materials may also be suggested by the scriptwriter for ensuring efficiency.

It is not desirable to show off the knowledge or use any technical jargons and very bombastic words. Simple language and style are to be preferred. Demoralisation or sermonising is to be encouraged.

Too many teaching points should not be in a script and too many facts and figures are to be discouraged.

Script being the basic framework of educational audio programme, utmost care should be taken to make it suitable for reflecting the above concepts and principles. In this context, the guidelines developed by the British Council Media Departments, London are found to be quite relevant as well as comprehensive. These are given below:

1. The script is the most important of an audio programme. Unless it is excellent, every other aspect of production is useless.
2. To be successful it must be written in the right language for the listener.
3. The right language is the language the listener can understand. So it must take into account the listener's background, education and interest. The writer must therefore think carefully about the structure he is going to use and the vocabulary.
4. The words the scriptwriter uses are not read by the listener-they are listened to. So the words must appeal to the Ear, not to the Eye.

5. Writing for the Eye relies on the conventions of writing-punctuation-paragraphs-type sizes-columns-headlines. The reader can go at his own speed. He can go back to check any point of difficulty. He can stop reading, put the writing aside and return to it later.
6. Writing for the Ear is quite different. The listener can not be given too many facts. He cannot be given too many figures. It is essential to sustain his interest — therefore the script must be presented in an interesting way. It must develop logically. The radio writer may have to repeat, expand and reinforce. He must use the form of language which is simple and informal. It is Spoken Language. The listener must be held — otherwise he switches off mentally.
7. How is the listener held? The radio writer must think of the listener as his personal friend....

He must talk with the listener, not at him.

He must hear in his mind all the tones of voice that will communicate the script.

He must visualise the listener.

He must read the script aloud to himself and ask ----

"What do I sound like?"

"What do I mean?"

As discussed earlier, the script is the basis of all work in educational media including radio or audio cassettes. It contains ideas and content to be presented in an interesting way on a particular medium - here, radio/audio. The script for radio/audio programme would be different from one for television. Script writing for any medium requires an understanding of the potentials and limitations of the medium, production and distribution processes.

In India, workshops are organised for developing scripts of various kinds with or without any knowledge of the medium, production and distribution technicalities. Even though they might not have heard good examples of audio programmes or audio materials like audio tapes/cassettes, the writers would be exposed to some good programmes/materials and production machines and processes. They, under the guidance of experts develop scripts of their own. They should ask and answer all the questions listed earlier before they start writing scripts.

It is natural that a few drafts would not be upto the standard, because the quality of an educational audio script is not judged merely by the correctness of its information/content. That is essential but more than that the format, use of sound/music effects, etc., are also of great importance. A good script might have undergone three or four revisions and modification before it emerges as the final script. A flow-chart of such exercise is given below:

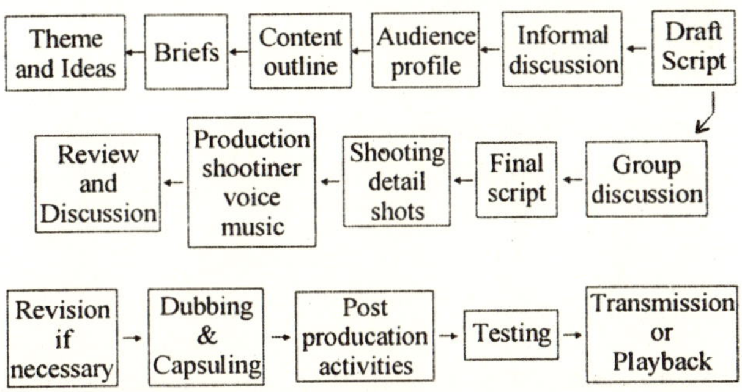

Audio programme is dependent on an aural medium quality of what is heard and clarity of recording is of paramount importance. Reception on short waves due to variable conditions in the ionosphere, can adversely affect speech clarity. R. L. Hilliard writing about school broadcasting observed, "The conscientious radio broadcaster aims to transmit sound in such a way that the listening public will be able to understand speech clearly and enjoy the reproduction of music— After leaving the transmitter, sound is subject to all sorts of losses and quality degradations before it reaches the listeners' ears. Therefore, it is necessary to keep the technical quality of the sound as high as possible at all times while it is under the control of the station."

John C. H Ball (Ibid) in this context said, "By quality here we mean quality directly in relation to audibility. It is of first importance then the producer of programmes is aware of the reception conditions in the area to which he is broadcasting and he takes them into account." It is therefore, necessary that proper recording of the audio programmes and their broadcasting or playback should be made under favourable and congenial conditions. Hence besides production quality, listening conditions need to be suitable.

Audio programmes should be interesting any way. Otherwise these cannot be heard at all or heard, not received adequately. Ball has aptly said therefore, "The class teacher may consider the programme useful and so switch on the radio, but unless it is also 'interesting' the children will switch off their ears." Besides, content and format of the programmes, the quality in production, broadcasting and playback has to be ensured for increasing effectiveness in the educational institutions and distance education system. In the AIR we have a quite well-developed infrastructure for production of audio cassettes/tapes.

Although Akash Vani is responsible for production of educational radio programmes, it depends on the outside resource persons for preparing scripts. However necessary editing of the script is made by the producer. A case-study of school broadcasts at Delhi revealed that "It is mostly of the nature of substituting some difficult words with simpler ones, and/or curtailing/adding the spoken matter. The accuracy of facts presented in the material is generally accepted, as no other subject matter specialist is consulted in the matter. This practice allows a material passed off for broadcast without providing a safeguard for checking its accuracy at the editing stage". This practice at New Delhi holds good for all the Akash Vani Stations and the instances of errors in educational programmes are also not rare.

Hence writing of scripts free from all errors thematic as well as linguistic is very important for success of the educational broadcasting. It may be regarded as a specialised job. The script-writers are usually appointed from among subject experts which does not always happen well. Therefore care should be taken for preparing fool-proof scripts for the purpose. It is better to get them approved by subject experts and then use for production of programmes in presentable form by the producer who is a media man.

It was thought desirable as well as more practicable to train the specialist to write scripts for educational radio. In order to write suitable scripts, besides content knowledge the writer should have knowledge about various formats, audience profile, different techniques for attracting attention and sustaining interests, ability in creative expression, proficiency in language and presentation styles and techniques. During a training course or workshop, the prospective scriptwriters should be exposed to these theoretical as well as practical aspects of the programme. It should be realised that good scriptwriters are not born, but made through sincere efforts, long practice, keen interest and love for the job.

At present a good number of institutions like IGNOU and UGC through their production centres are producing many kinds of educational audio cassettes/tapes. These are being produced by groups of subject experts, and media experts and the audio materials are sold at no profit no loss basis. Besides, some private firms are also engaged in producing audio tapes for various educational courses/ classes. They produce these audio tapes on commercial basis and the quality of their production is not always satisfactory.

Radio/Audio Vision

As discussed earlier, audio tape/cassettes and radio are aural media and these programmes have their own limitations. Some people have aversion to listening only. They dislike to hear only words, words and words. Again what is heard is fleeting and changing from moment to moment. That is why, radio/audio programme is called evanescent and taxing to its audience.

In view of these handicaps, attempts are being made to provide support to the spoken words. Illustrations are used to explain, to create interest, to motivate and to help concentration. That is, vision is supplemented with audio or radio. This is done in many ways - viz., by showing pictures or flash cards or by projecting slides or film-strips even by organising activities. France Berrigan and Anne Gibson (1978) have rightly observed in their paper "Radio and Audio - Vision in the British Open University: Towards Individualisation", "At the simplest level, having a visual support does seem to help concentration. It is easy enough for the mind to wander during a twenty minute radio talk or discussion. To support what is said by an illustration or an activity helps to concretise the subject matter."

Research conducted by Gallagher (1977) has revealed that students prefer radio-vision to radio alone and this justifies more of it in the advanced countries of the world. Radio-vision has become more popular day by day and the latest trend is towards more audio-vision in the field of educational broadcasting.

Abroad

The British Open University is a remarkable achievement in educational technology and has been using various kinds of media for providing its students with rich learning experiences. It has developed multi-media packages for various units in all subjects—arts, sciences, technologies and humanities. Particularly, its attempts to support radio-programmes with print materials, posters, coloured post cards, slides and film strips are really quite laudable and enlightening.

Since 1964 the BBC has started with radio-vision programmes systematically. In Sweden, Norway and Denmark, radio-vision series are specifically broadcast along with educational radio programmes in general. Even in Kenya, its Ministry of Education used to broadcast radio vision science programmes in conjunction with the Centre for Educational Development Overseas (CEDO), London. In 1976 the Audio-visual Media Research Group was asked to evaluate several programmes with special emphasis on a radio-vision programme. But it was found that there was a wide range of materials being used for radio-vision programming. At that time there was no record of the number of courses or programmes using radio-vision and no way of measuring the cost of this medium to the OU. It was therefore decided to carry out a study to discover the range, extent and cost of radio-vision in the university. According to the study undertaken by Berrington and others (1987) radio-vision described the simultaneous use of radio and vision which promotes better utilisation.

The extent of radio-vision showed that Mathematics made most use of the medium. The second most extensive use is in Science. The range of materials used for radio-vision includes diagrams or tables in broadcast notes, charts, maps, samples or specimens, film strips and transparencies. Radio-vision materials in the Arts Faculty consist of coloured or black and white photographs, colour postcards, drawings and plans, etc. It is interesting to know that 62% of all Open University courses in 1977 were making use of radio vision. But 23-33%, i.e., a quarter of all radio programmes made use of the technique in some way or other. Thus the innovation has made a headway in the visual area and has shown a significant development in the educational broadcast.

The experience in use of radio-vision of OU shows that much more effort has been devoted to the provision of elaborate visual support material for radio-vision than to the design of the sound component. Berrington and others have in their study rightly pointed out "Many radio-vision programmes overload students, requiring sustained concentrating as well as expecting a great deal of pre-broadcast preparation to assemble materials. Often programmes seemed to race through the material, allowing insufficient time for the detail to be located, or observed" (1977).

Besides, many radio-vision programmes are designed with a predetermined work pace, when broadcast makes no allowance for individual learning styles and varying speeds of comprehension. This is, of course, due to the very inherent limitation of the sound broadcasting. Once the listener fails to locate a reference, he is likely to lose concentration and miss valuable information.

In India

During the Satellite Instructional TV Experiment (SITE) period (1974-75) an in-service training course in Science was organised by the Centre for Educational Technology, NCERT in collaboration with the Educational Technology Cells of Andhra Pradesh, Bihar, Karnataka, Madhya Pradesh, Orissa and Rajasthan for the teachers of the elementary schools. A Multi-Media Package was developed by the CET for this course which included radio-vision programme in its sound broadcast component.

Explaining these radio-vision programmes to the teacher monitors who were to conduct the course, it was mentioned by the CET (1975), "Radio-Vision means a radio-programme accompanied by visuals which may be on flash cards as in this case (shadows) /or as posters as in the case of next programme "Vikas aur Vigyan" or on slides/film strips. A topic like "shadows" needs visuals. In the materials sent to you, have included "Sketches/ diagrams as eleven cards numbered serially. You should display these cards one by one, the programme will cue you for such display by announcing look at card no. so and so? Please ensure that the participants are made to sit in such a manner, at such a distance that where these sketches, they could easily see them while listening to the radio-feature. The teacher monitor here has to be alert to change the sketch when next sketch is referred to."

It was found that with the help of these suitable graphics accompanied by commentaries from radio, the principles of shadow in various situations were well-explained to the trainees. Similarly, few posters used in the other radio programme "Development and Science in Villages" helped to clarify certain difficult concepts and made the radio teaching interesting and meaningful.

The question "In the age of TV, has pedagogical Radio a future?" stimulated the Department of Education, South Gujarat University, Surat to take up a research project "Radio-Vision as a Partial Substitute to Educational TV." The experience of SITE programme provided further impetus for the venture. Although TV is considered to be a better medium of communication for the rural masses, the question arises, "Are we in a position to provide TV to all the inhabitations of our country?"

Secondly, "Have we been able to exploit fully the potential of Radio as an educational medium? "Loud thinking over these questions further stimulated to examine the "effectiveness of Radio-Vision as a medium of instruction." As reported in the Newsletter of the Indian Association of Programmed Learning (1978), the major aim of the project was to study the efficacy of radio-vision as a medium of instruction in formal and non formal education situations (1978). The findings of this study were quite encouraging.

Sharma (1980), Oberi (1981) and Sharma & Tripathy (1980) have conducted a good number of studies in the use and efficacy of radio-vision programmes. All these experiments have reported that radio-vision programmes produced significantly better results as compared to traditional classroom instruction.

Conclusion

Production of audio/radio programmes is a significant process. It assumes special significance when such programmes are educational. Although hardware and software are two wings of audio production, software is more important, because we can procure the machineries and equipment from the market if funds are available. But software materials need to be developed with the help of persons having adequate knowledge in psychology, pedagogy and content areas. Software is to be need-based and need-specific relating to a particular group of clientele.

Important features of audio production are instructional objectives, audience profile, content, format, sound and music effects. Importance of script writing cannot be overemphasized. A few basic guidelines should be followed in developing suitable scripts for radio/audio programmes.

In the AIR there is quite a well-developed infrastructure for production of audio programmes. Besides script writing which is quite significant a number of precautions need to be taken for sound recording, editing, broadcasting, etc., to ensure better quality and higher reception.

Some innovative measures have been taken for overcoming the deficiencies and limitations of audio programmes. Radio/Audio-Vision is one of such innovations for providing visual support to aural presentation through the use of slides, illustrations, maps, charts, etc. In India NCERT and South Gujarat University have made some notable experiments in radio/audio-vision while the BBC and some other agencies have done the same abroad.

Production of Videos

Both hardware and software are needed for video production as incase of any other media and these two components call for more or less amount of time and money according to the nature and quantity of these requisites. But software is given more importance than hardware due to the fact that the former is developed by the experts with adequate knowledge in pedagogy, psychology and content subject. Knowledge in learning strategies, reinforcement techniques, reading readiness, attention and interests and content is felt essential for developing suitable video programmes for the clientele groups. The software approach is often referred to behaviour technology aiming at modification of behaviour and enriching learning achievement. Maximisation of learning experiences can be possible through the adequate use of software inputs in man-machine systems.

Procurement of hardware, even production and transmission services are more or less one-shot activities, but software development is a continuous process and purely academic in nature. Software must be relevant to the curricular needs specific to the courses/ clientele. Teachers and students can interact and develop the material according to their capabilities and requirements. The entire process must be taken as integrated and interrelated. The objectives should be precisely identified and software has to be developed by educationists and academics. These useful material can be utilised in video production.

Software production for educational TV or video cassettes requires a combination of knowledge of subject matter, media production techniques and communication strategy to reach the target audience. Just recording a chapter of the book cannot make a good video tape. The video/TV productions are only tools for communication and some basic questions need answering and understanding before production. Some of these questions are:

i. Who is the target group?

ii. What is their socio-cultural background?

iii. What are their needs?

iv. What are their experiences?

v. Material to be produced by what means/medium

vi. By which agencies/personnel?

vii. What advance preparation is needed?

viii. With what infrastructure?

ix. What targets are feasible in terms of time and money to produce the material?

The production personnel, especially the scriptwriter should answer these and other allied questions and understand the production techniques before developing the software for the video programmes. The infrastructure for administration and production should be quite adequate and oriented to produce good quality video programmes without much hindrances and handicaps.

Objectives regarding Software

The objectives of such communication may be one or more of the following:

i. To impart relevant knowledge

ii. To inform

iii. To entertain

iv. To teach skills

v. To present concepts

vi. To generate curiosity and interest

vii. To stimulate creative and imaginative ideas

viii. To develop problem-solving ability

ix. To bring about change

x. To modify behaviour and attitudes

These objectives are to be realised through the scripts. Some objectives are very easy for realisation. These objectives are also not hierarchical. Media communication to be effective needs insight and understanding of the target audience and their needs according to which scripts and materials for video programmes are developed for realising the specific objectives.

Programmes Related to Video

Scripts are the basis of all production activities. These software materials need to be translated into action i.e. video programmes. Sometime scripts for educational video programmes are developed through workshops where writers of various abilities with experience and insight, discuss the programme briefs, objectives, audience profile and prepare drafts in a rough proforma. These drafts prepared under the guidance of experts are presented and discussed in the workshops. Again the scripts are revised, redrafted and utilised for video programmes. These scripts undergo several revisions before good quality materials are ready for video production.

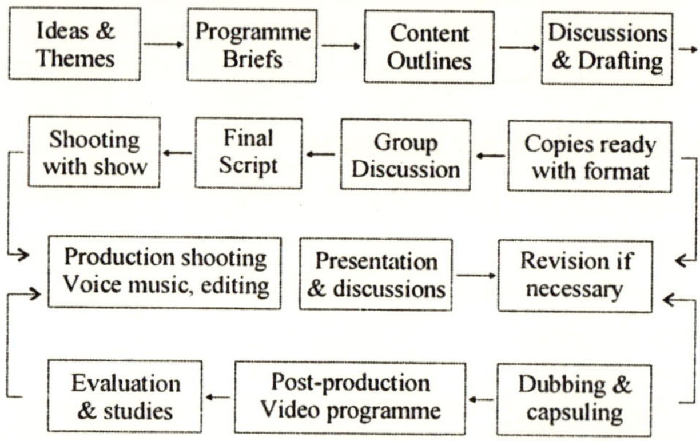

The process of writing a script for ETV and video programmes is essentially the same as designing any learning activity. But writing video scripts means using your "ideas and imagination in a different way." i.e., giving visual treatment to your ideas. The first thing, therefore, to understand and learn about video script writing is that it is not a process of writing words or sentences and thinking of pictures to accompany them. On the other hand, it is an imaginative and creative process and is essentially and basically an art of imaginative programme creation, using the available resources. It is because of this reason that it is said that television programmes are evolved from the combined or pooled talents of the producer, the scriptwriter and occasionally others directly involved, such as designer, graphic artists, etc. Satisfying success can be achieved in this exercises more conveniently and confidently, if we look upon the process of evolving an ETV video script as a cyclic process, as shown in the diagram below.

ETV Programme

Before going into the details of each of the steps involved in the process of evolving an ETV script, it is, however, essential to point out the two important facts that all scriptwriters must always keep in mind.

1. Television is a one-way medium
2. Television is a mass-medium

Both these factors exert considerable limitations on the

designing of ETV programmes. One has to bear in mind that there should be no gap in the content and the script should, as far as possible, be self-sufficient in communicating the desired messages. This limitation makes script writing a difficult job which demands special care and attention, better imagination and visualisation, mastery of the subject and mature experience in identifying the requirement of the viewers. So the script should evolve step by step and different steps be presented vividly and linked so smoothly and naturally, one after the other, that the average viewer understands and follows the total content without any difficulty.

Secondly, because television is a mass medium, an ETV programme will be viewed by a large number of students, including the talented, the average and the below average. It may be very difficult to cater to the needs of all the three categories simultaneously throughout a programme. Therefore, the programme has to be planned and prepared in such a way that all the three categories benefit to the optimal extent, providing involvement and satisfaction to each one of them. This can be achieved by devoting the major part of the programme to the average students and also offering some satisfying material for the talented as well as the below average ones, so that the interest of all the three categories is sustained and the programme attracts and serves viewers from all sections of audience.

Introducing the entertainment element in a television programme is useful, but a balance is to be maintained by the scriptwriter between entertainment and education. In case of younger age group audience, entertainment programmes are desirable but this element must be exploited cautiously and carefully so that children are not carried away by the entertainment part so much that the actual message is not at all received by them. Thus, a successful scriptwriter always keeps in mind the psychology, interests and needs of his target audience. He has also to remember that visuals are the main carriers of the message and sound effects and words have a role to play but only in support of visuals, Television script writing is thus the other name of thinking in terms of visuals to convey the intended message, combined, of course, with sound effects, music and words to make it a continuous programme in order to achieve the desired objectives.

Different writers follow different methods and techniques for writing scripts and it varies from writer to writer. However, for purposes of explanation and convenience of beginners, the process of script writing may be described under the following main steps:

Defining Objectives and Selecting Content Outlines

Once the topic for writing a script has been assigned, the scriptwriter should be informed about the target audience, their age-level and specific objectives and the programme.

This is to be followed by deciding the content to be presented in order to achieve the established objectives. Specifying objectives and visualising content in detail is an essential discipline in the production process. At this stage, the detailed visual ideas on which the programme will be based are evolved. "How can we convey that concept visually?" "How can we grasp the attention of the viewers?" This stage demands creativity and imagination. The success of the programme will heavily depend on the care taken at this stage.

Research and Selection of Materials

Research is important to all programmes. Finding information from books, periodicals, reports, atlases, encyclopaedias, dictionaries and from experts in the field, checking details, locating pictures, selecting film locations, etc., are the part of research. Once the materials have been collected after research, the relevant materials which match the content and lead to the achievement of the desired objectives, can be finally selected for making the programme.

Selection of Resources to Present the Content

The scriptwriter has to be very imaginative in his selection of resources to match the content and the objectives. It is the most important step in the process. Success of the programme depends on the imaginative use of visual resources, keeping in mind the time and money available for the programme. This process of selecting resources implies the conversion of the programme content into suitable and appropriate visual terms, i.e. how the content can be presented visually. It needs imagination, research and experience to accomplish this job successfully and to achieve the desired quality of the programme.

Organisation of Resources into a Programme Structure

This is the process of giving the programme a shape and a form-visual treatment. It includes deciding how the programme will vary according to the needs, interest and how the parts of the programme will be linked together and knit into a natural sequence, so that the programme may have varying interest levels and appear to be evolving from one sequence to another.

In this process, each sequence would have to be linked with the previous one in respect of content, visuals, sound effects and other demonstration materials. But at the same time, care may be taken to see that there is a good coherence in the whole programme, something to bind everything into one natural and effective unit. At this stage, it is helpful to draw a time-line of the programme, showing how much time is to be spent on each element of the programme keeping in view the way the selected resources are to be used.

Developing a Story-board/Draft Script and the Final Script

All the visual themes alongwith necessary links thought out and planned by the scriptwriter need to be communicated to the producers for understanding the shots and logical sequencing of the programme. This could easily be communicated if the scriptwriter presents his ideas in the form of a story-board.

For developing the story-board, the scriptwriter may divide the white sheet of paper into two vertical columns. Pictures in sequence may be described within different rectangles (ratio 3: 4) drawn on the left hand side of the paper. The supporting words, sound effects and music may be indicated in the right half of the paper.

From the story-board and final script, the producer writes the camera script which contains the technical information necessary for the production of the programmes.

To sum up, the following guidelines should be borne in mind by the scriptwriter while writing a script for an ETV programme.

1. First of all, the scriptwriter must realise and accept the

factual position that scripts are not written but they are evolved.

2. He should always keep in mind the target audience and their needs.
3. The script must be simple, direct and personal.
4. It must be written with full knowledge of and involvement of programme visuals.
5. It should constantly pick up, stress and reinforce its educational points using different resources.
6. It should involve the audience, as far as possible, actively.
7. The commentary should be informal and not book type.
8. It should not attempt to say too much in limited time and space.
9. It should end with a simple summary of the main programme points, with a different visual presentation.
10. It should have a variety of pace and rhythm and must give breathing space occasionally.
11. Above all, it should attempt to take its viewers/audience on a journey of discovery and not merely give information.

Television or video is primarily a visual medium. Naturally, therefore, the quality of any video programme will be determined by the quality and variety of visual and other resources that have gone into its making. A scriptwriter must, therefore, have a thorough knowledge of different visual and other resources of television which may be available to him to evolve a programme.

For purposes of convenience, the resources for video production can be classified into the following major categories:

i. Pictures: By pictures, here, we mean any kind of visuals that can be put in front of a video camera. These may include still photographs, slides, filmstrips, overhead transparencies, especially prepared graphics such as charts, diagrams, maps, outlines, summaries, pictures from books, cartoons, captions' with lettering on them. We call all such pictures or photographs as captions or photo-captions. Sometimes, we can prepare special captions in which things and words can be made to move, appear and disappear. These are known as animated captions. All drawn pictures and photo-captions are usually made in a standard size of 12" x 9", unless the camera is required to move about for showing different parts of the picture.

ii. People: Most television is about people, people telling us things, people being interviewed, people acting, people laughing, people weeping, people playing instruments and dancing, people singing, people playing games, people doing all kinds of things from mending bicycles to telling jokes, and people trying to persuade us to take to their point of view. They also include presenters, demonstrators, guests, teachers and class children.

iii. Things: The range of things shown on television is infinite, elephants, puppets, models, machines of all kinds, toys, furniture, bridges, buildings, aeroplanes, the sun, the moon and so on. Television provides a unique opportunity to bring together a huge variety of things, new and old, mundane and unusual.

iv. Drama: Drama is also classified by many as one of the important resources for television. It may be very simple with no studio set or very complex ones using several settings. Drama does have elements of people, things and sound included in it, yet it may be classified as a separate resource.

v. Film: Films constitute a very important resource for television. The film can be put on a projector and beamed straight at a television camera. Things that are impossible or impracticable to shoot on television - such as under-water photography and complicated cartoon work which we call Film Animatio4n - can be shot on film. Films can also be used to slow down or speed up actions, as you might have seen in programmes shown on games, sports and races. All such specially prepared films can be fed into a TV programme. (The technique of making films and television programmes are in themselves very different, of course).

vi. Set & Lighting: It is also an important resource of TV which gives it reality.

vii. Sound: Sound is an important resource for television though it is often under-utilised. Imaginative use of music and appropriate sound effects can certainly go a long way in making a good TV programme.

This classification of resources into Pictures, People, Things, Drama, Film, Set, Lighting and Sound, is particularly useful and convenient for beginners who, while trying to evolve ideas for video programmes, can refer to this broad classification.

Pictures are of paramount importance in video programmes. The Central Institute of Educational Technology, NCERT has identified the following, mostly related to pictures.

A video programme consists of a series of pictures, i.e., the pictures keep changing in quick succession. This change is not just for variety, but each picture has its own message. All the pictures must synchronies with sound.

Types of pictures (shots) depend on the focal length of the lens and the distance between the camera and the subject. Following types of shots are used commonly:

1. Single Shot - a shot including one person
2. Two Shot - a shot including two persons
3. Three Shot - a shot including three persons
4. Crowd Shot - a shot including a number of people
5. Wide Shot or Very Long Shot (VLS) - a shot which includes along with the principal subject, a large amount of the background in the picture.
6. Full Length Shot or Long Shot (LS) - a shot in which the subject occupies about 3/4 of the vertical height of the picture frame.
7. Medium Long Shot (MLS) or Knee Shot - a shot in which the subject is seen from the knee upwards.
8. Medium Shot or Mid Shot - a shot in which the subject is seen from the waist upwards.
9. Medium Close Shot (MCS) or Medium Close Up (MCU)- a shot which includes the subject's head and shoulders. It is also called the chest or Bust Shot.

10. Close Shot (CS) or Close Up (CU) - a shot which includes the subject's head and neck only
11. Big Close Shot (BCS) or Big Close Up (BCU) - a shot which includes only a section of the subject's head from chin to forehead.
12. Over-Shoulder Shot (OSS) - a shot of a subject or subject taken over the shoulder of person in the foreground.

For maximum effects, the change of pictures must be brought about in the right manner. The following are certain conventional methods of changing the shots.

1. *The Cut :* This is an instant change form one picture to another. It is used when the action is continuous in time. A cut should be motivated by an action, by the dialogue or both.
2. *The Dissolve or Mix :* This is a gradual change from one picture to another. While the first picture is vanishing slowly, the second one is gradually appearing on the screen. At a point both pictures are visible on the screen simultaneously. It is used when a lapse of time is to be indicated, when there is a change of screen, and in getting to and from captions or telecine.
3. *The Superimposition* : This is the imposition of one picture over another one which is already on the screen. It is used for showing written captions over persons or objects in order to identify them, in teaching to reinforce the visual with the verbal, and for special effects, e.g., to show a person dreaming or thinking.
4. *The Fade In and Out :* These are the gradual appearance of a picture on a blank screen and the gradual disappearance of a picture from the screen. These are used at the beginning and the end of a programme and instead of a mix when there is longer lapse of time to be indicated.
5. *The Pan :* Here the change of picture is brought about by panning i.e., moving the camera head left or right in the horizontal plane while the base of the camera remains static. It is used when following a moving person or thing

and for moving from object to object in order to build up a particular effect or to provide background for a series of captions.

6. *The Tilt :* Here the change of picture is brought about by swinging the camera head up or down in the vertical plane without moving the base of the camera.
7. *The Crab :* Crabbing is like panning except that here the whole camera is moved left or right from the base.
8. *The Zoom In :* Using a zoom lens, a wide shot of an object or person is changed to a closer shot. This is used for focusing attention on a particular part of the whole picture and for special effects (horror, surprise, excitement, etc.).
9. *The Zoom Out :* Using a zoom lens, a close shot of a person or object is changed to a wider shot. It is used for establishing the relationship between the object or person with the surroundings, when a person in close-up moves or is joined by someone else or is going to talk about something next to him but not visible at the moment.
10. *The Track In Out :* This has the same effect as the zoom in and out except that here in the absence of a zoom lens the whole camera is moved forward or backward from the base. This not only requires great skill on the part of the cameraman but a very smooth studio floor. It cannot be used for a quick change of shot and the range between the two shots would be limited.

Some Guidelines for Video Script-writing

1. Use active voice as far as possible.
2. Use specific words and examples, wherever possible, to establish specific relationships.
3. Try not to start with a negative sentence.
4. Sometimes, we may write just one sentence as commentary and then change three/four similar slides/ shots in succession.
5. There is no need to describe pictures which must speak for themselves.
6. Words should coincide with pictures where they make sense.

7. If you have a marvellous·speaker in your programme, let him do the job. It will give your programme some "credibility." So, let it come from horse's mouth.
8. Make your audience see the 'pictures' you want them to see in a long snot.
9. Use just one line of commentary and let the noises take over. Avoid too much use of words. Try to forget your bombastic vocabulary and get rid of words only.
10. In general, the less you write, the better it is. So, learn to get rid of your vocabulary and use simple words only.
11. Never cover all the really dull stuff like facts, figures etc., in commentary. These can be really handled much more amusingly when they are presented graphically.

Software is more important than hardware and is very local specific, objective based and academic in nature. It must be relevant to the curricular needs and is developed with the knowledge and skills based on pedagogy, psychology and content subject. The objectives of software are to impart knowledge, inform, entertain, and so on and learners' experience and interest are taken into account for suitable software development.

Script writing for video production is of paramount importance and is evolved through the efforts of the writer, producer and other associated personnel. In view of the limitations of the video programme, better visualisation and imagination, careful selection of content, appropriate format and language, etc., are used for script writing. A well integrated and interdependent process is adopted for developing suitable script and video production.

Various resources like pictures, content about people, things, drama, film, set, lighting, sound, etc., are utilised for video production. Since visuals are of crucial importance, great caution is taken for selecting spots and taking shots relevant to the content. Besides, producers and scriptwriters need to be acquainted with various technicalities including production strategies, terms and techniques used in video production. To write suitable scripts, particularly as regards language, teaching points, visuals, and so on, we need to follow several guidelines.

6

TECHNOLOGIES IN HARDWARE

Different Views

Audio-Visual aids, audio-visual material, audio-visual media, communication technology, educational or instructional media and learning resources — all these terms, broadly speaking, mean the same thing. Earlier the term used was audio-visual aids in education. With the advancement in the means of communication and that of technology, educators coined new terms, More specifically media refers to films, filmstrips, recordings, etc. The use of newer terms Educational Technology or Instructional Technology is primarily due to the dynamic expansion of programmed learning, computer assisted instruction and education T.V. This revolution in the field of audio-visual education is the outcome of the development in electronics, notably those involving the radio, tape recorder and computer.

Brief history of the use of Audio-visual aids : A Dutch humanist, theologian and writer Desiderious Erasmus (1466-1536) discouraged memorization as a technique of learning and advocated that children should learn through the aid of pictures or other visuals. John Amos Comenius (1592-1670) prepared a book known as *Orbis Sensulium Pictus.* (The world of Sense Objects) which contained about 150 pictures on aspects of everyday life. The book is considered to be the first illustrated textbook for childhood education. This book gained wide publicity and was used in childhood education centres all over the world. Jean Jacques Rousseau (1712-1778) and other educators stressed the need of pictures and other play materials. Rousseau condemned the use of words by teachers and he stressed 'things'. He pleaded that the teaching process must be directed to the learner's natural curiosity. Pestalozzi (1756-1827) put Rousseau's theory into action in his 'object method'. He based instruction on sense perception.

The term 'Visual education' was used as early as 1926 by Lelson.I.Green.

Eric Ashby : Identified four revolutions in education, education from home to school, written words as tool of education, invention of printing and use of books and lastly the fourth revolution in the use of electronic media i.e., radio, television, tape recorder and computer in education.

Burton : Audio-visual aids are those sensory objects or images which initiate or stimulate and reinforce learning.

Carter V. Good : Audio-visual aids are those aids which help in completing the triangular process of learning i.e., motivation, classification and stimulation.

Edgar Dale : Audio-visual are those devices by the use of which communication of ideas between persons and groups in various teaching and training situations is helped. These are also termed as multi-sensory materials.

Good's Dictionary of Education : Audio-visual aids are anything by means of which learning process may be encouraged or carried on through the sense of hearing or sense of sight.

Kinder, S. James : Audio-visual aids are any device which can be used to make the learning experience more concrete, more realistic and more dynamic.

Mckown and Roberts : Audio-visual aids are supplementary devices by which the teacher, through the utilization of more than one sensory channels is able to clarify, establish and correlate concepts, interpretations and appreciations.

Audio-visual aids or devices or technological media or learning devices are added devices that help the teacher to clarify, establish, co-relate and co-ordinate accurate concepts, interpretations and appreciations and enable him to make learning more concrete, effective, interesting, inspirational, meaningful and vivid. They help in completing the triangular process of learning viz., motivation-clarification-stimulation. The aim of teaching with technological media is 'clearing the channel between the learner and the things that are worth learning'. The basic assumption underlying Audio-visual Aids is that learning—clear understanding—stems from sense experience. The teacher must 'show' as well as 'tell'. Audio-visual aids provide significant gains in informational learning, retention and recall, thinking and reasoning, activity, interest, imagination, better assimilation and personal growth and development. The aids are the stimuli for learning 'why', 'how', 'when' and 'where'. The 'hard to understand principles' are usually made clear by the intelligent use of skilfully designed instructional aids.

According to Gandhi Ji, "True education of the intellect can only come through a proper exercise and training of bodily organs—hands, feet, eyes, ears and nose."

Commenting on the use of audio-visual aids, the Kothari Commssion 1964-66 observed that it should indeed bring about an 'educational revolution' in the country. It further stated that the supply of teaching aids to every school was essential for the improvement of the quality of teaching.

The National Policy of Education, 1986 and as modified in 1992 has laid a great stress on the use of teaching aids, especially improvised aids, to make teaching-learning more effective and realistic.

In the words of Edgar Dale, "Because audio-visual materials supply concrete basis for conceptual thinking, they give rise to meaningful concepts enriched by meaningful association, hence they offer the best antidote for the disease of verbalism."

Some of the important values of the proper use of audio-visual aids are given below:

Antidote to the Disease of Verbal Instruction : They help to reduce verbalism. They help in giving clear concepts and thus help to bring accuracy in learning. As observed by Raymound Wyman (1957) "We (teacher) tell students, and we provide them with written material so much of the time. Words are wonderful. They are easily produced, reproduced, stored and transported. But the overuse or excessive use of words can result in serious problem, chiefly, the problem of verbalism (using or adopting words or phrases without considering what they mean) and forgetting."

Best Motivation : They are the best motivators. The students work with more interest and zeal. They are more attentive.

Clear Images : Clear images are formed when we see, hear, touch, taste and smell as our experiences are direct, concrete and more or less permanent. Learning through the senses becomes the most natural and consequently the easiest.

Vicarious Experience : It is beyond doubt that the first-hand experience is the best type of educative experience. But it is neither practicable nor desirable to provide such experience to pupils. Substituted experiences may be provided under such conditions. There are many inaccessible objects and phenomena. For example, it is not possible for the pupils living in India to see the Eskimoe. Similarly, it is not possible for an average man to climb the Mount Everst. There are innumerable such things to which it is not possible to have direct access. So, in all such cases, these aids help us.

Variety : 'Mere chalk and talk' do not help. Audio-visual aids give variety and provide different tools in the hands of the teacher.

Freedom : When audio-visual aids are employed, there is great scope for children to move about, talk, laugh and comment upon. Under such an atmosphere the students work because they want to work and not because the teacher wants them to work.

Opportunities to Handle and Manipulate : Many visual aids offer opportunities to students to handle and manipulate things.

Retentivity : Audio-visual aids contribute to increased retentivity as they stimulate response of the whole organism to the situation in which learning takes place.

Based on Maxims of Teaching : The use of audio-visual aids enables the teacher to follow the maxims of teaching like 'concrete to abstract', 'known to unknown' and 'learning by doing.'

Helpful in Attracting Attention : Attention is the true factor in any process of teaching and learning. Audio-visual aids help the teacher in providing proper environment for capturing as well as sustaining the attention and interest of the students in the classroom work.

Helpful in Fixing up New Learning : 'What is gained in terms of learning, needs to be fixed up in the minds of students. Audiovisual aids help in achieving this objective by providing several activities, experiences and stimuli to the learners'.

Saving of Energy and Time : A good deal of energy and time of both the teachers and students can be saved on account of the use of audio-visual aids as most of the concepts and phenomena may be easily clarified, understood and assimilated through their use.

Realism : The use of audio-visual aids provides a touch of reality to the learning situation. By seeing a film show exhibiting the life of the people of the Tundra region, students learn it more effectively in about 2 hours than by spending weeks by reading.

Vividness : Audio-visual aids give vividness to the learning situation. A film on Buddha provides a vivid picture of his life and teachings.

Meeting Individual Differences : There are wide individual differences among learners. Some are ear-oriented, some can be helped through visual demonstrations, while others learn better by doing. The use of a variety of audio-visual aids helps in meeting the needs of different types of students.

Encouragement to Healthy Classroom Interaction : Audio-visual aids, through their wide variety of stimuli, provision of active participation of the students, and vicarious experiences encourage healthy classroom interaction for the effective realization of teaching-learning objectives.

Spread of Education on a Mass Scale : Audio-visual aids like radio and television help in providing opportunities for education to people living in remote areas. They also help in promoting adult education.

Promotion of Scientific Temper : In place of listening to facts, students observe demonstrations and phenomena and thus cultivate scientific temper.

Development of Higher Faculties : Verbalism promotes memorisation. Use of audio-visual aids stirs the imagination, thinking process and reasoning power of the students, and calls for creativity, and inventiveness and other higher mental activities on the parts of students and thus helps the development of higher faculties among the students.

Reinforcement to Learners : Audio-visual aids prove effective reinforcers by increasing the probability of re-occurrence of the response associated with them and thus render valuable help in the teaching-learning process.

Positive Transfer of Learning and Training : Use of audio-visual aids helps in the learning of other concepts, principles and solving the real problems of life by making possible the appropriate positive transfer of learning and training received in the classroom.

Positive Environment for Creative Discipline : A balanced, rational and scientific use of audio-visual aids develops motivation, attracts the attention and interests of the students and provides a variety of creative outlets for the utilisation of their tremendous energy and thus keeps them busy in the classroom work. In this way, the overall classroom environment becomes conducive to creative discipline.

Aid for Teaching

In addition to reading, vicarious experience can be gained from still pictures, films, filmstrips, resource persons, simulations, mockups, television, and the like. The more concrete and realistic the vicarious experience, the more nearly it approaches the learning effectiveness of the first level. Of course, unless the learner realizes that he is dealing with a substitute, his learning may not be comparable to that of real-life learning.

Interest in the role of the senses in learning was already there in educational circles when instructional media began their ascendancy. It has long been recognized that the various senses condition the reception of messages in the communications act. Research done by Cobun (1968) indicated that:

1 per cent of what is learned is from the sense of TASTE.

1.5 per cent of what is learned is from the sense of TOUCH.

3.5 per cent of what is learned is from the sense of SMELL.

11 per cent of what is learned is from the sense of HEARING.

83 per cent of what is learned is from the sense of SIGHT.

Retention of what is learned is likewise related to sense experience.

Observation and research by Cobun tended to show, holding time as nearly constant as possible, that people generally remember:

10 per cent of what they READ.

20 per cent of what they HEAR.

30 Per cent of what they SEE.

50 per cent of what they HEAR AND SEE.

70 per cent of what they SAY.

90 per cent of what they SAY as they do a thing.

Popular Sayings

I hear, I forget.

I see, I remember.

I do, I understand.

Characteristics

1. They should be meaningful and purposeful.
2. They should be accurate in every respect.
3. They should be simple.

4. They should be cheap.
5. As far as possible, they should be improvised.
6. They should be large enough to be properly seen by the students for whom they are meant.
7. They should be up-to date.
8. They should be easily portable.
9. They should be according to the mental level of the students.
10. They should motivate the learners.

Principle of Selection : Teaching aids prove effective only when they suit the teaching objectives and unique characteristics of the special group of learners. Following points may be kept in view in this regard :

(i) They should suit the age-level, grade-level and other characteristics of the learners.

(ii) They should have specific educational value besides being interesting and motivating.

(iii) They should be the true representatives of the real things.

(iv) They should help in the realization of desired learning objectives.

Principle of Preparation : This principle requires that following points should be attended to:

(a) As far as possible, locally available material should be used in the preparation of an aid.

(b) The teachers should receive some training in the preparation of aids.

(c) The teachers themselves should prepare some of the aids.

(d) Students may be associated in the preparation of aids.

Preparation of Physical Control : This principle related to the arrangement of keeping aids safely and also to facilitate their lending to the teachers for use.

Principle of Proper Presentation : This principle implies the following points :

(i) Teachers should carefully visualise the use of teaching aids before their actual presentation.

(ii) They should fully acquaint themselves with the use and manipulation of the aids to be shown in the classroom.

(iii) Adequate care should be taken to handle an aid in such a way as no damage is done to it.

(iv) The aid should be displayed properly so that all the students are able to see it, observe it and derive maximum benefit out of it.

(v) As far as possible, distraction of all kinds to be eliminated so that full attention may be paid to the aid.

Principle of Response : This principle demands that the teachers guide the students to respond actively to the audio-visual stimuli so that they derive the maximum benefit in learning.

Principle of Evaluation : This principle stipulates that there should be continuous evaluation of both the audio-visual material and accompanying techniques in the light of the realisation of the desired objectives.

While all these aids are becoming more and more popular day by day, there are still some problems to be faced and solved. These are :

Apathy of the Teachers : Teachers in general are yet to be convinced that teaching with words alone is very tedious, wasteful and ineffective.

Indifference of Students : The judicious use of aids arouses interest but when used without a definite purpose they lose their significance and importance.

Ineffectiveness of the Aids : Due to the absence of proper planning and the lethargy of the teacher and without proper preparation, correct presentation, application and discussion and the essential follow-up work, the aids do not prove their full usefulness. A film like a good lesson has various steps—Preparation, Presentation, Application and Discussion.

Different Classes

Classification Number 1: Projected and Non-Projected Aids

Projected Aids	*Graphic Aids*	*Display Boards*	*3-Dimensional Aids*	*Audio Aids*	*Activity Aids*
1. Films	1. Cartoons	Blackboard	Diagrams	Radio	1. Computer-Assisted Instruction
2. Filmstrips	2. Charts	Bulletin	Models	Recordings	2. Demonstrations
3. Opaque Projector	3. Comics	Flannel Board	Mockups	Television	3. Dramatics
4. Overhead Projector	4. Diagrams	Magnetic Board	Objects		4. Experimentation
5. Slides	5. Flash Cards	Peg Board	Puppets		5. Field Trips
	6. Graphs		Specimens		6. Programmed Instruction
	7. Maps				7. Teaching Machines
	8. Photographs				
	9. Pictures				
	10. Posters				

Classification Number 2: Audio Materials, Visual Materials and Audio-Visual Materials

Audio Materials	*Visual Materials*	*Audio-visual Materials*
(1) Language Laboratories	(1) Bulletin boards	(1) Demonstrations
(2) Radio	(2) Chalk boards	(2) Films
(3) Sound distribution	(3) Charts	(3) Printed materials with recorded sound system sets
(4) Tape and disco recordings	(4) Drawings etc.	(4) Sound filmstrips
	(5) Exhibits	(5) Study trips
	(6) Film strips	(6) Television

Contd..

Audio Materials	Visual Materials	Audio-visual Materials
	(7) Flash cards	(7) Videotapes
	(8) Flannel boards	
	(9) Flip books	
	(10) Illustrated books	
	(11) Magnetic boards	
	(12) Maps	
	(13) Models	
	(14) Pictures	
	(15) Posters	
	(16) Photographs	
	(17) Self-instructional	
	(18) Silent films	
	(19) Slides	

Financial Hurdles : The Central and State Governments have set up Boards of Audio-Visual Education and have chalked out interesting programmes for the popularization of teaching aids but the lack of finances is not enabling them to do their best.

Absence of Electricity : Most of the Projectors, Radio and TV cannot work without the electric current which is not available in a large number of schools.

Lack of Facilities for Training : Training colleges or specialised agencies should make special provision to train teachers and workers in the use of these aids.

Co-ordination between Centre and States : Good film libraries, museums of audio-visual provision to train teachers and workers in the use of these aids.

Language Difficulty : Most educational films are in English. We should have these in Hindi and other important Indian languages.

Not Catering to Local Needs : Little attention is paid in the production of audio-visual aids to the local sociological, psychological and pedagogical factors.

Improper Selection of Films : Films are not selected according to the classroom needs.

Today, the problem is not whether visual aids should have a place in education. Their place has been recognised long ago. The problem, now, is that of extending the benefits of these aids to all teachers and all children. The future can be bright if there is proper planning on the part of the Government and co-ordination between producers, teachers and students. Useful and effective aids can be produced after getting the reaction of the audience and doing research work in the field. A great deal is being done already but a lot more still remains to be done.

Big Media and Little Media

Big media include computer, VCR and TV. Little media include radio, films strips, graphic, audio cassettes and various visuals.

Three Dimensional Aids

(i) Models

(ii) Mock-ups

(iii) Specimens.

Three dimensional aids are the replicas or substitutes of real objects.

All the learning experiences which can be utilised for classroom teaching are shown by Edgar Dale in a pictorial device—'pinnacle form'—which he called the 'cone of experience'. If we go up the pinnacle from its base, we find that every aid has been arranged in the order of increasing abstractness or decreasing directness. In a simple language, it may be stated that the 'cone' classifies the audiovisual aids according to their effectiveness in communication—aid at the base of the cone as 'most effective'—relative effect gradually decreases.

At the pinnacle of the 'Cone', the direct, purposeful experiences are represented. At the pinnacle of the 'Cone', the verbal symbols are represented.

The experiences included in the cone are as indicated below:

Direct, Purposeful Experience : The experiences gained through the senses are direct and purposeful. It has been amply observed, "An ounce of experience is better than a tonne of theory, simply because it is only as an experience that any theory has vital and verifiable significance." This, direct experience is gained through the aids mentioned at the base of the cone.

Contrived Experience : When the real thing cannot be perceived directly, its simplification becomes necessary. Contrived experience is like a working model which is an editing of reality and differs from the original either in size or in complexity. The real object may be too small or too big, may be confused or concealed. In such a situation imitation is preferred for better and easier understanding.

Dramatic Participation : In dramatics, certain real events are presented through the play, the pageant (kind of community drama, usually based on local history), pantomine (actors do not speak, make movements), tablean (pictureline scene in which the characteristics stand still, silently), and the puppets.

Actual Objects : Actual objects and specimens are indispensable in science and other subjects. They are very vivid and impressive. They make a direct appeal to the senses of children. It is not possible for a child to have a clear picture of a river, a factory or a mountain unless he has seen these. The teaching of history and geography can never be effective without visitsing places of importance, valleys, lakes, old forts, monuments, etc. The students get a correct idea of various minerals when they are shown these objects. In framing the multiplication table, counting of beads and sticks prove to be very useful at the earlier stages.

Blackboard : Blackboard and a piece of chalk prove very helpful in illustrating concepts and ideas to the students. These can be used for drawing diagrams and sketches, etc. Blackboard is a simple and unique device which, in spite of new devices and techniques in teaching, is irreplacable as well as indispensable. It is the oldest and the best friend of a teacher. It is the mirror through which students visualise all about the teacher's mind regarding the lesson in hand, his way of explaining, illustrating and teaching as a whole. It is the cheapest teaching device and continues to be the '*sine quo non*' of our educational system. It is the most universally used aid. Writing on clay and sand was the ancient form of blackboard writing. It helps 'crystallizing' the main points, 'summarising' and 'reviewing'.

1. The teacher can illustrate the main points of the lesson on the blackboard.
2. Abstract statements can be clarified in the exposition stage and a summary containing the salient features can be given at the recapitulatory stage.
3. Questions and problems can be listed on the blackboard.
4. Pupils' interest in classwork can be stimulated by blackboard writings and drawings.
5. A teacher can use the blackboard for graphs, graphics, sketches, maps and statistics, etc.
6. A blackboard provides a lot of scope for creative and decorative work.
7. The teacher can erase writings and drawings and start afresh.
8. It helps the teacher to focus the attention of his students on the lesson. It takes heed of varying capacities and rates of grasp of the students.
9. A teacher can review the whole lesson for the benefit of the class with the help of the blackboard.

Types of Blackboards

Fixed Blackboard : Fixed in the wall facing the class and normally made of wood or concrete cement.

Blackboard on Easel : A portable and adjustable blackboard put on a wooden easel can be taken out of the classroom while taking classes in the open.

Roller Blackboard : Made of thick canvas wrapped on a roller mostly used for teaching higher classes.

Graphic Board : It has graphic lines and is used for teaching mathematics, science and statistics.

Magna Board : A board which enables teachers to make three-dimensional demonstrations with objects on a vertical surface. Small magnets are used to hold suitable objects fixed wherever they are put on this vertical surface.

Chalk Boards of Different Types of Surfaces

1. Paint-coated pressed wood.
2. Dull finished plastic surface.
3. Vitreous-coated steel surface.
4. Ground glass board.

	Colour of the blackboard	*Colour of the chalk*
1.	Green chalk board	White or Yellow chalk
2.	Grey board	Yellow
3.	Red chalk board	Green, Yellow
4.	Orange chalk board	Blue or light Green
5.	Yellow chalk board	Blue
6.	Rose chalk board	Purple, dark Blue
7.	Black chalk board	Any colour

Effective Use of Blackboard

Following points may be kept in view while using the blackboard:

1. Blackboard should be kept clean so-that writing on it could be easily read by the students from all parts of the room.
2. Writing on the blackboard should be legible.
3. Letters and drawings should be large enough to be seen from all parts of the room.
4. Writing should be started from the top left corner.
5. Writing should be in straight rows.
6. Extreme lower corner of the blackboard should not be made use of as writing on it cannot be seen easily.
7. Material on the blackboard should not be covered by standing.
8. Only salient points of the subject-matter should be written on the blackboard.
9. Diagrammatic visual presentation involving many processes should be prepared before the beginning of the lesson.
10. It should be ensured that blackboard is well lighted by natural or artificial means.

11. Everything needed for the blackboard should be got together before the class begins *i.e..*, collection of chalk, rulers, T. Square, Compass, Projector, etc.
12. While writing on the blackboard, the teacher should ensure that the class is attentive.
13. Duster and not hand or handkerchief should be used in cleaning the blackboard.
14. Occasionally students may be asked to write or draw diagram on the blackboard.
15. Teachers should develop the ability to draw freely on the blackboard. The map or chart or diagram that grows before the very eyes of the students is much more useful and valuable than a well finished map, chart or diagram.
16. It should be ensured that the blackboard is periodically serviced.

A chart is a combination of pictorial, graphic, numerical or vertical material which presents a clear visual summary. The most commonly used types of charts include outline charts, tabular charts, flow charts and organisation charts. Other types of charts are technical diagrams and process diagrams. Flip charts and flow charts are also being used. Ready made charts are available for use in teaching in almost all areas in all subjects. But charts prepared by a teacher himself incorporating his own ideas and lines of approach of the specific topic are more useful.

Purposes of Charts

Charts serve the following purposes:

1. For showing relationship by means of facts, figures and statistics.
2. For presenting materials symbolically.
3. For summarising information.
4. For showing continuity in process.
5. For presenting abstract ideas in visual form.
6. For showing development of structure.
7. For creating problems and stimulating thinking.

8. For encouraging utilisation of other media of communication.
9. For motivating the students.

How to use Charts Effectively?

1. Teacher-made charts should be preferred.
2. Students should be involved in the preparation of charts.
3. Charts should be so large that every detail depicted should be visible to every pupil in the class wherever he is sitting.
4. Charts should display information only about one specific area in a subject.
5. A chart should not contain too much written material.
6. A chart should not contain too many details.
7. A chart should give a neat appearance.
8. When a chart is to be used in the classroom, the teacher should make sure that there is provision for hanging the chart at a vantage point.
9. The teacher should have a pointer to point out specific factors in the chart.
10. Straight pins, staples, pegboard lips, gummed hangers, paper-clips, folded making tapes may all be used for fastening charts without damaging them.
11. Charts should be carefully stored and preserved for use in future.

Types of Charts

The following is a list of basic types of charts in terms of arrangements and the kinds of ideas which they may express :

1. The narrative chart, an extended left-to-right arrangement of facts and ideas for expressing: (a) The events in a process such as shoe making, oil cracking, or the like, (b) The events in the development of a significant issue to its point of resolution or to present status (sometimes a time limit). Example: the events leading to the separation of the Bangladesh from Pakistan, the events leading to the establishment of the idea that an individual should be free and that he should have a voice in his own government

and the events leading to increased regulation of business by government, (c) Technological improvement over a period of years such as improvement in transportation, communication, manufacturing etc.

2. The tabulation chart, a left-to-right, top-to-bottom arrangement of facts and ideas for expression: *(a)* Numerical data for making comparisons, *(b)* Lists products, mountains, rivers, or the like in selected areas.
3. The cause and effect chart, usually a limited left-to-right arrangement of facts and ideas for expressing: *(a)* Relationship between standard of living and such factors as economic system, availability of natural resources, level of technological advancement, *(b)* Relationship between a culture and neighbouring cultures, *(c)* Relationship between rights and responsibilities, *(d)* Relationship between a complex of conditions and change or conflict, *(e)* Relationship between the elected and the electors, (f) Relationship between community workers and the community which supports them.
4. The chain charts, a circular or semi-circular arrangement of facts and ideas for expressing: *(a)* Transitions, such as the transition from raw materials to useful products, *(b)* Cycles, such as the water cycle.
5. The evolution chart, a left-to right arrangement of facts and ideas for expressing: *(a)* Changes in specific item from beginning to date, perhaps with projections into the future. Example: origin of the automobile and its subsequent development, early basic homes and changes in basic homes to date, *(b)* Change in standard in food consumption, length of work, weak purchasing power of a rupee, or the like.

Diagrams : Diagrams are very helpful in supplementing vertical illustrations in teaching. Difficult operations may be explained with the help of diagrams. The parts of a flower or leaf can be suitably explained by means of sketches drawn by the teacher in front of the class on the black-board: Simple diagrarns can be used to explain different phenomena in geography and science. The diagrams of battle plans and forts can be drawn on the blackboard. The area and volume, etc., in mathematics can be illustrated through diagrams. A teacher is expected to possess the skill of drawing diagrams easily, neatly, rapidly and readily on the blackboard.

Epidiascope : The epidiascope is an instrument which can project images or printed matter or small opaque objects on a screen, or it can project images of a 4" X 4" slide. With the help of any epidiascope, any chart, diagram, map, photograph and picture can be projected on the screen without tearing it off from the book. No slide is needed for this purpose. An epidiascope serves two purposes.

It works as epidiascope when it is used to project an opaque object. It works as epidiascope when it is used to project slides (by operating a lever). It works on the principle of horizontal straight line projection with a lamp, plane mirror and projection lens. A strong light from the lamp falls on the opaque object. A plane mirror placed at an angle of 45° over the project, reflects the light so that it passes through the projection lens forming a magnified image on the screen.

Film Strip : A film strip is 35 mm wide and has a series of 12 to 48 picture frames arranged in a sequence so that they develop a theme. A film strip can be prepared by taking a series of photographs using a 35 mm camera and then by taking a positive print of the negative film on another 35 mm film.

Globe : Knowledge of map is unreal without the knowledge of globe-the true map. It is the true representative of earth's physical personality. A globe gives a true idea of the total environment at a glance in a classroom situation. It is through globe that a child can understand the concepts of time, space, wind's planetary relations and proportion. Hence, every school shall have globes. Four types of globes may be kept in every school. (1) Political globes, (2) Physical globes, (3) Washable projection globes, (4) Celestial globes.

Graphs : Graphs are flat pictures which employ dots, lines or pictures to visualise numerical and statistical data to show relationships or statistics.

Several Types of Graphs

Line Graph : In a line graph, data is represented with the help of simple lines horizontally or vertically drawn. For increasing the interest and readability of concepts, pictorial illustrations and cartoons are occasionally used on the line graph.

Bar Graph : A bar graph consists of bars arranged, horizontally or vertically from a 'zero' base. The colour, length and size of the bars represent different values.

Circle Graph : Data may be presented in a circle graph.

Magic Lantern : Magic lantern is the earliest invention in the history of audio-visual aids used for projecting pictures from a transparency (slide) on a wall or screen. When the figure or illustration is very small and it is required to be shown to the entire class, a transparent slide of the small figure is prepared. Then, this slide is placed into the slide carrier part of the magic lantern. This magic lantern device projects it on the screen by enlarging its dimension and making the vision more clear and sharp.

Significance of Map Study : In several subjects, especially social studies, the learning of many geographical, historical and economic concepts remains unreal, inadequate and incomplete without map media. A resourceful teacher by motivating the pupils will turn the fear of map into the genuine love for them. This, however, presupposes the invariable uses of maps at every possible opportunity by the teacher in the classroom, and the possession of individual atlases by the pupils. Every student should also know certain elementary aspects of map preparation such as copying, enlarging and reducing, symbolizing, colouring, and preparation of key. Most of the students develop an aversion to maps because they do not know skills relating to map preparation.

Meaning of Map : A map is an accurate representation of plain surface in the form of a diagram drawn to scale, the details of boundaries of continents, countries, of etc. Geographical details like location of mountains, rivers, altitude of a place, contours of the earth surface and important' locations can also be represented accurately with reference to a convenient scale with suitable colour scheme.

Identification of Various Aspects of Maps

1. Understanding and interpreting the key of index.
2. Understanding the lines-boundary lines, lines of communication, lines indicating the rivers, contours, meridians and parallels.
3. Understanding the colours, tints, shadows, symbols in a map or globe.
4. The top of every map is not north, but the direction of northern pole is north.
5. Distinction between the various types of maps such as relief, political, distribution maps, etc.
6. Understanding of the position of earth in the universe. Many students suffer from a notion that the earth leans in June towards the Sun northwards and in December southwards and thus the seasons are formed. Earth never dances that way. The student shall understand that the inclination of earth is constant and the learning effect changes due to its rotation around the sun.

Various Types of Maps

Relief Maps (regional and the world) : This requires the knowledge of colours, contours, symbols and the other connected ethics of map making.

Historical Maps : Maps in history reveal the changing times and the growth and decline of various kingdoms. Knowledge of lines of boundaries and other symbols is necessary.

Distribution Maps : Generally, the student shall associate with the following types of distribution maps: (1) Vegetation maps, (2) Population maps, (3) Economic maps, (4) Statistical maps, (5) Dot maps, (6) Pictorial maps, (7) Language, race and other human division maps, etc.

Geographical Maps : Contour maps, weather maps, seismological maps, archaeological maps, rainfall maps, geological maps, etc.

Microfilm : The microfilm and microfiche are used widely for storage and retrieval of information. Microfilms contain photographed reading material on 35 mm film, each frame being the reduced photograph of a printed page. Thus, printed matter of a book can be stored in *a* small loop of 35 mm film. When the microfilm is passed through *a* microfilm reader, an enlarged image approximately of the size of the printed page is formed on a ground glass (rear-view) screen and the observer can read the matter. By moving the film through the microfilm reader, images of different pages can be obtained and read.

Models : Models are substitutes for real things. A model is a three-dimensional representation of a real thing. Models are concrete objects to explain clearly the structure or functions of real things. A model is a replica of the original. Models enable students to have a correct concept of the object. Being three dimensional, models evoke great interest and simplify matters. Models enable us to reduce or enlarge objects to an observable size. It may not be possible or even practicable to make students see the whole of a large industrial unit or even a large machine unit, but a model will give the correct perspective. Preparation of models could, form a topic for project work.

It is essential to create interest in creative activity in students. Models are working as well as static. A working model will secure immediate attention and serve as motivation to learn. Model can be prepared with several kinds of materials like cardboard, plastic, plaster of paris, wood, clay, and thermocol etc. (See also under three Dimential Aids)

The Secondary Education Commission, on the role of school museums observed, "Museums play a great part in the education of school children as they bring home to them much more vividly than any prosaic lectures, the discoveries of the past and the various developments that have taken place in many fields of science and technology." Again the Commission observes, "We believe it is necessary from the educational point of view to establish such museums in important centres at least wherein both ancient and modern collections will be exhibited and in some cases even demonstrations given of the actual process of development of various scientific discoveries. Nothing can impress students in the formative age so much as the actual visualising of these experiments in a graphic manner,"

Museums are made up of materials used in classroom teaching which, in many cases, are collected, classified and exhibited by students, with or without the help of a teacher. The museum activities may be an extracurricular function of the class or the school or they may be incorporated into a scientific-experimental method of teaching. The objectives of this type of museum are:

(a) to form within the school or the classroom an embryonic community dedicated to the usual occupations reflected in the school life of adults;

(b) to permit visual instruction and experimentation with actual museum specimens;

(c) to stimulate enthusiasm for study and research among both teachers and students;

(d) to stimulate interest, co-operation and participation in the cultural activities and scientific research conducted by the larger museums;

(e) to instruct students in proper scientific methods of laboratory, research and museum conservation and exhibition techniques;

(f) to form, in the absence of larger museums in the community, a nucleus from which the classroom museum can grow beyond the limits of the. school to serve ultimately the community and the region as a whole.

Exhibit Programmes, Interpretation, Visual Communication : What then are some of the ways in which museums as cultural and educational centres of the community can communicate successfully with their transitory visitors of heterogeneous composition? Based on various audience-testing experiments the following media can be used to heighten the effectiveness of visual communication.

Dramatic Labels : Usually they are far too short in the museums or far too long. They actually frighten away rather than entice the average museum visitor. Experiments suggest that large letters placed at the focal point of the case or exhibit area will successfully headline the exhibit and catch the visitor's attention. Like a newspaper headline, the main label tends to direct the eye to smaller, less conspicuous letters that outline the most important points of the exhibit.

Dramatic Lighting : Light is a means of visual communication as well as an attention getter. Coloured lights that change, fade or highlight an exhibit can be used with great dramatic effect. Light can also be used to tell a story and to convey a sense of passing time. Light is particularly important in art museums.

Dramatic Utilization : Again experiments suggest that museum visitors should be given a chance to touch exhibits as well as to see them. Of course, much depends on the nature and expendability of the object involved but certain types of material-objects of wood, stone and metal and special "touch me" samples of animal skins and fabrics-can be used with great success to satisfy the visitor's urge to which while permitting a minimum of danger.

Dramatic Sound Effects : Sound, like light, can be used to heighten the dramatic effect of visual communication. For example, an Amazon rain forest exhibition can be made vastly more effective by adding the sound of tropical rain, the croaking of frogs, the chattering of monkeys, and the beat of drums. An exhibit of mediaeval art can be made more meaningful if it is accompanied by music of the same period:

Effective use of Space : Special concepts are also important in planning visitor traffic patterns within the exhibit areas.

Pictures' Use

Pictures are very much liked by children and especially of lower classes, pictures provide an environment of 'reality'. A lesson in history can be made interesting and stimulating by showing the pictures of kings and queens, costumes and dresses, forts and weapons, monuments and tombs, etc. Similarly in a geography lesson, we can show the pictures of animals, deserts, lakes, mountains and rivers, etc., and also the various aspects of lives of people of other lands with great effect.

Following points need to be kept in view while showing pictures to the students:

1. Child's point of view should be the main criterion in the selection of pictures.
2. Pictures should be relevant to the topic.
3. As far as possible, pictures may be coloured.
4. Pictures should be accurate and of a suitable size.
5. It is desirable if the teacher himself prepares the pictures and takes help from the students.
6. Pictures should be shown in such a way that all students in the class can easily watch.
7. Too many pictures should not be displayed in one lesson.
8. After showing the picture, it should be removed from the view of the students.
9. Sufficient time should be given to see the picture.
10. Students who are good at drawing should be encouraged draw pictures.

Project Per Person

Micro Projector : The combination of a microscope and a slide projector is an instrument called micro-projector. The microscope is used to see very minute parts of objects by magnifying the same hundreds of times. The minute part usually of a plant or an animal is put on a glass slide and a magnified image formed by a combination of leuses in a microscope which can be seen by an individual through the naked eye. The micro-projector attachment consists of a projection lens; a plane mirror fixed at 45 degrees to the vertical plane and a vertical ground glass screen. It is very useful in teaching science.

Overhead Projector (OHP) : Over head projector is a device that can project a chart, a diagram, a map, a table or for that matter, anything written on transparent plates, upon a screen or the white wall before students in a class. This makes teaching illuminative, illustrative and impressive. It also saves a great deal of the teacher's time used in drawing or writing. These transparencies can also be preserved by the teacher for future display while taking up the same topic. It is very simple to prepare such transparencies. All that a teacher has to do is to draw or write, as the case may be, upon transparent plates with any dark ink with a fibre tipped pen. Any material meant for display before the class while teaching can also be typed on such transparencies using a good carbon paper. In case transparencies are to be washed out for use, washable water colour can also be used for writing on the transparencies.

Slide Projector : With a slide projector, photographic slides can be projected on the screen or the wall before the class. Photographs of relevant matter meant for teaching in the class can be developed on celluloid slides and displayed with the help of such a projector. The teacher's lesson can also be recorded on an audio cassette and played with a tape recorder suitably synchronising with the slides by manipulating a remote control switch. Such an arrangement is called a tape-slide sequence. In case there are several slides to be shown in quick succession, the tape-slide sequence can bring as interesting an effect on the viewers as do the movie films. An ordinary slide projector has a frame containing two slits into which slides are put for focusing. They are manually and continuously replaced by other slides one after another. An improved type of a slide projector consists of a circular disc with more slits where even a hundred or more slides can be inserted in a sequential order which can be projected on the screen with the help of a remote control switch to be suitably manipulated by the teacher as he delivers the lesson.

Puppets : Puppetry is one of the old and popular arts in India. The use of puppets has been very popular in China, Egypt, Greece and Japan. Puppets can serve as an effective aid to learning. They can be made to illustrate lessons in civics, geography, history and hygiene. Puppets throw a lot of light in an interesting way on the life of historical personages if they are accompanied by effective narration. There should be plenty of dancing and music in the display of puppetry. While presenting puppet programmes, the age and tastes of the pupils should be duly considered. A short puppet play is always preferable to a long play. Puppets are of three types: (i) Hand puppets which fit in the hand like a glove and are operated from below by fingers. (ii) Rod puppets which are operated from below the stage by a combination of rods and springs, (iii) Marionettes or string puppets which are figures with moving limbs. These are operated from the above by means of strings.

The Reprography

Reprographic is a branch of technology dealing with methods of duplication or reproduction. Duplication involves making a number of identical copies of the original. Reproduction enables preparation of one or more identical copies of the original, same size or of different size in monochrome or colour. Equipment and processes, included are: duplicators, reflex printing and photography.

Player of the Record

Record players are a means of audio playback. They are older types of hardware using records of discs for the needed playback. Four sizes of records 7", 10", 12" and 16" are in common use. There are also high speed record player with standard stylus. The record players now in use are equipped with speed changer mechanisms permitting the playing of the slower long-playing 45, 33⅓ and 16⅔ r.p.m. records played by microgroove stylus. The use of recorded pieces in education has great value in language learning, appreciation of poetry and literature and presentation of brief dramatised episodes from history, from development of musical knowledge and discrimination. Long-playing records with 20 minutes of recorded information per side provide several diverse selections inscribed on each side and are very suitable for classroom instructional purposes. The needed selection for a particular learning situation can be easily identified by the specific microgroove ring it occupies on the record. 'Talking books' for the blind also consists of recordings of essential literature for the visually handicapped. The older, manually wound spring powered gramophone's place now has been taken up by electrically powered multi-speed record players and changers with built-in amplifying unit or linked to separate amplifying units and speakers. Likewise, the older mechanical recording has given place to electrical imprinting involving greater clarity and fidelity.

Tape-recorder : A tape-recorder in its own can be very effective for classroom instruction. Pre-recorded tapes consisting of lessons by eminent teachers on any subject can be played in the class.

Such instructions become impressive not only because of the novelty but also because of their being well-thought out and planned. The tape-recorder has proved to be a boon in teaching foreign languages like English. Pre-recorded tapes on English lessons can be played in the classroom to teach not only the contents of the lesson but also proper accent, pronunciation and intonation which an average English teacher very much lacks.

Video Tapes Played through TV : Pre-recorded video tapes can be played through TV in the classroom. Video films on educational topics shown through TV in the classroom have the same effect on the students as the ordinary cinematic educational films do. Video films have the added advantage over ordinary films in that the arrangement is compact and requires little space and time for manipulation. It is the most convenient of all audio-visual teaching-learning materials.

Video Cassettes

The potential advantage of video cassette lies in the fact that control of the equipment and the learning process is placed in the hands of the learner through control over the mechanics of the machine, i.e. stopping, starting, timing, reviewing and previewing and consequently the capacity to order the sequence of events, controls the rate of learning, and facilitates practice sequences.

The potential exists for providing the basis for learning a wide range of motor, intellectual and cognitive and interpersonal skills, as well as affective aspects. These are important aspects which printed materials cannot deal with adequately.

This facility could be particularly useful where distance education programmes are involved with updating skills and techniques of workers in the field. For example, new horticulture techniques can be transmitted to field workers to improve farming techniques. Mid-career retraining can also be catered for.

In some countries as a way of regionalizing a centrally produced programme, video cassette programmes are being built round the study centre concept, a location where several video machines are available to which students bring their study notes. The students run the programmes as individuals. Sometimes study centres provide for group sessions during which video cassettes are played. Unless some supplementary teaching is provided, this technique can become another version of broadcast technology.

In other countries some institutions assume that students can gain access to such equipment and make programmes which will be used on an individual basis as either supplementary learning material or integral to the teaching programme.

The problems associated with video cassettes are of two kinds: (i) cost; and (ii) production of programmes.

(i) Equipment costs cannot always be kept down by using lower quality equipment. Cheaper equipment formats do not enable technical material such as animal or plant tissue to be represented adequately or tapes to be reproduced in quantity without loss of fidelity.

(ii) Video production for educational purposes calls for new techniques different from the entertainment modes. Producers, directors, scriptwriters need to be knowledgeable about teaching and learning. Many of the old techniques of film and television will no longer be of use. For example, the very basic concept that programmes must have a beginning, a middle, and an end will no longer apply as a cassette could just as easily consist of a series of short video events which sets a problem, teaches a technique, or brings together a range of visual material to make concepts or principles clear.

Aids in Three Dimensions

Three dimensional aids serve as good substitutes for the real objects. There is no doubt that an encounter with real objects serves as an unmatchable source of learning. But on account of several reasons it may not be possible to bring the real objects in the classroom. The real objects may be too large to move or store in the classroom. It may be too small to be seen for a group of students. It can be too complicated in real form to be understood. Its movements may be too slow to be studied completely. It can be too expensive to be purchased by an educational institution. Being handicapped in such situations, a teacher has to search for some good substitute for the real objects.

Models diagrams, mock-ups and specimens are the important three dimensional aids.

Models : Models are the replicas or copies of the real objects. Models are usually of three types: solid, cross-sectional and working. Models are concrete objects, some considerably larger than the real object. Sectional models explain clearly the structure or functions of the original. In some cases working models of the original are used where the specific function of the original is duplicated and could be explained easily.

Following are the important functions of models:

1. Models simplify reality.
2. Models concretise abstract concepts.
3. Models enable us to reduce or enlarge objects to an observable size.
4. A model provides the correct concept of an industrial unit or a bridge or a dam like, the Bhakra Dam etc.
5. A working model explains the various processes of objects and machines.
6. Preparation of models could form a topic for project work. This is very helpful to create interest in creative activity in pupils.

Cardboard, plastic, plaster of paris, wood thermocol' and metal, etc., can be used in the preparation of a model.

Mock-ups. A mock-up refers to a specialised model or working replica of the object being depicted. In a mock-up, a certain element of the original reality is emphasised or highlighted to make it more meaningful for the purpose of instruction. While a model is a recognizable limitation of an object (though larger or smaller than the original one), a mock-up may or may not be similar in appearance. Mock-ups of aeroplanes, automobile engines, bridges, ships and tunnels, etc., may be demonstrated for explaining their structure and actual working. Mock-ups are often used in technical institutions for training purposes.

Dioramas : A diorama is a three dimensional scene in depth incorporating a group of modelled objects and figures in a natural setting. The diorama scene is set up on a small stage with a group of modelled objects kept on the foreground which is blended into a painted realistic background. Dioramas are very effective in the teaching of biological and social sciences.

Tools for Learning

The computer should be used as a learning tool within the student's college classes. Students need to experience how one learn via computer. At WOSC we are in our third year of a National Science Foundation Comprehensive Assistance to Undergraduate Science Education grant titled, "Infusion of Computer Science into Liberal Arts, and teacher faculty member per year concerning the potential of the computer as an educational tool. This is accomplished through a two week summer workshop during which time the faculty member defines a project to be implemented during the course of the following year with grant support. Through these activities we have begun to incorporate the computer as a teaching tool in several courses in various departments on campus. The most successful applications to-date have been in the Music, Dance, English Composition, Biology, Mathematics, Education, and Psychology areas.

Special Education/Psychology-computer-aided testing, software programmes for lab experiences, and student scoring of their own personality inventories.

Music : Pitch and interval ear raining and multi-voice score training.

Physics : Wave motion demonstration programme.

Mathematics : Intermediate Algebra competencies and data research on testing.

Chemistry : Organic compounds nomenclature practice.

English : Composition editing using word, processing.

Education : Application of on-line computer-administered testing.

Psychology /Special Education : Statistical teaching packaged.

Economics /Business : Record keeping system, simulations of running a profitable business, and fiscal management.

Biology : Use of pre-packaged programmes in General Biology and demonstration of various programmes to elementary teachers.

Mathematics : Graphing programmes for trigonometry and vocabulary.

Education : Collection and analysis of student data and transfer of that data to a statistical package.

For the education majors, additional training is required to lay the foundation for using computers as an instructional tool. Very few instructors write primary textbook materials, yet almost all instructors create supplementary materials.

The typical classroom instructor will not be writing computer programmes, but will be creating or managing supplementary materials. The focus is on helping the instructors learn to choose and use good application software in their classroom and to use the computer as a management tool. The following topics are covered in the foundation block for elementary and secondary educational:

1. Computer managed records—
    - (a) Grade book;
    - (b) Test banks of questions;
    - (c) Achievement records.
2. Drill and practice material—
3. Tutorials.
4. Entire curriculum packages.
5. Video/computer interface.
6. The computer as an exploratory tool.
7. Software evaluation and selection.

For students who wish to develop a computer science emphasis the following courses are available at WOSC.

First year

CS 101 Computers and Society 4 credits.

CS 133 Computer Coding - BASIC 4 credits.

Second year

Cs 211 Introduction to Computer Science 4 credits

CS 212 Techniques of Programming- PASCAL 4 credits

CS 215 Computer Organization 4 credits

CS 213 Symbolic Language- FORTRAN 4 credits

CS 217 Into to Data Processing -COBOL 4 credits

Third year

CS 311 Symbolic Language Programming 3 credits

CS 371 Applications Programming 1 3 credits

CS 372 Application Programming II 3 credits

Fourth year

CS 430 Data Structures and Management 3 credits

CS 406g Special Topics 3 to 4 credits

MTH 406g Extended BASIC 4 credits

Students who wish to become the managers and area specialists on computers within speed need to have much of the same basic training as any other computer science person on the lower division level. Their upper division work should be directed toward the area of teaching about computers or the development of instructional material. To provide for this need WOSC offers the following courses—

ED 451g Microcomputer Systems 3 credits

— The building of a working vocabulary dealing with microcomputers. Essential hardware and software components and their functions are studied. Applications of microcomputer systems within the classroom are investigated.

ED 452g computer Based Education 3 credits

— Characteristics of computer-based education illustrating

the advantages to be derived from using computer-managed and computer-assisted interactive systems. Most of the work in the class will be focused on the micro-computer. Prior classwork in ED 4518 and/or CS 133 is required.

ED 461g Computer -Assisted Instruction 3 credits

— The design of computer-assisted instruction lessons and interactive systems will be studied. Students will be asked to design a set of computer-assisted lessons for classroom use.

ED 466g Computer-Managed Instruction 3 credits

— This course is designed to introduce students to a computerized method of testing, record keeping, and decision making that will assist administrative, classroom, and individual learner management. The student examines how computer-managed instruction can solve the management problems of individualized instruction.

A revised education technology masters degree programming incorporating up to 18 credit hours in computer application courses has received committee approval and is in the process of being implemented. Supporting our underlying philosophy that the computer is an instructional medium available to all students, WOSC has one central facility consisting of 13 APPLE II microcomputers, 10 of which are connected to two CORVUS hard disk drives.

Two of the systems have printers attached to them. In addition there are three free standing units, one of which has a video interface. This facility is located in the college library providing, access to all. There are also six microcomputers located around campus for faculty development of programmes and classroom demonstration. During the course of the school year over 50 per cent of the college population interacts with these computers.

The CAUSE Grant has allowed us, as Western Oregon State College, to begin acquainting faculty and administrators with microcomputers. The faculty has begun to examine the curriculum to see how to make use of computers as a teaching tool and to determine the degree of exposure a beginning teacher needs to be prepared for tomorrow's classroom.

Public education is in a period of dramatic change; we believe that all aspects of teacher-education must be examined to insure that we can help future teachers not only gain skills in working with people but also gain the skills needed to use the developing educational technology. Curriculum must be continually examined and adjusted or teacher education risks being out of phase with both students and society itself.

Before listing some of the things being done for teachers using the resources of the School of Education at the University of Michigan, we should describe the basis for our interest in and approach to serving education through computers. In general, we strive for balance among teaching, research and service' we hope to develop, apply and share knowledge about the use of computers at all levels of education, elementary school through college. We choose to give special attention to school and community resources, and then make the most of the special resources of the University of Michigan and the School of Education.

Focus on School and Community Resources : The things most important to effective learning with computers are happening today in schools and homes, not in universities and the colleges. What we do for teachers using the resources of the School of Education must serve them well in their own schools and communities. Therefore the pre-service training, as well as in-service programmes and consolation, is carried out with an eye for the facilities and situations which will be found in the local schools.

Computers, Education and Teachers : Inexpensive computing facilities that are easy to use will be one of the more important things to happen to education in this century. We believe that she experience of teachers and the availability of technical support will be the most important factor in determining how well computers are used in schools. The need is now, and growing more rapidly than institutions are professional organizations can respond.

A Role for School of Education : Colleges and universities can translate interest in computers and education into actions to meet the needs of students, teachers and administrators by going out into the schools and communities to assist with operational programmes, by maintaining high standards for professional development and practice, and by nurturing appropriate interest in research, e.g., to increase knowledge about teaching and learning processes. More specifically, we recommend that schools of education provide practitioners with skills in teaching and administration of computer-related curriculum as well as information about computers, and arrange for continuing support of on-going programmes as well as one-shot training to get them started. Action-oriented research is appropriately included in all training and support activities, that is, professionals should get involved in planning for, collecting and interpreting data to aid in decisions in their schools.

Resource of the Colleges and Universities : Training and support offered to teachers through colleges and universities should take advantage of the special resources available there. Microcomputers are used throughout the University in many different ways—information systems, process control, laboratory equipment, specialized graphics, etc.

Students have a unique opportunity to learn about current and future uses of microcomputers, and as teachers they need to know about computing in their areas, in jobs, and in society, not just in the classroom. Exploration of microcomputer applications opens doorways onto the entire world of computing. The university of Michigan has been a leader in computers and education since a Food Foundation grant in 1956 for curriculum development in engineering education. Nearly all parts of the University have been involved, humanities and the arts as well as sciences and professions.

Various units provide courses as well as software and applications, Research and development throughout the University contributes to the quality of the programme in the School of Education, and education faculty help other units using computers in teaching give appropriate attention to matters of leaning and teaching. We believe the most effective uses of computers in education today are well based in the subjects taught and in supporting disciplines, so we do not treat "Computers in education" as a separate discipline.

Overview of this Report : The first section describes the academic programmes in the School of Education—degree programmes, courses, independent work, and cooperation with other teaching units. The second and third sections summarize service and research activities. The facilities for educational computing are described briefly in the last section, and we close with a brief statement about future directions.

The University of Michigan School of Education is organized in five large units: administration and policy planning; development, learning and teaching; higher science Computers are used in all the programmes, but they get particular attention in "development, learning and teaching" as part of literacy. Special topic such as problem solving, learning strategies and social relations are considered in all four areas of literacy. Computing in education is not treated as a separate degree programme because the University gives only one masters degree or doctorate in education, and more importantly, because computing in education is considered in context rather than as a separate subject.

Microcomputers and Education provides an overview of computers in education with special attention to instructional design, testing and evaluation. Microcomputer Programming for Educators serves as an introduction as well but leads to specific skills is one or more languages and the development of specific programmes for use in ones teaching. These two courses are offered every term and enroll about 30 students each time. Microcomputers in the classroom integrates programming, instructional design and classroom management. Seminar in the Use of Microcomputers in Education provides for advance project work. These two courses are scheduled once each year and are restricted to graduate students; typical enrollment is 20.

Because the field is growing and changing more rapidly that a school of education can respond with new courses, and because the student learning about computers in education come from varying backgrounds and situations, the College offers many opportunities for study of special topics by individuals and small groups in addition to regular courses. Typically students will define topics for independent reading or research, often derived from questions raided during one of the regular courses, and sometimes based on experiences in their own teaching, research of administration.

One or more faculty members will assist in redefining the topic and identifying resources for independent work. The results often are reported through informal seminars as well as in publishable reports. About ten students use this option each year. These opportunities for independent work provide some of the flexibility needed in a new area of study, and help determine what topics later students should study as a more formal programming is developed. That is, some of the following topics may become regular courses:

- Computer use in science, match, social studies, etc.
- Planning and administration of computer labs and programmes.
- Curriculum science and education.
- Information sciences and education.
- Social amplifications of technology.
- State and regional programmes for computers in education.
- Learning theories and technology.
- Research and evaluation.

The need for practitioners helping with computer applications and studies in schools is considerable and immediate. The linkage between research and practice is of immediate benefit to operational programmes as well as long-term research. Therefore, practical experience is very appropriate in a graduate study of computers in education. We encourage practicums and project experience, either in association with on-going projects in the School of Education or elsewhere in the University, or in the schools in which the candidates presently work. We know no better "examination" than that provided by experience in the field—managing a microcomputer lab, developing instructional applications in one's discipline, or helping teachers to use computers more effectively in their classrooms. We expect about ten students a year to enroll for credit in a practicum; presently the only students in this category are working on doctoral dissertations.

Undergraduates in our teacher preparation programme have ample opportunity to use computers in their regular classes or independent work. In addition to trying computer applications in the relevant discipline, students are likely to be signed other interesting activities, such as using a microcomputer to carry out a readability analysis of text materials and designing a computer-based learning activity. A microcomputer resource center provides machines, software, publications, and other materials for individual work, as well an opportunity to observe learners from pre-school to adult working with computers individually or in classes

Diffusion of computing through methods classes began with a grant from the "faculty development fund" at the Center for Research on Learning and Teaching. We went to the instructors with suggestions for computer use in the various disciplines, demonstrated the applications, and offered to assist. Virtually all methods courses now include computing activity directed by the individual instructors, with technical assistance form the staff of the resources center. Students can go on to teach themselves more about computers; some enroll in the undergraduate classes.

The School of Education draws on the resources of other units that work with computers and information systems, and also coordinates its efforts with others interested in computers in schools. The School of Library Science shares resources for demonstration and research; working together, education and library science prepare students for serving a support function in the schools. The College of Engineering has set up microcomputer classrooms for undergraduate courses in programming and applications. At scheduled times these classrooms are available for demonstrations, workshops and special classes.

The PET shop is available for other uses, especially for summer institutes since only a few chemistry lab sections are scheduled in the summer. The Department of Computer and Communications Sciences helps staff several courses off campus for teachers needing a sound basis in computer science. The Department of Psychology has several laboratories working on learning and instruction using computers, providing graduate students in education access to a wider variety of research opportunities. The Center for Research on Learning and Teaching helps provide the resources for demonstration and research, and in return, the School of Education helps faculty elsewhere in the University explore computer applications in their own teaching and scholarly work, a task beyond the resources of the Center. The communication among faculty using computers began with a series of workshops and "faculty seminars" organized by the Center for Research on Learning and Teaching. Later the same series was offered on the site of the resource center in the School of Education, establishing it as the new site of information and advice. The Apple users group meets regularly at the School of Education, further identifying the resource center as a focal point for communication.

The School of Education offers many lectures, demonstrations and consultation on the use of microcomputers for schools. These include;

— faculty orientation sessions;

— intermediate district or country school board sessions; and community meetings.

— At times faculty members help the staff in the planning of computer systems and curriculum to be used throughout a school or district. We are always conscious of helping share experience among organizations and agencies. For example, we helped establish a state task force on computers in schools, we work with regional resource centers in the public schools systems throughout the state, and, of course, we share software through professional associations and user groups.

The University also offers specific in-service programmes for schools system.

Researchers at the University are active in a variety of studies and plan a comprehensive research programme on the use of computers in education. A microcomputer research collaborative established in the summer of 1979 has encouraged and participated in research on attitudes and values; learning with computer assistance; social structures; and futures. CAI, per se is not given much attention, but the researchers focus instead on aspects of learning, procedures for curriculum design, social context for learning, or other disciplines which contribute to effective use of computers in education.

The realities of computer-use in schools for the next few years dominate research planning. For example, attention is being given to conceptualizing how a single microcomputer is best used with a group of students where the institution cannot afford enough machines for everyone individually or in pairs. The programme of research assumes more computers will be purchased for homes that for schools and so explores ways to exploit home computing for education. Research is encouraged in many innovative uses of computers in education. Such uses include but are not limited to attitudes that those using computers in education have towards:

— learning;
— careers;
— educational institutions;
— technology in education;
— lifelong learning;
— creative activities supported by technology;
— family activities.

Learning with Computer Assistance, Including Aspects of

— efficiency;
— effectiveness;
— long-term effects;
— thinking and problem solving;
— learning skills;
— skills for handling information.

Social Structure, Involving

— classroom structure and activities;

- — friendships;
- — interpersonal relations;
- — teacher-student relationships;
- — teacher role;
- — parent role;
- — implications for family.

Futures, Research, Including

- — anticipating new technology and its impacts;
- — assessing social implications;
- — shaping alternative futures.

Centre for Resources

The computer education resource center is housed in the Instructional Strategy Services unit of the School of Education, providing an appropriate context, technical support, and ready access for students, faculty and the teaching support, and ready access for students, faculty and the teaching community to explore a new technology in education. Other programmes of the Service unit provide links with graphics, video, curriculum review, information services, and the like. Of course, other units in the schools of Education also use microcomputers in their work; students use machines in the Statistical Laboratory, the Center for Evaluation Research Training, and a special programme in education and psychology. Both the manager and assistant manager of the resource center know the computer field well, along with their own specialities in library science. Workshops, demonstrations, and open access fit well within its domain, and the unit provides the larger context of teaching and learning.

The lab includes at least one of each common microcomputer along with documentation and a library of applications. About seven Pets, ten Apples, and a dozen Atari's can be assembled so that workshops and classes have one computer station for each of two terminals on time sharing systems, and one additional terminal is dedicated to special uses in graphics. Typically half of the machines are out in faculty offices or field research. The equipment kept in the resource center is arranged about the periphery of the space for individual work but it can easily be shifted for group use of classroom demonstration.

A second classroom is used when we call in extra machines. Group viewing is accommodated through use of large monitors: black and white monitors for applications which are primarily text, and colour where that is helpful to the demonstration. The same monitors are used for viewing material from videotape for more convenient use in group demonstrations as well as easy access by individuals The resource center also has two vediodisc players, one consumer model and one industrial for experiments with computer-controlled videodisc.

The staff person who handles other equipment for the Resource Centre also takes care of computer connectors, cables, and the like Some time is required for the cleaning and repair of disk and cassette media, the diagnosis of equipment problems, and minor repairs. This person also makes arrangements for outside repair as needed.

The computer lab maintains a large set of materials in cooperation with the Center for Research on Learning and Teaching. The center manages to maintain:

— a comprehensive programme library;

— a substantial reference library;

— most of the relevant periodicals;

— manuals for each of the machines;

— most of the recent textbooks;

— media materials:

1. video tape
2. tape-slide
3. computer programmes;

— annotations on programmes and applications;

— self-help posters.

The resources center is supervised by experienced library and media staff. The manager, assistant manager and laboratory aides together provide service to both faculty and students, comparison of equipment options, such identification and review of software, advice on development of applications—and assistance with preparation of graphics for use in papers and other presentations. That is, the resource center provides computer resources for any scholarly work by students, as well as a site for study of computers in education. In addition to the regular staff and faculty, undergraduates are hired as aides and programmers to extend the support staff to serve more people at modest cost.

The students use their work as a learning experience. About twenty undergraduate students benefit from this opportunity each term. Graduate students help with review application programmes and publications. Workshops, short courses and programme review are carried on by faculty members on a regular basis.

Service to other units, organizations and informal groups have proved mutually beneficial. For example, the University of Michigan Apple users group meets regularly, and typically some education students who happened by, get "hooked" and leave with some new ideas of software for innovation or use.

Graduate students have gained excellent experience staffing special courses for the University Children Center, and education classes have observed young children exploring computers. The resource center is a resource for local teachers, providing the full tango of information and examples maintained for University students and faculty, and offering demonstrations in an "open house" format and instruction through institutes and workshops. In addition, and academic programme for talented students offered by the Gifted Students Institute each summer since 1978 provides one example of the "computer camp" idea that has becomes so popular recently. "Properly designed, can allow students to formulate hypotheses, test them, analyze results, and refine their conceptions. Moreover, they can provide the student with a record of the course of his or her investigations, permitting greater self-awareness of thinking and, learning." There are, however, many barriers to realizing this potential, among them a lack of consensus on the definition of higher-order thinking and an incomplete understanding about the use of technology to promote it. We explore both issues in this chapter.

There are diverse views about the components of higher-order thinking and no adequate and agreed upon theory from which to derive a definition that would elicit consensus. Although a number of researchers have developed theories, definitions, and criteria for higher order thinking, a consensus remains elusive. For instance, Feurstein emphasizes "autonomous learning" and the importance of logical reasoning, recognizing relationships, classifying and comparing concepts.

Foshay stresses the importance of learning to learn, which he labels the "pursuit of meaning," and includes such components as learning facts and findings, learning techniques, learning sources and processes interpreting information. Zacharias is more practical, emphasizing heuristics such as determining whether a problem can be solved, pushing possibilities to the limit, even to absurdity, asking for help, changing scale to achieve a different perspective, and bringing in outside information. Each perspective is valid, but they do not combine to provide a consensus.

For the purpose of this chapter, we suggest that higher order thinking occurs when a person is engaged in active and sustained cognitive effort directed of solving a complex problem and when the person makes effective use of prior knowledge and experience in addressing the problem. The problem must be complex for the person; many problems will meet this criterion for some people but not for others. Problems may be well-structured with clear definition, rules, and goals or ill-structured with unclear definition, ambiguous rules, and subjective goals. By sustained effort we mean engagements requiring anywhere from ten minutes to many hours or longer.

Cognitive effort includes activities generally identified in the literature on problem solving, such as integrating and synthesizing different bodies of information, making critical judgments, and developing and testing hypotheses. We include the concept of effectiveness in our definition because an important overall pedagogical goal is to improve the student's capacity to succeed in solving increasingly complex problems. We believe that a novice problem solver, although engaged in active and sustained cognitive effort, may not use strategies of the same efficiency as those used by an expert.

On the other hand, an expert who very quickly reaches the correct solution to a problem that to other might be complex would not be engaged in higher-order thinking. We believe that effectiveness in higher-order thinking necessarily involves making appropriate use of prior knowledge and experience relating to the problem. This conception of higher-order thinking enables us to think about ways of realistically challenging students of different ages and with different levels of knowledge as they deal with problems they perceive to be intellectually complex.

Although we can not precisely specify the components of higher-order thinking, we have a good idea of what such thinking is not While higher-order thinking may be involved, it usually is not evident when the central activities of students are (a) memorizing, (b) learning isolated facts and findings (c) using algorithms rigidly or automatically, or (d) answering problems with solutions already known to them. Such activities do not involve higher-order thinking because they do not represent "complex" problems nor do they require sustained cognitive effort for most students.

Our definition of higher-order thinking suggests that much of what goes on in schools bears only an indirect relationship to higher-order thinking. Evidence of lack of instruction in higher-order skills comes from a variety of places. Studies of reading instruction find that 90 percent of instruction is directed at the learning of isolated words and only 5 percent is focused on understanding text. Surveys of textbooks indicate the tremendous emphasis on vocabulary learning and the superficial and fragmented nature of the material. Studies of mathematics instruction report that early instruction in arithmetic may even drive our some of the effective problem-solving strategies that students bring to school.

The nature of standardized achievement tests discourages teachers from focusing on higher-order skills. Items on such tests typically require responding with discrete bits of information in a multiple-choice format. Domains for these tests are often rigidly defined and rarely require students to synthesize information across defined domains. Recent work by a small group of educators and cognitive psychologists has resulted in school-based curricula designed to improve thinking skills. Like others, Sternberg has argued for the necessity for training students to think: Each program should provide explicit training both in the mental processes used in task performance and in self-management strategies.

Wide-range Options

Techniques for teaching these skills cover a wide range of options and philosophies. Glaser and Sternberg have described and analyzed several of the more touted instructional programs and their reported successes. These programs range from teaching ways to structure problems and generalizable heuristics in a nearly content-free environment to training strategies within a specific content domain.

Generally, computer software for the schools is similar to other instructional material in its focus on imparting factual information and on low-level algorithmic skills. There is evidence that students can learn factual information effectively by using computers in academic subject areas. For instance, the effectiveness of computer-aided instruction has been consistently demonstrated in foreign language and in science.

Across subject areas, computerized instruction is associated with greater or equal gains in learning when compared with traditional instruction. Furthermore, this achievement is obtained in equal or less time than is needed for regular classroom learning. An experiment carried out in the Los Angeles Unified School District shows some of the potential for computer-assisted instruction.

In conjunction with the Educational Testing Service, the district conducted a five-years longitudinal experiment using the Computer curriculum Corporation's drill and practice software that was originally developed by Patrick Suppes. The purpose was to determine whether these computer programs could improve performance of students in compensatory education programs in mathematics, reading and language arts. Compared to a control group, students using the CAI materials showed large and significant gains.

The use of CAI curricula helped students to improve standardized test scores significantly. Nearly all the research on effects of computer-assisted instruction in schools focuses on knowledge development programs similar to the programs in the Los Angeles schools. Such programs account for the greatest use of computers in elementary schools. There is little evidence however that computer software stimulates higher-level thinking. This lack of evidence is one of the reasons that software to promote higher-order thinking is used in schools only to a very limited degree. Another reason is that few programs are available, even though the quality of such programs is beginning to improve.

7

COMPUTER-AIDED INSTRUCTION

Learning Method

Chemistry is an experimental science. It is a collection or experiments, observations and inferences as compiled by various scientists, researchers and philosophers scattered all over the world. The development of science and technology is more or less dependent upon the advancement of chemistry. Its applications are spread over not only to earth sciences, but also to life-sciences. The study of Chemistry is the study of various experiments and observations as reported by scientists and researchers. The study may conveniently be divided into three classes: (i) minor, (ii) major, and (iii) futuristic.

The minor-class is meant for students upto postgraduate or pre-research level. The major class is meant for researchers while the last futuristic class is meant for philosophers and thinkers. At present the minor class has been further sub-divided into various courses of study based upon stepwise progress (slow process) such as X class, XII class, B. Sc., M. Sc., and M. Phil. This study has been progressively divided into career-class division, commonly popular by the name academic qualifications. This minor class level study is generally available in the form of (i) books, (ii) charts and (iii) films, which comes under the first phase—Near Education.

One has to see and hear these materials when one reaches these materials (going to library, book-shop etc.) or materials reach the student (purchase of books, etc.) in order to be acquainted with the knowledge of the subject. In both of these processes, not only investment is required but also duplication/frequent edition of library stock and books becomes necessary, which increases the budget on education many-a-time more than stipulated, but without advancement of knowledge. In the computer-aided instruction, no doubt, per-set expenditure is must in the form of a super computer, having stored knowledge, satellite communication system, based upon sometimes scattered micro-wave receiving/ transmitting mobile systems and video cassette players/recorders-cum-coloured T.V. system at the receiving ends, whether in schools, colleges or Open universities. This is the second phase known as Distance Education.

In this distance education, the quality of education can be maintained much more easily compared to the near-education. In the near-education system, the quality of reading material is difficult to maintain and also the lack of interest by the teachers will result in the deterioration of the quality on imparting standard education to all. On the other hand in the distance education, quality of education can be improved continuously, as a result of comments of viewers/ open University students more easily and the question of lack of interest of teachers does not come in the picture at all.

The span of human life is very much limited but the extent of education is infinite. To be familiar with at least a few knowledgeable materials, the slow-stepped education, as it is imparted in schools, colleges and universities, has to be improved. Probably at present the best course will be "viewing," "listening" and "evaluating" the retention of understandable material through the distance-education system.

In the past, each branch of knowledge was linked very smoothly to the other and one person was wise enough to understand gists of varied subjects. Now-a-days, the resolution of knowledge has been so much that even a segment of knowledge has so many sharp peaks. And it is rather impossible to jump from one peak to another without falling into the lowest precipice.

Another aspect which rests upon the autonomous state of educational institutions, no doubt, is curbed in the distance education system but there is ample scope for those who want to set the path for others to follow in this system. Such persons may come forward with suggestions and improvements underlying the basic aims and objectives of the system. In this system, lethargic persons are eliminated in the sense that they have to fall in line with the queries posed by viewers/distance education students. One can learn a number of spikes of knowledge in the short span of one's life.

Once students after the minor level training enter the major level, they will be better equipped to make use of the already stored knowledge in the form of reported experiments and results to become futuristic philosophers and thinkers. As has been mentioned earlier, Chemistry is an experimental science, therefore computer-aided instruction must provide experience to familiarise the students with various experimental techniques and also to develop theoretical and manipulative calculations. Actually, Chemistry is not a precise and a mathematically 'finished' discipline, but requires new experiments based upon law of probability rather than on the law of singularity. Instruction involves teaching and learning. In the usual chemistry curriculum viz. lecture, laboratory, problem-oriented sessions, tutorial and sessional assignments and examinations ; all may be programmed by computer methods. Moreover, transferability is possible not only at the computing level but also from the point of view of the environment in the class for which the programmes have been designed.

At present, a vast literature on computers in Chemistry is available but a serious time lag exists between the development of computer science and the application in the natural sciences. It will be appropriate to list some of the elementary programme languages viz., PIL, Pitt's Interpretive Language, CATALYST/PIL, Pitt's CAI language and Fortran IV and PIGS.

The computer-aided instruction (CAI) provides information, presents question and problems and provides hints if help is requested just as the student in the class-room poses any query to the teacher. A dialogue between a student and a teacher exists in this CAI system. It also sharpens dull arithmetic skills of the students. The programmes are written in CATALYST/PIL—a lesson designer-oriented language which may be accessible to students nearly 24 hours a day from public terminals. CATALYST uses the symbol whereas PIL uses for the prompting character. The following are the two examples :

(1) Now Let's Calculate the Atomic weight of a Hypothetical Element. The Element has two Isotopes :

Isotope	*Exact Mass*	*Percentage Natural Abundance*
43	42.9637	51.27
45	44.9752	41.73

What is the Atomic Weight of the Element ?

help

Help

Need A Hint ?

The atomic weight of an element can be found from the exact mass and the abundance of the isotopes according to the expression :

(Exact mass) (% abundance/100) for isotope one + (exact mass)* (% abundance/100) for isotope two + ...—atomic weight of the element now try it !

42.96 37*, 5127 + 44.9752* .4873 VERY GOOD

(2) What is the (Approximate pH of A 0.147 Molar Acetic Acid Solution ? (Ka + 1.8E-5)

Calc

Ready:

Type—the log of the square root of (0.147* 1.8e-5)—the log of the square root of (0.147* 1.8e-5)—2.788705 return

Return to last question

Very Good : Another important feature of CAI system is the branching capability which is a powerful teaching aid. The CAI lessons contain CATALYST as well as PIL Statements.

For Example

Which of the following acids dissociates to the greatest extent in Water ? Type the name of the Acid.

Carbonic acid (h_2co_3)	k 1 = 4.6 e-7
Acetic acid ($h_2c_2o_2$)	k 1 - 1.8e-5
Boric acid (h_3bo_4)	k 1 = 5.8e-10
Oxalic acid ($h_2c_2o_4$)	k 1 - 6.2e-2

*Frame 423

? ? Frame 40 type 2 help

? Frame 46 type 2 boric

? Frame 100 return 4 type 2 oxalic

Sorry, that's not the answer I am looking

For. Try again or ask for help.

Set c (4) = c (4) + 1

? Frame 41

- Frame 46
- Set c (4) = c (4) + 1

No, you have chosen the acid which dissociates the least. Are the exponents troubling you?

100	10	0.1	0.0001
1.0e2	1.0e1	1.0e-4	

Remember: The greater the dissociation constant, the greater the number of ions in solution.

Try it again. ? Frame 423* frame 501

A number of CAI lessons are available now-a-days comprising atomic structure, bonding, periodic trends, descriptive chemistry, analytical chemistry, structural techniques, physical chemistry, numerical analysis, etc. etc.

Another important feature of CAI is the simulation programme which may be displayed graphically without being burdened with detailed numerical calculations.

The last part of the present education is the examination which involves huge administrative expenditure and wastes so much time. The computer-generated repeatable examination system will give students the opportunity of taking examination on a repeatable basis. Students may be allowed to take examination up to five times and the answer-sheet with missed items indicated will become input to an item-analysis programme. The examination will also serve a diagnostic purpose. Bright students will relatively score more and may concentrate more intellectually stimulating topics in Chemistry. Computer-aided instruction can be broadly further sub-classified into computer-assisted instruction, computer-evaluated instruction and non-interactive computer applications.

Computer-Aided Instruction (CAIDI) : Is there a continuing, on-line student-computer dialogue in which the machine is asking the student questions and subsequently checking his responses, and/or is the machine directing the logical development of a new concept ? In other words, is the communication pedagogically interactive or tutorial in nature ?

This entire branch is sometimes called Computer-Augmented Learning (CAL)

Yes	No
All Canned Programs Computer-Assisted Instruction (CAI)	Is the principal role of the computer in the development and grading of course assignment and examinations ?
NO	YES
The principal role of the computer must then be to assist in problem solving, to expand the course content via simulation, to provide student programming experience, or to merely expose the student to the various ways in which the computer can be utilized in Chemistry.	ALL CANNED PROGRAM Computer-Evaluated Instruction (CEVIN) includes computer-generated repeatable tests (CGRT)

Canned and Student-Written Programs : Non-Interactive Computer Applications (NICA) includes on-line classroom computing.

The broad-line configuration for on-line classroom computing is presented.

Outside Inside Classroom

Classroom Hardware Transmitting Viewing

Link Medium

CRT Equipped Teletype

Signal-Generating CRT Terminal Video Adapter with Keyboard Video Adapter TV

Monitor(s)

COMPUTER Teletype TV Camera Terminal

OR Mini "hard copy" Computer on transparency Overhead Projector Opaque Screen

Opaque Projector

A number of programmes have been used for on-line classroom computing viz. prediction of electronic configuration of atoms and ions in s, p, d terminology, VSEPR theory, X-ray crystallography, etc.

Chemical information and results lead to further research and development. Today chemical information can be generated, processed, stored, managed and retrieved and used in new ways and methods for the futuristic class. The computer generated data—in either human readable or machine readable form, in black and white on paper, magnetic tape disks, drums, chips, data cells or micro form —has become now-a-days a part of a vast, varied and disperse data bank or reservoir. Research efforts have promoted automatic indexing from full text. Many data bases are available for lease or license by individual companies, Universities and national bodies.

In India, this facility is now being initiated for the benefit of major and futuristic class.

Computer-Assisted Instruction

Ministry of Education under the Government of India has launched a pilot project for introducing Computer Literacy and Studies in Schools (CLASS) in collaboration with the Department of Electronics. At the first instance, 250 schools all over the country were brought under the purview of this project and training courses were organised for teachers in the selected Resource Centres. Gradually all the schools would be covered in a phased manner. This has raised a wave of discussion in the country: Why computer in the field of education also? There has very often been hue and cry when computer has entered into the arena of industry, business, banking, examination, and so on. It is usually complained that computer will replace the man and unemployment will be rampant as a result of this.

Computers in spite of strong opposition are now extensively used in various fields of human activity. Application of the computer in industry and business is considerable. It is used in traffic control and in police investigation. But for its help, space journey would be impossible. It is utilised for student guidance as well as for marriage counselling. It assists the universities and Boards of Secondary Education in tabulating scores and grading students. Now it is also useful in sports and games at the national and international levels.

In data-processing, efficiency of the computer cannot be over-estimated. It can make very complicated calculations in a split second. It has proved its wonderful capabilities and is regarded as the most important invention after the birth of the printing process. It may be said that as the printing machine has enlarged the scope of communication, the computer has broadened the field of information and data processing. Its impact on food and material production, defence and remote sensing, scientific research and education is enormous in most of the advanced countries. The scientists and researchers having confidence in computers claim that no teacher ever born, no method ever adopted and no media ever utilised, can match the computer's efficiency.

In view of such increasing importance of the computer, students, the future citizens and employees in various walks of life, cannot afford to keep themselves aloof from this potential medium. Education even at the school stage has to provide for computer instruction. Profound technical knowledge and positive attitude as well as interest in the computer are essential prerequisites for the successful citizens of the coming decades. Besides, some of the challenging job opportunities will be available to the young in near future.

The Ideas

The computer is an electronic machine working on the principles of prolonged learning that aim at individualised instruction to meet the special needs of individual learners. The computer is a flexible as well as powerful devise which can cater to these needs by storing, processing and retrieving information.

The computer is equipped with electronic circuits, keyboards recording and storage facilities. Although it is called "a dignified calculating machine", or a "glorified calculator", it has a unique capability of "memorising heaps of information and reproducing or retrieving" them whenever necessary. The procedures and languages used for recording and retrieving information are specific and peculiar. Hence, programming involves great knowledge and skills which call for training and experience for manipulation and translation of the information.

Application Approach

The computer usually has five important components: (i) input system, (ii) output system, (iii) a memory storage, (iv) processing equipment, and (v) a control system.

The input system converts our information into computer's language form and the output system retrieves the information into our language. The memory storage retains all the information that is fed into it through the input system. The processing system processes the data through manipulation and selects the information as required. All these functions are controlled and co-ordinated by the control system as per a particular programme.

Two kinds of information are normally fed into the computer and a programme consists of a set of instructions and an amount of information. Both sets of information are preserved in the memory storage.

Educational Role

The computer is now regarded as a super teaching machine. Its use in education has been tried as an innovation and it has proved its teaching efficiency in many developed countries. The computer has been helping the teacher in the following areas:

(i) Evaluation of students performance and classification of children according to abilities;

(ii) Preparation of timetable and schedules;

(iii) Allocation of learning materials according to individual needs and interests.

(iv) Maintenance of progress cards efficiently and confidentially.

(v) Providing information/data for guidance and reference.

(vi) Provision of direct interaction between pupils and subject-matter.

(vii) Engaging students in tutorial work;

(viii) Providing immediate feedback to students for better interaction and motivation.

Computer Assisted Instruction or briefly known as CAI is an interesting innovation in educational technology. Its marvels have been demonstrated and seem to revolutionise the whole spectrum of education. It has better flexibility and more versatility than any of the teaching machine. It can cater to the individual needs of many students at a time and record all the responses of all the pupils with reliability. The time taken by individual student in responding to a question and extent of correctness in the same are also recorded by the computer. All this helps the educator in planning instruction and providing relevant materials.

The CAI can deal the problem of quality in education more effectively and more flexible kind of branching is possible on the part of the computer according to the student's performance. A learner can make progress at one's pace, receive and choose the material, sequencing and level of instruction freely. Since each learner's performance is automatically recorded and can be fed back to the teacher, learner's performance can be evaluated and education be provided according to the strategy that is best suited to the individual. The teacher can be relieved from the daily routine and monotonous drilling activities. It has been experimentally proved that any lesson in any subject can be programmed for CAI if the objective is clearly defined and learning materials are represented in words, visuals and experiments.

The CAI installation usually consists of individual learning booths each with a console. Every student sits in front of the console with a television screen displaying information, etc. A complete learning package suiting to his individual needs is presented, sequentially. This package may consist of video as well as audio tape-recordings, films, slides, film strips, and so on. The student may make queries to the computer by means of a type-writer key-board and get answers in printed forms. The student may write the answers directly on the cathode ray tube display screen with a "light-pen" which can be evaluated by the computer. On completion of a programme, the computer records his progress and prints out a report for the teacher.

Points in Favour and in Opposition

Although CAI is developed on the principles of programmed learning, it also utilises the concepts of audio-visual education, communication theory, system analysis, data processing and learning theory. CAI produces learning experience effectively and efficiently. A good amount of information stored in the computer is made available to the learner more readily than by any other media. The interaction between the student and instructional programme is made more dynamic and more individualised in CAI than in any other system. But judicious pre-planning and careful programming are essential for this.

CAI is, however, extremely expensive. It is also mostly mechanical and deprived of human touch. Therefore, it is criticised on the ground that this innovation will dehumanise the educational system and the teaching-learning process will be lifeless and mechanised.

Educational technologists, therefore, suggest system approach representing an integrated, sequential and multimedia learning package. This systems approach should also consist of all relevant media, material and methods. It will not replace the teacher, but will relieve him of drudgery and dreariness. The Computer Assisted Instruction will rather bank upon the teacher heavily for constant analysis, curricular revision, better planning human guidance and counselling. A creative and committed teacher is more in demand than anything else when computer is available in education.

Policies at National Level

The provisions under the NPE, 1986 and POA, 1986 remained intact in the NPE, 1992 but more emphasis was given in the latter on Computer Education. In the beginning the coverage of schools under the CLASS Project was modest. But with a view to increase awareness of computer literacy among students, teachers and parents, more schools were taken up and more agencies were involved in the process. A notable initiative was triggered by the CLASS Project as private schools were allowed to charge fees for the said facility and professional agencies were contracted for providing the hardware and teaching inputs. The CBSE pioneered Computer Science Programme at higher secondary stage and some State Boards followed this lead. The UGC also started the Computer Education Programme by providing PCs, starting certificate, diploma and degree courses in universities and by giving computers for Central Institutions for research and higher studies. IITs and engineering colleges acquired computers and started computer science programmes in many institutions. The World Bank assisted the project for strengthening and modernising polytechnics and giving other facilities.

The CLASS Project expanded and covered many thousands of senior secondary schools and many advanced schools which implemented the CLASS Project effectively. Computer education with adequate facilities was encouraged in secondary and higher secondary schools. Access of students to computer facilities in universities, colleges and technical institutions was encouraged and computer facility was made available to students and researchers round the clock. With the resources available, computer platforms for MCA students and researchers were upgraded. The polytechnics and professional bodies were accredited by the Departments of Electronics. UGC formulated a concrete programme for motivating and encouraging teachers of Computer Science to commercially link up with the professional agencies for mutual benefit. The UGC set up effective training arrangements for college teachers and initiated the programme for starting a support paper at Master's level.

The MHRD worked with the Ministry of Information & Broadcasting, Department of Space, Department of Electronics, and Finance Ministry for augmentation of transmission facilities for educational programmes and opened a new educational channel. The CIET & UGC continued a co-ordinating role and assisted the State agencies more meaningfully both financially and academically.

As reported earlier, computer education has assumed immense significance in the education system of the country. But it is found that people are more interested in acquiring hardware, particularly computer sets and not in developing and utilizing software suitable for the various groups of clientele. The MHRD, UGC and even the foreign agencies have come forward to finance the projects relating to computer education. But necessary steps need to be taken for giving training and providing necessary facilities for developing and using software in the teaching-learning process. Many educational institutions at school and higher education stages are now equipped with computers. Prof. S. K. Khanna, Vice-Chairman UGC rightly pointed out that there is need to look at computer education in its totality starting from school education to higher education keeping pace with changing technology. He stressed that for imparting proper training, the educational institutions must posse necessary hardware and software.

Prof. M. Mukhopadhya has aptly observed that in the CLASS Project computers were provided with a few CAI software, while colleges were provided with computers without any software. The CAI software is almost absent, and lack of provision of suitable software has led to gross under-utilisation or no utilisation of computers.

The manpower requirement in computer education is wide

ranging i.e. from data entry operator and technician to designer and engineer of computer configuration and programmes. It goes without saying that computers can be used effectively for providing good quality education and for removing disparities between slow and bright learners as far as possible. Besides teaching various subjects, there can be versatile use of computers in research experiments and innovations for enriching curricula and improving the standard of education. Unfortunately there is lack of imagination and co-ordination in the planning, management and utilisation of computer education and unless this is removed there would be huge wastage of resources both material and human and instead of computers becoming functional and useful would be ornamental and great wastage. Therefore, the need of the hour is to take concrete steps and utilise all available resources and equipment to greatly improve our education system.

8

LEARNING PROGRAMMES

The Conception

Programmed learning is one of the important invocations of the 20th century in the teaching-learning process. It is a self-instructional technique for providing individualized instruction or learning experience to the learner. In programmed learning, the subject matter or learning experience is logically sequenced into small segments. The learning experience is self-corrective.

The English writers prefer to use the term programmed learning and the American authors prefer the use of programmed instruction.

It is held by some educators that 'Gita' is the first example of programmed learning. They hold that the text of the 'Gita' has several ingredients of programming: initial behaviour, small steps, active participation of the learner, terminal behaviour, immediate feed-back and self-evaluation by the learner.

Several educators regard Socrates as the earliest programmer. Socrates used to guide his followers to gain knowledge by conducting them conversationally along a path from fact to fact and insight to insight.

Programmed learning emerged in the beginning of the 20th

century from the efforts of American psychologists. E. L. Thorndike (1874-1949) was the first psychologist whose findings bear direct relevance to programming. Other important psychologists who have made significant contribution in the field are Sidney L. Pressy, Robert M. Gagne, Robert Mager and B. F. Skinner.

Programmed learning is related with the 'Law of Effect' as explained by Thorndike. Sidney L. Pressey, a psychologist of Ohio State University, is credited for developing in the middle 1920's practical machines which could teach as well as test. The teaching machines as developed by Pressey present a series of questions to a student and inform him immediately whether his response is right or wrong.

In 1943, Skinner and his two other colleagues started programming by teaching a pigeon to roll a small bowling ball by operant conditioning. By 1954, Skinner and James G. Holland devised the auto-instructional methods which have served the present generation as the basis for present work in programmed instruction. In Skinnerian programmed instruction, whether mechanised or otherwise, the learner is initially asked a question which he can easily answer correctly without any previous study of the particular lesson. The learner is taught by the sequence of questions. He is asked more and more as the lesson proceeds in very small steps.

In 1955, Norman A. Crowder developed what he calls "automatic tutoring by intrinsic programming" as against "extrinsic programming" developed by Skinner.

Robert Mager (1958) gave a new concept known as "Learner Controlled Instruction" which is a kind of Socratic dialogue in reverse, in which the learner led the instructor. The instructor remained silent until the learner himself stimulated the instructor with questions that suggested the needed illustrations, demonstrations, practice or some other help.

Stoluron, at Illionis, aimed at developing a process which should provide for greater individualization by measuring needs and developing programmes that require a computer to assist instruction.

In 1962, T. F. Gilbert gave formalized expression of his technology of education called Mathetics. Pennington and Slack expressed in 1962 further detailed methods of preparing lessons from mathetic principles.

Programmed learning is a process of arranging material to be learned in a series of small steps designed to lead a learner through self-instruction from what he knows to the unknown of new and more complex knowledge and principles. A programme takes the place of a tutor and leads the learner through a set of frames of specified behaviour designed and sequenced to make it more probable that he will behave in a given derived way.

In programmed learning, it is said that the most efficient, pleasant and permanent learning takes place when the student proceeds through a course by a large number of small, easy-to-take steps. Wilbur L. Schramm (1962) lists the essential elements of programmed instruction as: (*a*) an ordered sequence of stimulus items, (*b*) to each of which a student responds in some specific way, (*c*) his responses being reinforced by immediate knowledge of results, (*d*) so that he moves by small steps, (*e*) therefore, making few errors and practicing mostly correct responses, (*f*) from what he knows by a process of successively closer approximation, toward what he is supposed to learn from the programme.

Following definitions provide a comprehensive view of programmed instruction.

Dale, Edgar (1962) : Programmed learning is a systematic, step by step, self-instructional programme aimed to ensure the learning of stated behaviour.

Das, R. C (1993) : Programmed instruction is a method of individualised instruction where each individual learns by himself at his own rate. Programmed learning consists of elements of new knowledge called 'steps' which are arranged in a sequence in such a way that a student can easily learn by himself.

Espich, James E. and William B (1965) : Programmed instruction is a planned sequences of experiences, leading to proficiency in terms of stimulus response relationship.

Gulati and Gulati (1990) : Programmed learning as popularly understood is a method of giving individual instruction in which the student is active and proceeds at his own pace and is provided with immediate knowledge of results. The teacher is not physically present. The programmer, while developing programmed material has to follow the laws of behaviour and validate his strategy in terms of student learning.

Jacobs and Others (1966) : Self-instructional programmes are educational materials from which the students learn. These programmes can be used with many types of students and subject-matter either by themselves, hence the name "self-instruction" or its combination with instructional strategies.

Kampfer (1970) : Programmed learning is a device which presents an exercise or a problem to a student, inducing him to respond; and revealing to him whether or not his response is correct.

Leith, G. O. M (1966) : Programme is a sequence of small steps of instructional material (called frames), most of which require a response to be made by completing a blank space in a sentence. To ensure that expected responses are given, a system of cueing is applied, and each response is verified by the provision of immediate knowledge of results. Such a sequence is intended to be worked at the learner's own pace as individual self-instruction.

Luonsdaine Arthur, A (1964) : An instructional programme is a vehicle which generates an essentially reproducible sequence of instructional events and accepts responsibility for efficiently accomplishing a specified change from a given range of initial competencies or behavioural tendencies to a specified or terminal range of competencies or behavioural tendencies.

Marke, Susan (1969) : Programmed learning is a method of designing a reproducible sequence of instructional events to produce a measurable and consistent effect on the behaviours of each and every acceptable student.

Navi, N. S. (1984) : Programmed instruction is a technique of converting the live instructional process into self-learning or auto-instructional readable material in the form of micro-sequence (the segments of subject-matter) which the learners are required to read, make some right or wrong response, correct wrong responses or confirm right responses and attain the complete mastery of the concept explained in the micro-sequences.

May, K. O. (1965) : Educational programming is the scheduling and control of student behaviour in the learning process.

Smith and Moore (1962) : Programmed instruction is the process of arranging the material to be learned into a series of sequential steps. Usually it moves the student from a familiar background into a complex and new set of concepts, principles and understandings.

Stolurow (1966) : Programmed learning can be described as a process in which a teacher presents (*i.e.*, communicates), a subject matter to a learner so that he responds to it (i.e. communicates to the teacher) the next item of information to be presented.

From the above mentioned definitions of programmed learning, following characteristics may be derived:

1. It is a method of individualized instruction.
2. In this technique, instructional material is logically sequenced and broken into suitable small steps or segments of the subject matter called 'frames'.
3. For sequencing a particular unit of the instructional material, the programmer has to pay due consideration to the initial or entering behaviour of the learner.
4. In actual operation, the beginning is made by presenting a 'frame'. The learner is required to read or listen and then respond actively.
5. Programmed instruction system has an adequate provision for feed-back.
6. The interaction between the learner and the learning material or programme is very important.
7. Programmed learning provides self-pacing to the learner.
8. Programmed learning provides for continuous evaluation.

Theories and Application

There are three basic types of programmed instructional material—The teaching machines, the programmed textbook and scrambled textbook.

The Teaching Machine : A teaching machine is intended to function as a private tutor. It is simply a mechanical devise or piece of apparatus designed to present to the student a sequential programme of learning activities comprising instructional items which requires the student to make an overt response and which provides the student with immediate knowledge of the accuracy of his response. It represents the practical application of laboratory technique of education.

Programmed Textbook : Each page of the programmed textbook consists of usually four or five panels. The student begins with the top panel on page one, responds to it, turns to page two to get his answers confirmed on the top panel, goes to the top panel on page three, responds to it, confirms the answer by turning the page, and so on.

The Scrambled Textbook : In a scrambled textbook, branching or intrinsic technique is used.

Principle of Small Steps : It is shown by experiments that even the dullest students can learn as effectively as the brightest students if the subject matter is presented to them in suitable small steps. When we divide the task to be learnt into very small steps, and ask the students to learn only one step at a time, then probably all the students will be able to learn one small step at a time and sequentially learn all the steps. It is a difficult task to climb a mountain but once steps are built even a child can climb the mountain very easily. This is known as the 'Principle of small steps'.

Principle of Active Responding : The second psychological principle is that the students learn better and faster when they are actively participating in the teaching-learning process. In our classroom teaching the teachers to ask a few questions and the students respond. But is not possible for the teachers to ask all the students to respond at each small step. A teaching machine text or a programmed text contains a large number of questions—one question at each small step and the students respond actively. The principle of active responding is used for the programmes. The teaching machines and programmes have proved to be superior because they provide opportunity to every learner to respond at every small step.

Principle of Reinforcement **:** Every response even approximately correct must be reinforced immediately. Delayed reinforcement fails to work. This is possible only when a teacher has to teach only one student at a time. The most ideal situation is when the teacher can cater to the needs of his students individually. But in classroom teaching this is hardly possible. No teacher, however efficient and sincere he may be, can reinforce each correct response of each of his students as soon as it is made in a classroom situation where he has to teach abut 40/50 students. The teaching machines and the programmes do the job more efficiently.

Principle of Self-Pacing **:** The programmed instruction is based on the basic assumption that learning takes place effectively if the learner is allowed to learn at his own pace. Therefore, a good programme of the material always takes care of the principle of self-pacing. A learner moves from one frame to another according to his own speed of learning.

Principle of Student-Evaluation or Student Testing **:** Continuous evaluation of the student and the learning process leads to better teaching-learning. In the programmed instruction, the learner has to leave the record of his responses because he is required to write a response for each frame on response sheet. This detailed record helps in revising the programme.

Important stages in the Development of the Programmed Instruction

Preparation *:* This is the first stage in the development of the programme. It includes:

(*i*) Selection of the topic.

(*ii*) Writing assumptions about learners.

(*iii*) Defining objective in behavioural terms.

(*iv*) Writing the entry behaviour (present status) of the learner.

(*v*) Developing specific outline of the content.

(*vi*) Preparing a criterion test.

Construction or Writing of the Programme : The programme is written under these heads (i) Writing draft frames in a sequence i.e. from simple to complex. (ii) Editing the draft frames by a team of experts usually comprising a subject-matter expert, a skilled writer and the programmer.

Try Out Revision : It includes (i) Trying out the programme on a few individual learners and finding out their reactions and making necessary changes in the light of reactions, (ii) Trying out the programme on a group of learners and making necessary changes on the basis of their reactions; and (iii) Trying out the programme in the field.

Evaluation : This implies finding the success or the failure after implementing a programme.

Illustration Programmes

CIVICS-CLASS X

Introduction : This a programme meant for you for the study of salient features of the Constitution of India.

In this programme you will find paragraphs which are called frames. Study each frame carefully and write down what is required. Answers are given at the end. After stating your answers, check them. If your answer is wrong or you do not understand anything, you can again go back to the frame. It is not a test but instead it is a self-study programme.

Frame 1 : The Constituent Assembly of India was set up under the provisions of the Cabinet Mission Plan to frame the Constitution of India which was formally adopted on 26th Nov. 1949 and came into force on 26th January 1950. It took nearly three years to complete the work.

(i) What was the work assigned to Constituent Assembly?

(ii) Under whose provision was it formed?

(iii) When did our Constitution come into force?

(iv) When was it adopted?

(v) How much time did Constituent Assembly take to complete its work?

Frame 2 : The Preamble of the Constitution has a great significance but is not a part of the Constitution. The Constitution was framed by the people of India through their representations. It stresses the fact that the reign of the land lies with the people of India.

(a) Is the Preamble a part of the Constitution?

(b) By whom was the Constitution framed?

(c) In whose hands does the reign of law of India lie?

Frame 3 : The Preamble of our Constitution is as under:

We the people of India having solemnly resolved to constitute India into a Sovereign Socialist Secular Democratic Republic and to secure to all its citizens:.

Justice, social, economic and political;

Liberty of thought, expression, belief, faith and worship

Equality of status and of opportunity; and to promote them all;

Fraternity assuring the dignity of the individual and the unity and integrity of the Nation.

In our Constituent Assembly this twenty-sixth day of November, 1949, do hereby adopt, enact and give to ourselves this Constitution.

Note—Three new terms—Socialist, Secular and Integrity were added to the original text of the Preamble when it was amended in 1976 with the 42nd Amendment.

The Preamble stresses the democratic basis of the Constitution by stating that the People of India gave to themselves this Constitution. It also states objectives like justice, liberty, equality and fraternity.

(i) Who has given the Constitution of India?

(ii) What kind of justice has been ensured by the Preamble?

(iii) What type of Republic is to be constituted?

(iv) What kind of equality has been given to its citizen?

(v) How many types of liberty can a citizen enjoy?

Frame 4 : Another important feature of the Preamble is that the people themselves adopted and enacted the Constitution. Thus, the representatives of the people frame the laws of the country and they have the power to change or amend the Constitution.

(*a*) Who frames the laws of the country?

(*b*) What has the power to amend the Constitution?

Frame 5 : The Constitution of India has many unique features which distinguish it from Constitutions of other countries. The framers of the Constitution freely borrowed ideas but took care to adapt these to the needs of the country.

The Constitution makes India a Sovereign, Socialist Secular, Democratic Republic. The word Sovereign means that India is completely free from external control. No outside power has the right to interfere either in her internal administration or direct her in the conduct of her foreign policy.

This was emphasised to ensure that India was no longer 'dependent' on the British Empire as she had been before Indian Independence Act 1947 or 'dominion' as she had been from 15th August, 1947 to 26th January 1950.

(a) What kind of status did India enjoy during 15th August 1947 to 26th January 1950?

(b) Was India sovereign between 15th August 1947 to 26th January 1950?

(c) What is the meaning of the word 'sovereign'?

(d) Does the Constitution of India have unique features?

(e) Did the framers of the Constitution borrow ideas?

ANSWERS

1. (i) To frame the Constitution of India.

   (ii) Provision of the Cabinet Mission Plan.

   (iii) 26th January 1950.

(iv) 26th November 1949.

(v) Nearly 3 years.

2. (*a*) No.

(*b*) People of India through their representatives.

(*c*) People of India.

3. (i) People of India.

(ii) Social, economic and political.

(iii) Sovereign Socialist Secular Democratic.

(iv) Equality of status.

(v) Five.

4. (*a*) Representatives of the people.

(*b*) Representatives of the people.

5. (*a*) Dominion.

(*b*) No.

(*c*) India is completely free from external control.

(*d*) Yes.

(*e*) Yes.

The Assessment

Merits of Programmed Instruction : 1. A well-programmed instruction is a great thrust in the direction of individualised instruction, as it is tailored to the needs of the individual learner in the class. 2. It permits individual learner to progress at his own speed. An intelligent learner needs no longer to be bored or allowed to lose interest on account of his slow progress of other learners of the class. He can make progress as he is capable of. 3. Since a programme requires continuous response from the learner, it overcomes the inertia and passivity on the part of the learner. 4. The teacher can give explanation in the classroom if the error is common or he may arrange individual conferences on specific points. 5. Learning material in a programmed instruction is presented in such a way that learning becomes an interesting game and the learner is motivated to meet the challenges set by his own capabilities. 6. Programmes are developed by experts. They are empirically tested and modified till they are standarised. A number of learners can use a single good programme and thus evade textbooks. 7. In programmed instruction the learner is immediately reinforced to correct his response and this reinforcement sustains the motivation of the learner. 8. The self-instructional technique presents material in which its complexity is simplified through the analysis of the subject-matter into small and more easily assimilated segments of information. 9. The introduction of programmed instruction is of great significance for developing countries which are set on the path of educating millions of learners and are short of teachers. 10. Good teachers are freed from the boredom of routine classroom teaching and they are in a position to devote more time to more creative activities. 11. The programmed instruction has been used more successfully in teaching the discernment of the logic of various disciplines and inspiring students to creative thinking and judgement. 12. Certain motor skills and intellectual abilities normally taught by frequent drills and rote memorisation can be very efficiently taught by self-instructional devices. 13. Self-instructional materials have been found to be very useful in the West in revolutionisng the social setting of the classroom. Problems of discipline have been solved and a new hope for eliminating emotional and social problems has been generated. 14. Programmed instruction enables the teacher to diagnose the problems of the individual learner. 15. The introduction of programmed instruction is very helpful in certain situations where human instructors are not easily available in the required number, for instance small schools in the isolated or hill areas.

Programmed materials have been severely criticised as a threat to replacing the teacher.

It is also argued that there is too much emphasis in learning facts and very little emphasis on the mastery of principles and concepts.

Some critics of programmed instruction maintain that the user of a programme does not now where he is headed to.

They also point out that the learners are not aware of the

organisation and programmed instruction is unrelated to other aspects of instruction.

It is also argued that the programmed instruction material is very costly and only rich nations can afford it.

It is also stated that the development and use of programmed instructional material require expert knowledge and training. An average teacher finds it very difficult to make use of this device.

As a result of experimental studies and research, following types of programmed instruction have emerged.

1. Linear or Extrinsic Programming
2. Branching or Intrinsic Programming
3. Mathetics Programming
4. Rules System of Programming
5. Computer Assisted Instruction (CAS)
6. Learner Controlled Instruction. (LCS)

The first three styles—linear, branching and mathetics are the basic formats. The rules system represents the deductive and inductive approach to teaching. The other two types, Computer Assisted Instruction (CAI) and Learner Controlled Instruction (LCI) are not the basic format of Programming. They are, infact, the ways and means of providing instruction. Here we have taken up only the basic type of programming.

Linear Programming

B. F. Skinner is the originator of linear programming. It is also called a single tract programme. According to Skinner, a creature, a bird or a human being can be led to a desired behaviour by means of a carefully constructed programme consisting of small steps leading logically through the subject-matter from topic to topic, provided each step is reinforced by some kind of favourable experience or reward. The increments in information which the learner is expected to absorb are small. The favourable experience or response increases the probability of the same response to occur again in the future. The process of rewarding the correct response to a stimulus increases the general tendency to give a response.

The sequence of frames and path of learning in programmed learning is systematic and linear. That is why, this type of programming is referred to as linear programming. Hence all the learners have to proceed through the same frames and in the same order.

In a linear programme, learner's responses are controlled externally by the programmer sitting at a distant place. Hence linear programming is also termed as extrinsic programming. In branching programming, learner's response is controlled by the learner himself internally. It is, therefore, also called intrinsic programming.

Merits : 1. Immediate knowledge of results acts as a great motivator and releases anxiety and tension. 2. The smallness of the frames brings the sub-goals within the reach of the learner and thereby facilitates secondary reinforcement. 3. Repetition strengthens the responses and ensures learning. 4. Easy nature of the programme provides 'success experience' to the learner.

Limitations : 1. In linear programming, the learning process becomes quite dull on account of the following reasons (*a*) Subject matter is broken into very small pieces, (*b*) Responding is quite mechanical and restrictive, and (*c*) The learning process is quite slow. 2. The use of linear programming is limited to some subjects and topics. 3. Linear programming cramps the imagination of the learner and initiative for creative, integrative and judgement learning. 4. Linear programming encourages guessing. 5. Linear programming does not develop the discriminating power of the students.

Intrinsic Programming

Branching or intrinsic programming was developed by Norman A. Crowder (1954) an American technician. According to Crowder, branching or intrinsic programme is one which adopts to the needs of the learners without the medium of any extrinsic device such as a computer. It is not controlled extrinsically by the programmer.

Norman A. Crowder was a technician who was working in the United States Air Force. He was faced with the problem of efficiency of vocational training. His programme is based on intuition. His approach at the most is practical. This type of programme employs multiple choice response patterns. The learner is required to select one right answer out of several responses presented to him.

Merits : 1. Big size of a frame as well as the branching minimises unnecessary repetitions and responding, thus reducing the amount of learning time and fatigue. 2. The pitfalls and consequences of erroneous logic are usually explained in the remedial frames so that the learner not only gets the correct responses but also understands why some other response is not correct. 3. Instead of simple response it provides alternatives in the form of multiple choice. 4. Through its broad frames, branching programme provides for more freedom to respond and scope of choosing one's path of learning according to one's need. Thus, it helps in maintaining the interest and initiative of the teacher. 5. Branching programme is helpful in the development of the power of discrimination of the learner. 6. Branching programme helps in the development of creativity and problem-solving ability. 7. Branching is most useful in the areas beyond facts, definitions and basic skills. 8. The frames being of a large size contain a good deal of information and this may enable the programmer to enrich the style and expand his ideas.

Limitations : 1. The multiple choice questions provided in this programming may lead to guess work on the part of the learner and he may not understand the subject matter of the frame. 2. The setting of appropriate multiple choice questions suiting to the entire material of the frames proves a difficult task. 3. No branching method can provide infinite branching to take care of all possible needs of every individual student. 4. The cost of branching programme is very high when compared with traditional teaching approaches. 5. The branching programme is not suitable for small children as they are unable to express symbolisation. 6. The programme needs revision after every five years. 7. It is difficult to cover the entire subject matter of the curriculum in the stipulated time. 8. The diagnostic questions framed by the programmer may or may not suit the needs of the individual learner. 9. The programme cannot shape the behaviour of the learner.

Teaching Instruction and Programmed Instruction : According to Edger Dale, "Teaching' is a broad, vague, ill-defined term and instruction' is a purposeful, orderly, controlled sequencing of experience to reach a specified goal. 'Programmed instruction' is a sub-head under instruction and represents a more rigorous attempt to develop a mastery, over specified goals to secure 'insured' learning."

Programmed Instruction	*Traditional Method*
1. It is an individualised technique of instruction.	1. It is a group technique.
2. It is based on the teaching principles that have been known for years.	2. It becomes difficult to apply teaching principles in crowded classrooms.
3. It presents the instructional matter step by step in logical order.	3. It presents the instructional matter as a whole.
4. The size of the unit of information presented to the pupils is a small bit of information.	4. The unit is a lengthy one. There is very little provision for response from the students in the form of answers to questions.
5. Immediate feedback is given to the learner.	5. The learner does not get immediate feedback.
6. Objectives are defined very clearly in operational terms.	6. Objectives are not well-defined and are usually vague.
7. The programmer prepares his programme with care and precision.	7. Very little preparation is made.
8. Programme is prepared in such a way that the student automatically participates actively by making responses continually.	8. The student usually remains a passive listener and the teacher himself does the summarising and reviewing.

9. A programme is developed empirically through a series of tryouts and refined gradually. Effective sequences students reaction of frames are retained and ineffective ones discarded.	9. It is usually found to be very difficult to modify traditional instruction.

Role of the Teacher

Programme learning cannot replace the teacher. Any innovation in the school programmes and practices must remain in the hands of the teachers. The radio and T.V. did not displace the teacher. Similar is the case with programmed instruction. It is upto the enlightened teachers to take up the challenging task of preparing programmes. We have got a wide market. The programmes can be sold all over the country. A student who is convinced that he can learn better, achieve more with the help of this programme, will definitely prefer instead of buying this programme to buying a text book. By taking up this challenging task we will not only help the cause of education, help our fellow teachers by setting them free from the routine task of information, giving help to the students to achieve more, but we will be helping ourselves also.

It may also be remembered that these gadgets can be used mainly in the cognitive field and possibly in the psycho-motor field to develop certain abilities and skills of the students as an individual. A teacher is something more than all these gadgets put together. He has to bring about socialization of the individual; he has to promote socially desirable attitudes and interests and mould the personality of the students. The effective domain is almost reserved for his care. At present the teacher is not able to devote his energy and time to this important task as most of his time and energy is consumed by his routine job as an information giver. We always talk of education for three 'H's'—the head, the hand and the heart. But it has almost remained a mere slogan. Programmed learning teaching machines and other gadgets will set teacher free from routine work. These are labour-saving devices for the teacher so that he may function more effectively in a field of his own choice.

Technique involved in programmed instruction can be used in teaching different subjects. Teaching of mathematics, science, social studies and elements of Indian languages can be done effectively with the help of this new technique. The teacher has to formulate objectives of teaching a particular subject, undertake content analysis of the subject matter in the light of objectives, frame a chain of questions which will lead the pupils in the direction of the objective and present the questions to his pupils who are expected to try their hand at answering the questions independently. The teacher will have to play the role of a friend, guide and philosopher in the class when the pupils are engaged in solving the riddle and at the same time acquiring knowledge or skill. The question of class discipline may not arise as the pupils will be found busy doing the task assigned to them by the teacher. The teacher will have to do remedial or corrective teaching as the weakness of his pupils will be located in the very act of learning. The pupil will also undergo a process of self-evaluation as he completes his work.

Role of the teacher in the changed context of Programmed Learning may be stated as under :

1. Teacher as an advisor in helping students in the selection of programme learning material.
2. Teacher as a discussion leader for focussing the attention of the learners on important points.
3. Teacher as a guide to clarify doubts and elaborate on various points asked by the learner.
4. Teacher as an evaluator of the learning outcomes.
5. Teacher as a consultant to the various agencies engaged in production of programmed material.

The programmed learning approach can be adopted in normal classroom teaching in the following ways:

1. A teacher can make use of the principles of programmed learning such as active responding, minimal errors and confirmation while teaching various subjects in the conventional manner.
2. A teacher can define behavioural objectives in advance of teaching.
3. A teacher can validate the instructional systems of a class

in terms of the performance of learners immediately after teaching is over.

4. A teacher can regulate questions and answers. The answer of a learner can be immediately reinforced by informing or telling whether it is correct or incorrect.
5. A teacher can plan the entire instructional programme of a classroom and can treat the terminal behaviour, the pre-requisite skills and content analysis in advance.

Komoski (1960) an expert has observed "Two thousand years ago the world's first public administrator, a gentleman by the name Quintilian wrote what might be called a handbook for teachers." In it he has one bit of advice which will serve as an excellent starting point for a discussion of programmed learning and its potential uses. His advice is: "Do not neglect the individual student. He should be questioned and praised."

Programmed Instruction

Programmed instruction is still in its infancy in India. Programmed instruction as an optional or elective paper has been included at the B. Ed./M.Ed. level in a few universities in India. It also forms a part of the paper of Educational Technology/ Educational Innovation. However, as regards its classroom use, it may be observed that it is almost nil. As far back in 1966, the Kothari Commission suggested to develop programmed material in different subjects to test the suitability of the technique in Indian conditions. An Association of Programmed Instruction has been formed to coordinate the research being done at different centres in the country. The association also disseminates the information on new studies through its journal issued from time to time. The National Council of Educational Research and Technology has also done some work in the field. In spite of all these efforts, it may be stated that the application of programmed instruction has not yet made an appreciable impact on our classroom teaching. Our methods of teaching still remain traditional, by and large.

Literacy regarding Computer

Assuming that the societal changes wrought, by microelectronic technologies would have greater implications for changes in educational programs than would the instructional potential of these technologies. Second, since future scenarios about life in the developing computer culture will, in the final analysis, be written by individuals, the capacities of schools to enhance self-realization will become increasingly significant. Third, all of the important issues related to uses of microcomputers ultimately reside beyond technology in human and social domains. Finally, the objectives of computer literacy programs cannot be permanently fixed; they change as societal values and technology change.

Concept Variations

At a general level, differences in the conceptual and practical meanings of computer literacy exist within and across nations, at a specific level, they are found in the multiple programs offered in given school. Diversity expresses itself through the scope and depth of computer literacy programs, the objectives they seek, the outcomes they produce, and the places they occupy in curricula. Computer literacy programs now found in schools are not easy to classify, in part because they are usually defined in general terms. In addition, those describing programs often fail to distinguish clearly between concepts and their uses, and the resulting obscurities make classification difficult. Nevertheless, the categories of literacy elaborated below do help document and clarify the diverse expressions of current programs.

Those who have acquired "operational" literacy can define the basic components of hardware and software and can demonstrate the machine-related skills needed to make computers work. Designed to introduce students to the computer, this approach is often implemented through daily exercises during a period of several weeks. When the exercises are effective, students understand such concepts as "monitor", "keyboard," and "central processing unit" and how the components labeled by such concepts work together with other parts to make computers function.

Students are also able to turn a computer on and off, load software, show proficiency at the keyboard, demonstrate the use of storage devices, and acquire "minimal" troubleshooting techniques. Operational literacy, then, emphasizes "hands-on" experiences and simple concepts. Directed at elementary understandings and skills, the approach demands neither extensive teacher training nor substantial amounts of instructional time. Nor does it require much change in existing curricula or major investments beyond those made in hardware and software.

The minimal demands of the approach may account for the fact that many school districts have opted for it in their initial literacy efforts. The approach, while limited, provides an entry into the world of the computer and a potential bridge to more significant learning experiences; more easily than other literacy alternatives; operational literacy can be made available equitably to all students. Learning produced through operational literacy, critics argue, are both trivial and subject to quick obsolescence. They might contend, for example, that teaching students how to turn computers on and off is just as trivial as teaching them how to turn television sets on and off. Both activities squander valuable time. Critics also argue that operational literacy outcomes are immediately out of date, hardware and software are changing so fast, they say, that today's operations are obsolescent tomorrow.

In addition, future computers, with their enhanced "friendliness," intelligence, and simplicity, will require only the most elementary skills. Why waste students' and teachers' time, critics ask, by providing trivial and obsolescent learnings? Is the assumption about obsolescence as sound one? Since students of technology typically underestimate, often substantially, the time required to realize new developments, a note of skepticism is in order. Put differently, projections made about impending achievements in intelligent and friendly computers by critics of operational literacy, especially the highly optimistic ones, are likely to be in error. If the new technologies have potential for enhancing learning, then a pertinent question arises—why wait years for more powerful computers while immediately closing the door on opportunities for all students to acquire potentially useful entry skills and concepts?

Is the "triviality" argument sound? If the learnings acquired through operational literacy offer no foundation for new learnings, they can be classed as trivial. However, if the elementary and first-stage learnings facilitate the attainment of more advanced ones, they are not necessarily trivial. To be sure, research is needed to determine if the "operational" learnings acquired in fact enable students to realize more sophisticated learnings. Further, do students from diverse backgrounds actually use the initial learnings to acquire more advanced ones?

Instrumental literacy approach to literacy computers are used as instruments for acquiring stipulated learnings or bodies of subject-matter. In Sweden, for example, leaders have used computers in high schools to teach mathematics and civics. They chose these subjects in parts because they "are taken by all compulsory school pupils, and they are included in most lines of upper secondary school". The approach enables all enrolled students to learn to use computers as they acquire content or skills; in addition, the computer can be used as an instrument for "modernizing" subject-matter teaching.

In the Swedish plan, for example, computer-supported projects produced, according to one observer, a variety of subject-related outcomes among which were new insights by students into mathematical relationships, into "connections" among subject matters, and into the analytical aspects of mathematics. In addition, teachers coordinated instruction in physics and mathematics more effectively. The Swedish approach reflects the instrumental use of computers in selected subjects. Some high school leaders have aspired to use computers in all subjects taught. Those taking clerical courses, for example, might acquire word processing skills; some social studies students, insights into environmental problems through simulations; science students, understandings of physics from computer-based demonstrations; language arts students, enhanced vocabulary and spelling skills, and so forth. In each subject, in other words, the computer would provide a tool for advancing learning.

The instrumental concept of computer literacy is not without its critics. Some detractors maintain that this alternative provides "low level" types of learning only. Others are skeptical about whether the quality of future software will exceed significantly that currently available in today's drill and practice programs. On the one hand, school systems do not have the material and human resources to develop effective software, they maintain; on the other, the private sector, with its press to produce programs for mass markets, will continue its "least common denominator" stance toward software. In describing the low state of software development, critics pinpoint a major difficulty.

However, the conditions they describe are not sufficiently compelling to justify the elimination of the instrumental approach to computer literacy. Information presented in this volume suggests that computer-assisted instruction, when compared to other approaches to the improvement of student learning, already offers one viable option to educators. Undoubtedly, future improvements in software will come slowly and incrementally, and the cost of hardware will diminish less rapidly than in the past; nevertheless, comparisons of CAI with competing strategies of instruction are likely to become more rather than less favourable over time. In the meantime, CAI provides students some computer skills and provides staff a stimulus and a medium for assessing traditional modes of instruction.

Algorithmic reasoning, perhaps the most controversial concept of computer literacy, is acquired through computer programming. A.P. Ershov, a member of the USSR Academy of Science, has called programming the "second literacy". Literacy in reading and literacy in programming both have their origins in technologies-the printing press and the computer. Both support basic functions; "communications work, the contemplation of nature and the struggle against it", and they "supplement each other, forming a new harmony of human mind". Ershov suggests that the "acceptance of books blew up the integrity of word and action; it separated the process of knowledge accumulation from its application." Programming, with its emphasis on problem solving and on the clear comprehension of how to carry out what is to be done, helps rejoin, at least in certain types of tasks, what the book rent as under. To become programmers, students must make effective use of algorithmic reasoning, Kemeny writes:

We have to learn to think in terms of algorithms, which are precise recipes for solving problems or for accomplishing a task. A computer program describes an algorithm; it tells us "how to get there." Although algorithms were used and studied in mathematics in the past, there is today a strong prejudice in favour of formulae-that is, achieved results. But computers are forcing us all, even mathematicians, to readjust our thinking.

Algorithmic reasoning skills, Kemeny admits, are not easily articulated. Nevertheless, he suggests that programmers need—(a) to be able to express thought in very simple language (the small number of concepts available in a language like BASIC makes the task a demanding one); (b) to explain to the computer how to solve the problem (c) to divide complex tasks into small, clearly understood components; (d) to break down a procedure into simple steps and seek the logical relations among them; and (e) to find programming malfunctions and "debug" them. While recognizing that programming can teach "procedural" thinking, Seymour Papert has stressed its potential for providing fundamental insights into mathematical and related abstractions.

By using algorithmic reasoning to make the computer do their bidding, students can gain special insights into thinking and into the nature of knowledge. Put another way, learnings gained from programming can help students become their own "epistemologists". Not only can programming develop generic reasoning skills, it can, its advocates contend, improve the quality of learning. Students, as programmers, are active and involved-preconditions for significant learning. Papert has also suggested that computers can bring constructive change to "sluggish and conservative" school systems. When teachers and students become skillful programmers, they move the posits, beyond passive contexts to richer and more self-actualizing ones. Some advocates of programming cast a critical eye on instrumental literacy because it places students in a passive role. As programmers, students can use computers in the active pursuit of their own learning objectives. If their responses are limited to those in programs developed by others, their imagination and learning are sharply constrained.

Papert and Kemeny, as advocates of programming, speak and write as trained mathematicians. Algorithmic reasoning, an offspring of mathematics, can resolve precisely defined problems. It has repeatedly demonstrated its capacities to resolve technical problems associated with the development and use of microelectronic technologies. In fact, the expansive array of digital artifacts that lies at the heart of the computer culture is in one sense the product of algorithmic thinking. However, the task teaching students computer programming differs markedly from that of teaching them to address effectively the human, social, occupational, and civic problems created by microelectronic technologies. These latter problems lie outside the rational world of computer programming and in the emotion-laden contexts of political organizations, work settings, family milieus, and other locales.

Surrounded by conflicts, these formidably complex problems cannot be fully resolved through algorithmic reasoning. The contentions that all students should acquire computer programming skills, then, should be viewed critically. To make computer programming a literacy standard for all students reflects a questionable strategy. Even if the standard is one which can feasibly be met by all students-a proposition that is far from self-evident-major investments in time and resources would be required to produce a narrowly based set of skills.

Noble has identified "consumer literacy" "worker literacy," and "citizen literacy" as the major role-related concepts. Although writers do not always define these terms in the same way, the concepts do accurately reflect prevailing views about which roles are being altered by computers and which ones can serve as foci for developing computer literacy. Consumer literacy carries two meanings, one linked more to hardware and the other more to software. The first stresses that individuals should be effective acquirers and users of computers and associated hardware.

Since almost all families will eventually spend large sums of money on home computers and peripheral equipment, advocates of consumer literacy reason that schools should teach all individuals how to handle such expenditure wisely. The second meaning of consumer literacy centres upon the "applications" individuals will be making "as part of their strategies for information retrieval, communication and problem solving". Advocates of this view optimistically project rapidly increasing flows of information out of, into, and through home computers. Individuals using the expanding sources of information will need requisite knowledge and skills. They will need to learn, for example, how to enhance their education through electronic media, exchange ideas through computer networks, and use shared databases to solve individual and community problems. Schools, then, should provide students with the literacy skills required to function in tomorrow's microelectronic environments.

Worker literacy is defined, on the one hand, as the skills needed to perform specific jobs and, on the other, as generic cognitive and information skills. The first definition presumes that the trend away from industrial jobs and toward information jobs will continue and, further, that career and vocational programs should teach individuals to perform such specific information jobs as computer repairing, systems design, and data processing.

The second definition of literacy presumes that future job requirements will always be changing and that schools, more than ever before, should provide students basic skills which they can apply as their jobs undergo change or as they move into new ones. Workers in information-related jobs, in other words, need higher-level mental skills than industrial workers traditionally have had. During the last decade, the impact of computer technologies on political environments is so far-reaching, some argue, that new approaches to citizen literacy are sorely needed. Today space and time no longer constitute barriers to national and international communication.

However, television and satellites are increasingly communicating political events through images, leaving it to citizens to search for the deeper political meanings behind appearances. Further, as the new technologies take over an ever-expanding number of government and business functions, they are posing far-reaching questions related to the privacy of individuals, equity of citizen access to the new media, and the role of computers in politics. All of these conditions, proponents of computer literacy argue, highlight the need for citizen literacy. Actual descriptions of well-developed programs directed at consumer, worker, or citizen literacy are not as prevalent as are descriptions of other types of computer literacy programs.

For one thing, they are more difficult to design and implement than are operational, instrumental, or algorithmic reasoning programs. Since the definitions of role-related needs are still ambiguous, organized content to support instruction is not yet widely or conveniently available. Finally, support for the idea that schools should provide students generic or higher-order learnings for use in consumer, worker, citizen, and other roles is growing. Role-related literacy has not escaped criticism.

Recent Technologies

Computer enthusiasts, some contend, have exaggerated the impact of the new technologies on job requirements, consumer demands, and citizen responsibilities. Levin and Rumberger, for example, suggest that the number of "information" workers required will be relatively small as compared to the number of janitors, cashiers, secretaries, and other service, workers needed. Others contend that school and community leaders have launched literacy programs without adequate reflection. Some have blamed an "uncritical press" not only for exaggerating the need for literacy programs but also for providing "free advertising in the guise of objective reporting".

Many educators have tended to accept the claims of computer enthusiasts uncritically. Thus, criticism is needed to develop more realistic views about the educational significance of the new technologies. However, the claims of the critics can be accepted as uncritically as those of enthusiasts. Stated another way, criticisms that lack logical or evidential support need to be viewed skeptically.

Critics of role-related literacy may be correct within an immediate time frame and incorrect within a longer-range time frame. Expanding computerization is changing consumer, worker, and citizen functions, even if slowly. Thus, today's critical messages about role related literacy not only may prove to be errant; even worse, they may reinforce outmoded patterns and stifle the creation of needed new ones.

Advocates of computer literacy, then, have stimulated considerable thought about the concept during the last decade. Witness, for example, the analyses that increasingly dot the educational literature. By aggressively defining and diffusing multiple definitions of literacy and by skillfully linking them to diverse learning objectives, they have contributed significantly to the development and diffusion of literacy programs. However, the mixed messages elicited by computers have slowed the diffusion of the concepts.

Some, seeing nothing new in computer technologies, indifferently dismiss them; in so doing, they rule out the "Whither" question. Others, sensing a computer-created "revolution," urgently call for major adaptations in school programs and a thorough answer to the "whither" question. Given such disparate views, the first question facing those studying computer literacy is whether or not computer uses in schools indeed reflect another passing fad.

The indifferent, who "have seen it all before," believe firmly that the microcomputer is just another in a series of technologies without impact. They point to the high but disappointed hopes past educational leaders have had for programmed texts, televisions, and related innovations. They conclude that after a period of uncritical use the microcomputer will have an uninfluential ending as have past instructional technologies. Since it is only one more in a long series, they ask why one should assume that it has more than passing significance. The "passing fad" argument is erroneous because it is based upon a false assumption, namely, that the capacities and effects of microcomputers are similar to those of previous technologies.

Microcomputers in fact differ substantially from past technologies. Because of their greater versatility and flexibility, they can be put to many more instructional uses. In additions, they can help manage instructional processes; versatility access subject-matter from libraries, information utilities, and other electronic sources; and facilitate the development of programs by students to meet their own objectives-feats that past technologies could not perform.

Computers differ from past technologies in a more fundamental way, namely, in their far-reaching effects on society. The impacts of programmed texts, for example, were confined to educational contexts. Even television, with its widespread influence, has not moved as deeply into society's institutions as has the computer. Microcomputers populate homes, work places, business enterprises, government agencies, social agencies, and other non-school organizations. Having spawned a powerful array of novel industries, computers are now stimulating new dreams and aspirations, redefining human-machine relationships, shaping cognitive psychology, and altering modes of thinking.

As computers change society, they create new educational needs, as already noted. Microelectronic technologies, then, represent much more than new educational means, they are surfacing profound questions about the ends of education. Therefore, they cannot be blithely dismissed. The conclusion that the computer is not another passing fad does not imply that school purposes and programs will change rapidly. Powerful barriers constrain technological change. The new technologies do demand much more learning and change on the part of school personnel than have past technologies.

The high costs of implementing literacy programs will slow diffusions processes. The clashing tides of positive and negative opinion, which surround decisions about computer uses, will complicate adoption decisions. Finally, it is significant that much larger private-sector investments are currently being directed at 'offices of the future' than at 'schools of the future', and 'at functions performed in business, military, telecommunication and government agencies in contrast to educational ones."

The new technologies have evoked both dark and bright scenarios. Optimists, emphasizing effective uses, see computers producing beneficial outcomes; pessimists, emphasizing misuses, see destructive and even dire consequences. While enthusiasts make expansive claims, skeptics decry these claims and cast them aside. Hope, optimism, and enthusiasm clash with fear, pessimism, and skepticism. The result is bifurcated views. That these views impinge directly upon the 'whither' question can be shown with some specific examples. The first set of examples is linked to current computer uses; the second, to presumed future impacts of computers.

Sherry Turkle has referred to the "Computer as Rorschach." The phrase is an apt one; computers do tap deep human emotions and elicit contrasting perceptions about their meaning and significance. Applications of computers in the political arena, for example, bring dissonant views. Some examples relevant to citizen literacy can help clarify the point. Some have probed the impacts of the new technologies on individual liberty and privacy and have discovered an "electronic nightmare." Others, after studying national experiments in "teledemocracy," have concluded that the new technologies can help citizens influence public policy decisions.

In a similar view, some have observed that the power of "technological elites" constitutes a threat to democratic decision making; others see in the diffusion and use of microcomputers a new means for advancing decentralized communication and democratic action. Or while some argue that linear thinking can be effectively applied to political problems, others contend that intuitive thinking will be required to solve these problems. Some believe that expanding international databases will enable leaders to address worldwide political problems more effectively; others contend that leaders from developing nations will suffer even greater inequalities in political opportunities because they will be unable to access the data.

While the less sanguine stress that large technological systems, with "lives" of their own, cannot be controlled through political processes, the more cheerful contend that humans, as creators and users of these systems, can control their effects. Contrasting positive and negative views, such as those just noted, have implications for research. Inquiry is needed to shed light on actual in contrast to presumed outcomes of computer uses.

Some of the differences in view can be explained by the fact that scholars, in drawing their conclusions, use data about different but related phenomena as, for example, the computer's impact on a process (learning) in contrast to its impact on a value (privacy). However, a more fundamental problem is that the factual premises to support generalizations tend to be weak; effective research could uncover unreliable findings and false conclusions.

Perceptions about future consequences differ just as much as do those about immediate results. Thinkers often hold antithetical views, for example, about the long-range impacts of computers on the economic sector views which have implications for "worker literacy" programs. Some, looking at the steady infiltration of robots into industrial settings, conclude that the result will be a permanently unemployed "underclass"; others, examining the impacts of past technologies on unemployment, assert that the new technologies will create at least as many jobs as they eliminate.

Some contend that the new machines will inevitably dehumanize work; others argue that computers, by taking over the routine, will bring shorter work weeks and that this, in turn, will lead to more educational, social and other humanistic activities. While the optimists believe that ongoing research will make it possible for robots to perform increasingly "intelligent" functions, the least hopeful maintain that research break-throughs in artificial intelligence will be extremely limited. The act that leaders and scholars hold such sharply divided views about the immediate and long-range significance of new technologies signals in still another way the powerful forces unleashed by computers. By surfacing conflictive and vital issues, the forces are stimulating and encouraging proactive throughout.

The precious discussion has stressed that computer literacy is a young concept, that educational leaders have defined and implemented it in diverse ways, and that sharply clashing views surround its uses. At this point an important issue arises, namely, what framework can be used to analyze the newborn, diversely, interpreted, sharply contested and complicated concept of computer literacy? Since the history of the concept is short and relevant research is scarce, analogies offer one framework. Thus, acquiring computer literacy can be compared with the learning of a foreign language or the attainment of "book" literacy. Book literacy offers one fruitful analogy for probing the "whither" question.

Notably, book literacy and computer literacy are both similar and interdependent. The various symbols on the keyboard used to write this chapter are immediate indicators of the reciprocal relationships between written literacy and computer literacy. Other symbols, which appear from time to time on the screen are additional reminders of the interdependencies between books and computers. These linkages underline a significant fact, namely, that individuals cannot acquire computer literacy without literacy in written language. Since one-fifth of the population of the United States is illiterate in written language, when more demanding measures are used, millions are locked out of computer literacy.

The linkages between computers and books, then, suggest an important policy generalization, namely, that when school leaders make commitments to computer literacy they should not do so at the expense of traditional literacy programs. Those comprising today's large illiterate population tend to be members of disadvantaged social, economic, racial and other groups. Since as a rule they have had limited access to written materials in their homes, they have long experienced unequal learning opportunities. Such inequalities, which still persist 500 years after the invention of the printing press, offer another lesson to those concerned with policy related to computer literacy.

The opportunities available to students pursuing computer literacy will undoubtedly be more inequitable, at least for the foreseeable future, than will those available to students pursuing book literacy. Since computers and associated peripherals are much more expensive than books, educational agencies and parents will find it more difficult to provide children and youth the equipment needed to ensure equal opportunities. In addition, there are already public institutions that can diminish inequities in reading opportunities; however, public institutions to nurture computer literacy are not yet widespread.

If support for the concept of computer literacy continues, equity issues will increasingly find their way onto the agenda of school boards. Some educational leaders are already addressing the issues. Affirmative programs directed at computer literacy during the summer, after-school scheduling to expand computer learning opportunities, and the use of such concepts as "student-access ratios" all reflect responses more random than widespread and more inchoate than well developed. The concept of "public information utilities" highlights the access question in the larger context of society. According enable all interested individuals to use large electronic databases to pursue educational, citizenship, and related purposes.

The implementation of this idea is at best a long-range possibility. It could not be realized until more advanced technologies are achieved, new information norms and habits are developed, and the transmission of computer-based information becomes much less expensive, nevertheless, the adjective "public" that stands before "information utilities" denotes an already emergent sensitivity is society to the equity issue. Given the very slow diffusion of reading skills during the last 500 years, public funds to support electronic information exchange will likely come slowly, if at all.

The first to achieve new skills are usually not eager to transfer them to others. Thus, when individuals, centuries ago, acquired written language skills, they became members of an elite group; as elites, they opposed the broad sharing of literacy skills. For example, the reading elite in England in the nineteenth century "viciously criticized" the idea of free libraries for the common people. Arguing that such libraries would cater to the "popular passion for light reading, above all for light fiction," the elite contended that the mass reading of such books would deter human progress, the common people would simply read the wrong things. It is possible that even today those who have acquired highly sophisticated computer skills tend to look down upon the use of games and drill and practice routines in schools..

Those opposing and those supporting the mass diffusion of literacy skills have confronted one another for centuries. Leaders on the side of the people, including the most disadvantaged, have prevailed, even though their struggle is not yet ended. Aided by powerful institutions, especially governmental agencies, they have repeated and acted upon a simple message, namely, that if individuals are to be enlightened and effective, they must be literate. If computers fulfil their educational promises, the struggle to eradicate inequitable learning opportunities will continue. As computer-utilities, and international promises, the struggle to eradicate inequitable learning opportunities will continue.

As computer-driven interactive cable, electronic universities, information utilities, and international networks are increasingly used, equity issues will become more salient. Since microelectronic technologies are more complex, expensive, and mutable than books, the equity issues they raise will likely be even more difficult to resolve than those associated with written language.

The five-century story about book literacy is broader than that of ever-expanding learning opportunities; it also encompasses a long struggle to define and redefine the goals of literacy in ways that reflect changing societal values. Thus, Patricia Graham, writing about literacy skills in the early 1980s, observed: "literacy... is what everyone needs in late twentieth-century America, both for their own good and for society's good." However, Horrace Mann argued, from a nineteenth-century perspective, that if students acquired literacy, vice would be reduced and morality would be improved a view that in today's climate would strike many citizens as incredible. In Mann's time, however, morality was such a salient value that school leaders could not easily ignore it. Given the secularized public schools of today, Mann's definition of literacy is no longer highly relevant. Definitions of computer literacy will probably follow in the footsteps of traditional literacy; they will, in other words, be temporary and impermanent.

Rather than, policy makers will need to seek definitions and objectives that mesh with the needs, of their time. Since the information society is much more mutable than previous societies, computer literacy objective will likely undergo more frequent changes. Given the many fearful messages about robots and related machines and their deep cultural roots, computer literacy decisions will also likely be more controversial. Witness, for example, the currency of the dark omens expressed a century and a half ago in Shelley's Frankenstein.

Given the long evolution of book literacy, what features best describe its patterns of growth? For one thing, literacy definitions over time have become more complex—a pattern already reflected in computer literacy. For example, the simpler concepts of operational and instrumental literacy are associated more with the 1970s while the more complex concepts of computer programming and role-related literacy are linked more to the 1980s while the more complex concepts of computer programming and role-related literacy are linked more to the 1980s.

The move from the uncomplicated to the more complex can be seen as follows: operational literacy requires minimal machine skills; instrumental literacy requires minimal machine skills; instrumental literacy, the skills to learn from programs developed by others; algorithmic reasoning, the skills to create one's own programs; and role-related literacy, the skills to perform as competent consumers, workers, and citizens in the developing information society. Given the pattern just noted, another question arises: What features best denote literacy's developing complexities? For one thing, more varieties of radiant skill are now assembled under the literacy tent; for another, the functions served by literacy have multiplied.

Why are the meanings of literacy more encompassing today than they were earlier? Today's meanings stem from a multicentury trend toward an ever more varied content disseminated in a widening array of books, monographs, newspapers, magazines, and journals. When Martin Luther translated the Bible into the German language in the sixteenth century, he provided a powerful new stimulus and a popular means for the citizens of his nation to acquire literacy. At that time, however, literacy was by necessity defined largely in relation to one book.

With the spread of the printing press and the growth and popularization of diverse types of knowledge, literacy expanded to include the skills needed to read more diverse materials. In the nineteenth century, when individuals were pressed to understand the world around them by reading the newly invented newspaper, they had to expand their literacy skills. As reading skills have expanded, literacy functions have become more differentiated. "Scientific", "mathematical," "esthetic," "technological," and "language" denote some of these literacy functions. They also symbolize bodies of knowledge that go substantially beyond those in Luther's day or, for that matter, in Horace Mann's time. Significantly, they imply high expectations for schools, and they help to explain the emergence of compulsory education.

Computer literacy has already undergone considerable differentiation. Inherent in Previous descriptions of operational, instrumental, programmatic, and role-related concepts of literacy are such functions as word processing, computing; programming, information processing, and participation in teledemocratic arrangements. On the other hand, Marvin and Winther, through a study of computer specialists, have arrived at a different set of functions. Employing an electronic mail questionnaire sent to users of the Advanced Research Projects Agency Network (ARPANET), a large computer network, they obtained perceptual data from respondents about "the major types of skills and levels of knowledge that organize computer users into major classes." After analyzing their data, Marvin and Winther posited five levels of users. These classes of users, along with pertinent functions and skills, are described here:

1. Many individuals each day come in contact with microwave ovens, candy machines, cash registers, and related devices; since they perform passive rather than active functions, they do not require particular skills.
2. Members of the next group are called "tourists" or casual end-users. Professors, who rely upon experts for data analysis, fall into this category. The skills "tourists" need are very limited.
3. Programmers constitute the next group. They range from those who have written one workable program to those who have written model programs. The skills required by programmers, as already noted, are specialized ones.
4. Near the top of the hierarchy is the fourth group, called "hackers," who deal effectively with computer "logiams" and "bottlenecks." Their skills, which they express inventively, are, highly technical.
5. At the top of the pyramid are "wizards." Noted for their capacity to perform "amazing feats," they can effect results seemingly by "passing their hands over circuit boards." Their skills are of the highest order.

Marvin and Winther concluded that "the definition of literacy and its proper objects is at any time not only a standard of skillful performance but also a social sorting procedure for labeling certain tasks and domains of knowledge as worthy of social attention and effort."

If computer users at IBM, the New York City public Schools, and the Pentagon had filled in the electronic questionnaire, their lists of functions and skills would likely have differed from one another and from those identified by ARPANET users. Given the diversity of their missions and "social sorting" procedures, they would, in other words, have arrived at different skills. Obviously, schools cannot prepare individuals to perform all computer functions; rather, they must concentrate on basic skills relevant to many differentiated functions.

If computer literacy skills are arrived at through processes of social construction which go on in highly specialized organizations such as ARPANET, the following question becomes pertinent: How are current definitions of literacy, as described above, likely to be reconstructed in the decades ahead? the expanded and interrelated uses of micro-technologies provided one context for examining this question. Since the microcomputer is the most visible of all microelectronic technologies, thinkers have understandably concentrated on computer literacy during the last decade. This approach to literacy has provided a useful focus for designing new learning experiences. However, "computer," as the modifier of literacy, may prove to be an impermanent concept. To be sure, microcomputers are pivotal points in the processing of information; however, they are only part of a much larger and more extended communication complex. The microcomputer is, to use concepts from gestalt psychology, a small "figure" against a more encompassing and expanding "ground."

9

ROLE OF ELECTRONIC MEDIA

The Backdrop

All through the history of mankind, education has provided a continuing basis for the evolution of human society. This role of education may not have been consciously recognised at all stages, nor education organised into a largely formalised activity as it is today. It is nevertheless true that education, through developing human capabilities—their knowledge, skills, attitudes and values—has provided the strength and resilience needed to respond to changing situations and to enable the people to seek and contribute to societal development.

The concept of societal development includes economic development for furthering the material well-being of people, social and political development for living harmoniously and promoting a democratic and just society, and the intellectual, cultural and aesthetic development for enrichment of the quality of life.

To enable the education system to play its due role in the process of development, while it is essential to ensure that all people get the benefit of education, it should also be necessary to arrange that the level of educational attainment among people would not be too disparate between sexes, among social groups and across geographical regions.

At the time of its conception, the Indian Constitution envisaged free and compulsory education for all upto the age of 14, by the year 1960. At other levels of education, and in other sectors like technical, vocational and other professional areas, high expectation come to be associated with education. Today, nearly four decades later, inspite of many impressive achievements, the gap between the goal and the reality in education remain substantial. In order to narrow this gap, it would be necessary to take bold steps. An analysis of the more important statistical data in the field of educational development in India since independence will adequately bear out this thesis.

Indian System of Education

Elementary Education : Universalisation of elementary education has been an important concern of the national policy makers since independence. About 110 million children comprising roughly 76 per cent of population of the relevant age-group are in the elementary stage. The country has reached a gross-enrolment level of 93.4 per cent at the primary level. These national aggregate figures, however, hide many disparities between states, sections of populations and sexes. For example, in Assam enrolment is as low as 62.9 per cent. In some districts of Rajasthan, the enrolment of girls is as low as 19 per cent as against national average of 75.5 per cent. Enrolment of girls is especially poor in rural areas and among scheduled castes and scheduled tribes.

Primary education facilities have not reached all corners of the country. About 1,91,000 habitations comprising nearly 20 per cent of the total are not served by any primary school. 35 per cent of schools have only a single teacher to teach 3 or 4 different classes and cannot, therefore, look after the diverse educational needs of students. There is a need to equalise educational opportunities across all schools in some way.

Then there is the question of wastage. It is disturbing to note that only 23 per cent of the enrolled students reach class VIII. This is mainly because these schools are deficient in resources, for example, inadequate number and quality of teachers, curriculum not relevant to the needs, poor physical facilities like class-room, blackboards etc., and more importantly lack of wall —designed instructional material. With emphasis on mass education, student population in a class-room has become heterogeneous—with different social, cultural and economic background. Their educational needs differ and call for individual attention by the teacher.

Secondary Education : There has been phenomenal expansion of secondary education from some 4000 schools in 1947 to 52,279 schools by 1982-83-a 14 fold increase. Along with this there has been twenty fold increase in the enrolment from 7 lakhs in 1947 to 140 lakhs in 1982-83, but with only ten-fold increase in teachers from 93,000 to 9,93000. This pressure for expansion will certainly continue and will indeed increase as the country progresses in its task of universalisation of elementary education. Today, only 22 per cent of students in the age-group corresponding to classes IX and X are in the school ; this percentage would rise substantially with increasing success at the elementary stage. Ever larger number will join higher secondary schools.

Here again the problems of disparity in states, sexes and sections of society manifest itself. Rural areas in general are deficient in the number of secondary schools. So are educationally backward states like Rajasthan, Madhya Pradesh, Assam, Himachal Pradesh and Punjab. Enrolment of girls in general, and of both girls and boys from rural areas, scheduled castes and tribes, is still not adequate. Enrolment of girls is as low as 20 lakhs against 60 lakhs for boys. Removing geographical disparities and also equalising educational opportunities in all rural and urban schools need urgent attention.

Higher Secondary schools are saddled with the unenviable task of receiving cohorts from less than satisfactory system of elementary education and preparing students for entering the next stage—be it higher education of the world of work. Adverse student-teacher ratio, outdated methods of teaching, poor physical facilities, deficient management system, which discourages innovations, are factors which militate against the task of developing requisite level of competence among school students. The importance of improving the quality of instruction and individualisation of instruction cannot be overemphasised.

Vocational Education : Vocationalisation of higher secondary education was a major objective of the reforms envisaged in the Education Policy adopted in 1968. Attempts made in the past till today have not borne sufficient fruit and enrolment in this stream which was expected to cover 50 per cent of students at the +2 stage has remained marginal and confined largely to few states.

Radical reconstruction with appropriate financial backing is now necessary. The National Working group of AICTE (1985) has drawn up the following numerical profile for 1990 which should be the concern of the vocational education system.

Target Group requiring SUPW/WE or Vocational Education (in Lakhs)

Sr. No.	*Target Group*	*Within General Education Schools*	*Institutes, Schools of Vocational Education*	*Out of School*	*Total Per Class*
1.	(a) Class I-V	200.0	—	—	—
	(b) Class VI-VIII	74.0	—	110	184
	(c) Class IX-X	49.0	—	115	164
2.	Higher Secondary	24.5	—	115.5	140
3.	Certificates and	—	5.0	—	—

Diploma Courses : Besides, tertiary level vocational education will have to be designed for about 45000 to 60000 students of the higher secondary vocational stream. Also, some 30,000 of the ITI and polytechnic output will have to be provided opportunities for higher education.

In addition to the student population within the formal education stream, there is a large working population with the following characteristics which also needs vocational education inputs :

(i) Over 50 per cent of the workers in public sector in occupations requiring technical knowledge and skills do not possess relevant education and training.

(ii) 94 per cent of the workers in occupations requiring general education do not possess formal education.

(iii) Employment in professional and technical categories is growing at a fast rate particularly in service sector, and appropriately qualified people are not available.

(iv) Even those who have received adequate formal education before entry into the world of work, need continuing education and training for another 30 years of productive life in view of the ever changing nature of technology.

In view of its importance in the economic development of the country, the task of expanding vocational educational facilities for school population, out of school population and working population is both large and demanding.

On the basis of previous experience with elementary and secondary schools, one can expect vocational schools in rural areas to suffer from unequal resource provision—poor physical facilities, inadequate informational resources, large student-staff ratio, and poor curriculum processes. The impact is further aggravated since vocational education is more expensive than elementary and secondary education. Unless the system is well supported by the government and employers, wastage is going to be high. The complexity of vocational education is multiplied by the variety of courses for different occupations, the need for modular courses, and the necessity to permit multiple point entry into the vocational stream.

Expanding educational facility to remote areas, equalising educational opportunities in all institutions and enriching class-room instruction for qualitative improvement are concerns which apply with equal force in vocational education.

Higher Education (General and Technical) : The single most important indicator of a country's developmental potential is the state of its higher education. In terms of absolute number we have a large system of higher education. But only 4.8 per cent of the relevant age-group is enrolled in higher education. The corresponding percentage in developed countries is much higher and could be a clue to the future size of the higher educational system. In any case, success in universalisation and improvement in qualitative processes resulting in lowering of drop-outs and failures, will push up the quantitative dimensions. Other factors which impinge on the system are :.inadequate enrolment of women and SC/ST ; rural areas touched only marginally by quality higher education ; heavy orientation in enrolment to general education ; not enough opportunity for quality education in science and technology at different levels etc.

On the front of equalisation of opportunities, the extent of physical facilities, instructional material, the quality and number of teachers vary widely. Internal efficiency of the higher education is low as evidenced by 59 per cent of students enrolled failing or dropping out. A large number pass under third division. Major national inputs for Research and Development having gone to laboratories outside the universities, there is a general deprivation of research facilities among institutions of higher learning.

Trends Today

In recent years, in the sector of technical and management education, polytechnics registered a 6.8 per cent growth rate, reaching a figure of 515 polytechnics in 1982-83 from a base of 325 in 1975-76. The number of engineering colleges increased from 108 to 200 during the same period. With further pace of economic development expected during the next five years, there may be a need for expanding technical and management education system even in conventional areas like civil, mechanical and electrical engineering. Major challenge, however, will be in providing educational facilities in emerging areas like electronics, computers, bio-technology, energy and rural development.

There is a wide variability of standards among different types of technical and management institutes. Even though IITs/IIMs and Regional Engineering colleges receive some what better financial support in comparison to other institutions they all need in varying degrees to modernize their equipment and remove obsolescence in teachers, curriculum and instructional material. Teacher shortages are endemic. Even in conventional areas, teacher shortage is acute as there are 20 to 30 per cent vacancies in majority of the technical and management institutes. In emerging areas, the situation in respect of both teacher shortages and the availability of instructional material is considerably worse.

Improvement of quality of instruction is an urgent necessity. Industrial sector is coming under increasing pressure of international competition. It has to change rapidly for sheer survival. This process can be accelerated and supported only if, besides being provided with relevant equipment, and technology, urgent measures are also taken to augment the human resources in numbers as well as in quality and they are equipped with new knowledge and skills on a continuous basis. These have direct implications for preparing appropriate instructional material, text-books and introducing new educational technologies.

Taking the benefits of the modern technology to common man in rural areas, throws up yet another dimensions of the educational task.

Consequence of Knowledge Explosion and Continuing Education : Research and development in science and technology is responsible for generating ever larger amounts of knowledge and changing technologies at an ever-accelerating pace.

James Martin quotes the following data in the book 'Tele-matic Society—A challenge for Tomorrow' on the dimensions of knowledge explosion—

— The number of scientific journals is increasing by factors of ten every fifty years starting from 1750. The figure was 100,000 journals in 1950.

— The sum total of human knowledge was estimated to be

— doubling every 10 years by 1950.

— doubling every 5 years by 1970.

— By the year 2040 there will be 200 million different books.

As a result, the formal schools and colleges cannot impart all the needed knowledge and skills, within the confines of the classroom. It is just not possible to change text-books and other structured instructional material at the same speed with which knowledge advances. Neither is it possible for the teacher to keep pace with this change through conventional means.

Continuing education, extending over one's life-time, is an imperative of this knowledge explosion. Continuing education for all has therefore to become an integral part of our education system.

Design of continuing education is, however, a far more complex assignment for the educationist than designing initial education within the formal school system. There are many reasons for this. Firstly, unlike the initial education students are not available full-time or even at fixed times. Secondly, the learning needs are greatly varied and highly specific because they are related to their immediate job requirement. Thirdly, the learner has greater responsibility for organising his learning. Consequently the need for independent study skills and support from a diversified information and learning resource system.

The special characteristics of continuing education system are :

(a) It should meet the variety of diverse and highly specific needs.

(b) It should be flexible enough in terms of location and time convenient to the learner.

(c) It should depend more on learner taking the responsibility for learning.

(d) It should not depend on a high degree of teacher availability.

(e) It should provide for a diversified information system which is easily accessible and retrievable to the learner according to his needs. The support system should also support interactivity so crucial for proper under standing and internalisation of knowledge.

Non-Formal Education : The efforts of spreading education widely cannot be realised fully if confined only to formal schooling. Non-formal education has been called upon to play an important role since the Sixth Five Year Plan.

Non-formal education was organised for elementary and middle level age groups through the learning centres. Out of 14.7 lakhs of students enrolled, ninety-two per cent have been at the primary level and remaining at the middle level. Literacy which is the major concern of non-formal education, increased from 16.67 per cent in 1951 to 36.23% in 1981. But there is a glaring disparity between males and females (46.9% and 24.8%) and rural areas are less well served than urban areas.

Adult education programme, particularly in the productive age-group of 15 to 35 years has covered 58 lakhs through nearly two lakh centres. However, only Maharashtra, Tamil Nadu and Karnataka have registered high rates of enrolment. At the end of Sixth Plan the total enrolment was 2.3 crore ; some 8.7 crores remain to be covered. According to World Bank estimates, India would have the largest concentration of illiterate population by 2000 AD. This shows the urgency that should be attached to removal of illiteracy.

Philip H. Coomb in his "World Crisis in Education" has analysed the experience of non-formal systems worldover. He identifies that insufficient motivation prevents illiterates from continuous participation in adult education programmes. Other factors which contribute to failure of non-formal systems are : inadequate professional support from developmental agencies and marginal involvement of grass-root agencies/schools.

Most of these programmes are small, they operate in limited geographical areas, serve a limited clientele. There is no one agency to co-ordinate the non-formal programmes. The country lacks competent professional support services such as programme design and evaluation staff-training, preparation of training materials and various types of technical assistance to ministries organising non-formal programmes.

Inspite of the fact that the non-formal programmes are as important as formal system, the conventional methods have not been able to cope with problem of expansion of these programmes and qualitative improvement.

The Feedback

The study of the facts and figures for the quantitative expansion and the qualitative improvement of the total educational system in India highlight three major issues which need our attention :

(i) Expansion of educational system to reach geographically scattered area, to remove disparity of educational facilities to disadvantaged groups—rural poor, women, handicapped, culturally and economically backward areas of the society and to meet diverse learning needs of the population.

(ii) Qualitative improvement of educational process through individualization of instruction to reduce wastage and produce high quality manpower for both economic and social development.

(iii) Continuing education system to meet the consequences of knowledge explosion.

The task of finding solutions to the above problems is not only vast, but also exceedingly complex, it is also obvious that it is not possible for the conventional methods and organization to cope with those problems. The present method of teaching is teacher dominated whose reach to a large number of students is limited ; instruction is mainly verbal and its effectiveness is limited ; information storage, and retrieval system for selective dissemination is manually operated. Any expansion which is thought of in terms of increasing the number of teachers, building additional schools, purchasing more equipment, is very costly and beyond the capacity of the nation to pay. As a consequence student-staff ratio remains high. In view of all these limitations, attempting quality improvement through individualization of instruction is an impossibility.

We need now to go in for a bold and imaginative solution to the problem. We must tap the potential of technology for meeting this challenge. An examination of the educational reforms project in India and abroad, gives one reason to hope that electronics is capable of providing just such intervention. Let us briefly see how electronics can play an important role in each of the three issues mentioned earlier.

Expansionary Phase

As stated earlier this aspect has to be seen from the point of view of—

(a) size of expansion,

(b) diversity of needs of the student population, and

(c) removal of disparity.

Size of Expansion : As pointed out earlier 20 per cent of the habitation are still to have even elementary educational facilities. These habitations are remote and many a time located at inaccessible places. Even if school buildings are constructed, teachers of right quality and inadequate number are not likely to be available. The only way is to depend on the local talent to teach but to support them in terms of information and instructional material through distance education. This system can reach large number of people, in accessible pockets and diverse groups. The distance education system, using electronic media, can help equalize disparities in the quality of instruction. One good example is the SITE programme designed by SAC for Kheda District, Ahmadabad.

Diversity : While thinking about the geographical expansion, we have to take into account the diverse learning needs of the population. Learning needs of the population change according to age, sex, social and economic status, occupation and ethnic diversity. It is often impossible to meet the wide diversity of these needs through conventional means, since the numbers involved for a localised effort become too small to set up expensive infrastructure. The needs therefore go unattended and a uniform system meeting the needs of only the dominant groups can at best be conceived. However, if electronic technologies are deployed to set up a distance education effort it is possible to combine the numbers of similar scattered groups to a critical level where it becomes cost-effective to set up adequate educational programmes.

Disparity : For upgrading the quality of instruction uniformly, across all schools, irrespective of their location in urban or rural areas they have to be equipped with adequate learning resources—teachers, books, equipment etc. Since all these resources are costly, alternative methods of teaching through electronic media will have to be adopted. In India, this has already been experimented by Delhi University (in 1964-65) in which about 22,000 students in 227 Delhi schools were studying science with the aid of television. In Thailand, today, about 800,000 students in schools are receiving lessons through radio-broadcast. Subjects chosen are social studies and music.

Individualisation of Instruction and Qualitative Improvement : Quality of instruction can be improved through (a) improving teachers competencies—skills, presentation skills etc., (b) improving the quality of instructional material—the content of lecture, supplementing print material by motion films animations, simulations, still picture etc. (c) improving support system through specially well designed information storage and retrieval system to make information readily accessible to teachers and students.

CCTV plays an important role in modification of teacher behaviour. A combination of media—television, radio and computer can be used to enrich class-room instruction, provide interaction and support independent study. Electronically operated information processing systems (dial access system, or integrated computer video system) enable teacher and student to individualize instruction. Individualization of instruction means a teaching process in which the teacher organises educational experiences for every student according to his need, at his pace and at time and place suited to him. Starting point for any learning can only be the stock of knowledge, skills and attitudes the student actually possesses before learning a new task and not some prescribed norm. Furthermore knowledge acquisition will be based on a solid foundation only when the concepts, principles and procedures are acquired and enforced through all types of experiences i.e. enactive (through physical manipulation of real world) ; iconic (through pictures - still or in motion—representing models of real world) and symbolic (through sound and written symbols). Teacher takes into account the type of experience the student already possesses and his level of integrated body of knowledge, and then provides relevant further learning experiences to aid his learning. It must be recognised that every student, whether in formal system or distance education system is different from the others in this respect and therefore needs different type of educational experience.

The second important aspect of individualisation is the pace i.e. the rate at which these experiences are presented at a time. Some students are slow learners, some grasp quickly.

The third aspect of individualisation is time and location of learning experience. School based system which forces all students to learn the same things at the same time is now being criticized in the educational circles. But no alternative to the present system has been found as yet, as individualization of instruction poses a highly complex and logistic problem. However, experimentation with distance education system like British Open University has demonstrated that electronic media like computer, television, telephones, dial access system etc. can be advantageously used by the teacher in individualisation of instruction in the school-based formal and non-formal education systems. Computer assisted instruction, computer-video link up for information, storing and retrieval etc. are some of the techniques which are now finding greater use.

Individualization of instruction is an important strategy to reduce drop-out rates and improve the quality of learning. This will help provide quality manpower which.the nation needs for economic and social development and electronics media can play a dominant role in this innovation in education.

Perusing Further

As stated earlier, life-long education has become a necessity for all. The characteristics of continuing education effort are : meeting diverse learning needs, shift of learning responsibility to the learner, flexibility in terms of time and location, and special attention to cater to the needs of scattered population for improving information accessibility.

Use of radio and television broadcasting can easily cover scattered population. Establishment of study centres at selected institutions and at homes, and availability of VCR, audio cassette recorders, projectors videotex/teletext, etc. may help learner to meet his individual learning needs. Dial access system, video-computer link up will improve information accessibility.

To sum up, electronics media can play an important role in meeting the challenge of education.

Before we look a bit more into the roles electronic media play in education, it is perhaps pertinent to ask the following questions :

(i) Is it going to replace the teacher ?

(ii) Can the country afford to invest in such expensive infrastructure ?

(iii) Is it cast-effective ?

(iv) Can we expect corresponding better educational outcome ?

(v) Do we have expertise to install, maintain and run the system efficiently ?

It is necessary to clarify at the outset that electronic media even in the developed countries, where these have been used on a wider scale, have never been used to replace teacher but to complement the efforts of teacher, extend his reach beyond the immediate class-room, and to improve his capacity to retrieve information resources.

As regards cost, it is true that the country has to prepare itself for significant initial investment, but with extensive coverage possible through broadcasting media and communication satellite, it is possible to bring down the cost per student. In terms of long range benefit in view of education's capacity to shape public opinion, change attitudes, skill formation among output of—school population, enhanced, facilities for continuing education, etc., there will be ample justification for such investment.

There is no doubt that to maintain and run the educational system with electronics media, a variety of skilled manpower is required : teachers with skills to manage learning, hardware specialist, software specialist, media managers, etc. It also demands total commitment of the educational system as a whole including educational policy makers at the national and state level, educational administrators, teaching community and students. But precisely this aspect of the electronic media will also be its strength. The entire educational system will then be involved in educational reform which is so necessary for any innovation to succeed. Piecemeal and isolated efforts in educational reform no matter how good are not able to create any nation wide impact and tend to prove too costly both in terms of cost, time and human-effort.

Let us now look into the nature of use of electronics media in school-based formal and non-formal systems, distance education system, and informal education system.

Role of Media

Enrichment of Instruction : In the formal education system individualisation of instruction and optimum utilization of teachers capabilities is a major problem. How to make the best use of a teacher, so that he can attend to the needs of an individual student and at the same time his expertise is available to the largest number of students ? The formal education system imparts certain basic knowledge (consisting of concepts, principles and procedures), basic skills (both physical and verbal), and basic attitudes to function effectively within a given working environment. In the present formal education system the teacher gives a lot of stress on verbal instruction using lecture as the predominant way of imparting instruction. In order to make instruction more meaningful, students also need both enactive as well as iconic experiences in addition to the symbolic presentation of information through lectures. Enactive experience is gained through actual participation of the learner in learning events. In case it is difficult by provide direct access to such experience, the learner should at least be provided the opportunity to see the actual sequence of events. This is possible through motion-film and video tapes. Iconic experience is presented through pictures or graphics which represent real world through models. These are made possible through video displays. Bringing of enactive and iconic experiences in the class-room requires the use of motion films and video displays.

Effective presentations of graphics for providing iconic experience can be done by projection media and video display. These media can also be used advantageously for explaining certain basic concepts particularly those concepts which can not be demonstrated in real life e.g. the movement of atomic and sub-atomic particles, and working of biological cells. Enactive and iconic experiences are also needed in order to change the attitude of students. Developing positive attitudes in inter-personal relations, sympathy for the poor and disadvantaged sections of society, respect for honesty, passion for quality and justice, needs simulation techniques, case study techniques, or bringing into the class-room examples of model behaviour. These are some of the gaps in conventional instruction rectified through technological aids with great success.

Educational psychologists emphasize that in order to achieve specific educational objectives every student needs different types of educational experiences depending on his entry behaviour. The teacher, therefore, should produce/acquire, and organise variety of resources and use them in the class-room to suit individual's learning needs.

It is also now recognised that mere provision of information through lectures does not suffice to equip students with certain critically important skills like the ability to critically analysing one's environment, develop solutions on one's own, and communicate effectively. A student can learn these only when he is motivated to set his own learning goals, chooses his own learning experiences and is allowed to learn at his own pace ; all of which are integral part of independent study skill. Technological aids can be used to strengthen independent study skills among learners.

Increasing Effectiveness of Lecturing : The presentation can be enriched by using multimedia information and resources. Now-a-days, lectures are supplemented by type recordings, filmstrips, set of slides and transparencies, OHP transparencies, etc. With the advent of video and computer, real-life events can be brought into the classroom through video-films. It is also possible to supplement the lecture by bringing the best available presentation in a particular subject into the classroom. Computer has made the use of animation and simulation techniques much easier and thereby helped the teacher in explaining complex concepts.

Increasing Effectiveness of Laboratory Instruction : The student-teacher ratio in a normal laboratory class varies between 10 : 1 and 15 : 1. This is because the operation and demonstration of the laboratory experiments by the teacher cannot be done effectively to a large class. Secondly, intermittent individual guidance by the teacher during the course of experimentation also requires a smaller student to staff ratio. The need for teacher involvement can be reduced somewhat by the use of self-instructional print material. But print material alone is not capable of reducing the load of the teacher or to ensure individual guidance. It is now possible to prepare 8 mm films or video-tapes to explain the total sequence of laboratory experimentation including explanation of procedure, and thereby permit the teacher to help larger number of students. Furthermore, stimulation plays a very important part where discovery learning is the objective of laboratory instruction i.e. where students are expected to discover for themselves certain principles and laws through laboratory experiments. In this Computers can play an important part by allowing quick and extensive exploration of the simulated experimental system.

Increasing Effectiveness of Independent Study : Independent study in the institution as well as at home is normally done with the help of print materials. Its effectiveness can be greatly increased if additional experiences can be provided through non-print media and the student is in a position to access a variety of experiences and information. For example, he should be able to listen to the lecture of an expert, retrieve textual and pictorial information from motion films or any other source, and process information. This is possible if he is supported with television set, VCRs, micro computers, film projectors, radios, etc.

Increasing Reach of the Teacher : Since teacher is the costliest resource in any educational venture, it is necessary to ensure that the teacher is accessible to as many students as possible without affecting the individual needs of the students. In USA it has been shown that with the help of interactive television a professor can successfully teach 200-300 students at a time. The difficulties of student-teacher interaction due to larger number can be overcome by electronically operated feedback system.

Establishment of Resource Centre : In its traditional concept a library is a place where only print material are stored for use by students and teachers. There is a need to extend the scope of library to production, acquisition and storing non-print information resources as well. In modern terms a library which stores a variety of information resources is a Resource Centre. A typical Resource Centre uses micro-film and micro-fiche for storing large amounts of documented information thus reducing requirement of storage space. It provides space for hardware needed for projecting retrieving, and recording information. The Resource Centre also stores, in addition to text-books, a variety of other print material like monographs, Journals, Articles, Newspaper clippings, etc. It also stores audio cassettes, video cassettes, films transparencies, and slides. But storage and retrieval through these information resources are being managed at the moment, largely manually which is too inefficient, and slow. With increase in the use and variety of A. V. aids in course of time, electronically operated system of information storage and retrieval will have to be introduced.

Various Researches

Wilber Schramm has described the experiences of five national reform movements in both developed and developing countries, whose aim was to bring swift reform in the formal education system. The countries are Niger (1964) for upgrading first five grades of elementary education ; American Samano (1964) for reforming all primary and secondary grades, plus pre-school and adult services ; Et Salvador (1969) for primary school, teacher training and out of school education ; Ivory Coast (1971) to cover all primary school grades ; and Korea (1973) for elementary and middle school with related teacher training. The reform movement in each case was built around ITV as the major medium of instruction.

In general the study indicates that introduction of education centered around ITV created improvement not only in the class-room instruction, but also brought about many positive changes in the entire system at the national level.

The size of effort involved in instructional television and the demands of logistics require a major commitment to change by authorities at all levels. At the national level and state level, it requires a policy level commitment to educational reform. With such a commitment and policy direction to the Ministries of Education both at the national and state level concomitant changes follow throughout the system in translating the policy into action plan. Educational reform through instructional TV, requires long range planning and preparation. It imposes specific time-schedules for curriculum revision, and arrangement of financing. It requires detailed advance planning of training of professionals for hardware installation, software preparation, maintenance, teacher preparation to develop new skills in lesson planning, script writing and team work. This also requires actual participation, of principles and teachers in the preparation of instructional materials, testing its reliability and validity and generates nation wide interest in such reforms and particularly stimulates the participants. Television can be used as an important tool of national reform. The major prerequisite for introducing such a project of national reform is the availability of a strong financial and professional support and the commitment of the nation at the highest level. The same author also describes further case studies on the use of media for (a) enabling schools to share expertise of the best teacher (b) expanding in-service training facilities (c) solving the problem of over-crowding.

Haggerstown school in America used imaginative and highly articulate teachers as tele-teachers who developed courses with the help of other teachers ; their lectures were televised in primary and secondary schools. The study showed that such televised lectures in the class-room were rated high especially in the primary schools ; students performance in general was better in comparison to classes without the benefit of these tele-lectures. In the wake of these tele-lectures the nature of classroom instruction changed from mere exposition to participation by the students through questioning and discussions. Additional preparation for such tele-lectures and better visuals helped to improve the quality of presentation.

In Japan, effort was mounted to equip schools in isolated areas with ITV programme. The study claims that televised lectures improved the performance of lower ability students in science courses.

In Columbia, introduction of televised lectures persuaded teachers to introduce questioning in the class-room to ensure students participation in place of frontal teaching.

In Thailand, radio was used as medium to supplement teachers activities. The report says the radio students scored higher than those students without radio facilities.

Role in Distance Education

Introduction : Since 1960 onwards many colleges and schools in UK and USA stretched themselves beyond the campus and the classroom to bring learning opportunities to students in their own locations. Initially this extended education—"distant teaching" was done through correspondence. The thrust in distant teaching was not merely to lake the formal education but also non-formal continuing education to these distant students. There are varying patterns of use of instructional media in distant teaching. For example USA in 1969 built distance education Programmes wholly around radio for regular college courses. France began in 1963 with radio coupled with correspondence ; practical work experience was provided at a University for. students who could not attend regular classes but wanted to pass state examination entitling them to teach in a school or university. East Germany started in 1961 a variety of adult-education programmes in cultural and vocational subjects. The courses are built around television and some print material. RTS promotion of France offers, through television and print material, non-credit courses for broadening the knowledge base and contributing to vocational and professional skills.

The survey of such distance-education courses indicates that such education has been found to be valuable to population of all ages in meeting the variety of their learning needs. For example, enrolment of German Telekolleg consist of 44 percent under the age of 25, 38 percent between 25 and 35 years of age, and 18 percent still older. Television courses addressed to working people in Austria attract 86 percent male, in Poland 79 percent, but in Chicago TV College, 75 percent of those enrolled are women. 80 percent of credit audiences of Austrian, German and Japanese and British Programmes come from people working full time.

The distance-education system with the aid of electronic media can provide immense help in taking education to a wide variety of population of different age groups, sex and situated at widely scattered areas, and catering to variety of learning needs both for initial formal school programmes as well as continuing education programmes. Some of the important problems of initial programmes of learning through correspondence alone, were the isolation of students from the teacher, the lack of schedule to encourage him to keep his work up-to-date and the limited nature of educational experience. These factors contributed to the high drop-out rate from such courses. Television, telephone, interactive-video can now break this isolation. Broadcast television and radio impose a certain schedule of study. Enrichment of experience is provided through television, video-recording, audio-recording, computer assisted instruction, etc. Further more self-pacing can go a long way to reducing drop-out rates.

The Limitations

As mentioned earlier, the formal school system offering formal and non-formal courses for a variety of target population has its own limitations. Recognising this and for providing educational facilities to large number of people, like working population, women, rural population who for some reason or other cannot attend to formal types of courses, there is a need to design a distance education system. The Government of India has already started the Indira Gandhi National Open University for offering courses at different levels and in a variety of disciplines. The electronic media will play an important role in this system of distance-education.

It will be interesting to examine the working of the British Open University since this will provide an insight into the use of media in distance education. The Open University system, if run on the lines of British Open University, does not prescribe any entry qualification and there is also no age restriction. It provides instruction at the door-step of the student through the combined use of correspondence texts, home experimental kits and suitably located study centres which use electronic media like audio-tapes, video-tapes fete. The British Open University was conceived to teach out of school population primarily through television and radio broadcasts. Initially when it started functioning, correspondence was used as the priority media for teaching. Subsequently, this effort was supplemented by teaching through television and radio broadcasting and video-recordings sent to individual homes. Still later, the concept of study centres located in universities, polytechnics and colleges was evolved in which students could go (i) to see video and audio cassettes (ii) 16 mm or 8 mm film and (iii) get the help of part time tutors on subject matter which was hard to comprehend only through correspondence text.

British Open University has lately started experimenting with computer assisted instruction, use of two-way television link, use of telephone for telephone tutorials and conference, and tele-writer. Computer is being used by the BOU in managing distance learning especially for recording a variety of student data such as names of students, their tutors, results of assessment, material distribution, fees collected, etc.

The major steps in designing any distance education system are : course creation, course production, course distribution, and course evaluation.

Course Creation : Because of the distance between the teacher and the student, the distance education system has two special characteristics. Firstly, the total course has to be designed for students whose individual characteristics are not known to the course designer. Every possible learning experience, therefore, has to be taken into account while designing a course. It is here, that the concept of integrated learning package consisting of a suitable combination of structured material, structuring material and unstructured material, both print and non-print, has been evolved. The selection of the type of instructional material to be used, and its format, depends upon the user facilities available to the learner at his place of study. The course creation therefore, normally takes into account the electronic media available in the community study centres as at homes.

The course designer must consider the working of the mass media organisations, postal departments, tele-communication organisations for designing an effective delivery-system. The course design is therefore a collaborative effort between the educational technologists, the subject matter experts, electronic hardware personnel, and software specialists.

Course Production : Because of the wide spread use of video-based education system, sometimes in combination with the computers, the production stage needs the services of script writers, supporting technical staff like graphic artists, visualisers, and video film producers. Production requires collaboration of the educational technologists, subject matter specialists, system designers, system engineers, system programmers, etc.

Course Distribution : Course 'distribution is concerned with ways and means of carrying the message of the course designers to the students and helping them in organising their own learning. The course distribution system should also have ways and means to obtain feedback from the learner as quickly as possible so that the teacher may reinforce his learning. In order to help the student in organising his own learning a wide range of video based information systems is now available. To mention some of them : television-displays, video-disc systems, video-cassette systems for interactive learning, cable-television systems, direct broadcasting technology, video-based information system for storage and retrieval, dissemination of documents by libraries, video-conference systems etc.

Course Evaluation : In the distance education system the number of students is large and course evaluation requires a complex data base for accessing student performance on a continuing basis. Course evaluation is quite a complex process and needs an electronic support system which will do the work speedily. Various types of video-based information systems connecting geographically scattered students with the teacher to ensure continuous evaluation are possible only with electronic aids. Thus networking of all the student centres as well as linking course production, course distribution, and assessment of students learning needs a careful system design based on electronics.

Some Case Studies : Several advanced and developing countries have already introduced distance education systems. India started in a modest way in 1962 ; radio and TV broadcast were used by Delhi University to support its correspondence course. Recently, Indira Gandhi National Open University has been established by the government. As far back as 1963 Australia introduced radio courses to provide primary and secondary education in remote areas. Paris University introduced radio instruction in 1963 to supplement its correspondence text for formal education. UK and West Germany have established full fledged Open Universities. In USA, University of Nebraska has established a regional university system by making use of TV and textual material. Stanford University is offering many of its engineering courses to employees of engineering firms through distance education. Israel has established an 'Everyman's University.'

Most of the countries who have experimented with the distance education system have realised that it can be used successfully as an extended schools system for every level of academic and vocational studies and that distance education can be an important strategy for life-long education. They have also realised that the use of TV and Radio makes the learning process lively, and these " media can ably support correspondence text and tutors. If properly supported by computer and home study kit, it can ensure active participation of the student in the learning process. A well designed distant education system has been demonstrated to be at least as efficient as the classical formal education system.

Following are some of the broad conclusions from the case studies on distance education :

1. Distance teaching, well conceived and well supported with proper media really works. Students in these media-supported programmes learn at least as well as students in the same curriculum in traditional class room.
2. With proper choice of electronic media, the unit cost can be brought down to an acceptable level even for remote areas.
3. Distant education is effective only if big media (TV and Radio) are further supported by other print material, home-study kits, assignments, two-way communication, occasional class, summer terms, study groups, telephone consultation, and tutorial classes.

Role in Formal and Non-formal Education

Non-formal Education with Case Studies : Non-formal

education is the motley assortment of organized and semi-organized educational activities operating outside the regular structure and routines of the formal system. It is aimed at a great variety of learning needs of different sub-groups in the population, both young and old. These learning needs relate to for example, health, nutrition, family planning, developing good character traits and positive attitudes, increasing economic productivity, improving family incomes and employment opportunities, strengthening local institution of self-help and self-government and broadening participation in them. Most of the programmes are aimed at benefiting particular sub-groups in the local population—farmers, craftsmen and entrepreneurs, women, young children, unemployed youth, members and leaders of community organisation such as cooperative societies of farmers. Non-formal education has assumed importance precisely because of the inability of the formal school system to meet all educational needs of the society.

Schramm describes how the non-formal education takes different forms ranging from localized schools to development campaigns such as family planning, agricultural improvement, and better health. Non-formal education system uses all sorts of media ranging from radio to print, posters and puppets and includes personal contact with field staff. Amongst the big media, radio has generally become the main medium of predominant use. Recently films and video tapes have found increasing use.

The localised school experiment of Litowa, Southern Tanzania, built around active community participation, was set up to produce students who would meet the developmental needs of a subsistence agricultural economy.

Initially, in the localized school system, media played a very small part. But once the participation increased, media was asked to play its part in the development and reconstruction of the village. The district training centre where local leaders come for guidance and instruction, is supposed to have a library/Radio/Information room. Visiting extension workers bring films and film-strips for instruction.

Development campaigns are the combination of information and persuasion. In these campaigns all types of media from television to traditional inexpensive media like puppet are used. Inter-personal communication is, however, integral to the use of such media.

Zaire has used radio a good deal in non-formal education for health and nutrition integrated with local participation through organised group activity. Ghana introduced a project of group listening for farmers. This programme was designed to increase agricultural production, improving marketing of crops, better harvesting, and practical training. Similar programmes were also instituted in India, Research indicates that group listening through such rural radio farms, followed by group discussion, is quite influential in changing attitudes, beliefs and promoting positive attitudes for adopting innovations :

Informal Education : Informal learning is defined as "spontaneous unstructured learning that goes on daily in home and in neighbourhood, behind the school, on the playing field, in work place, market place, library and museum and through various mass media, all of which constitute a person's informal learning environment." What an individual can learn from his or her particular environment, however, is confined to (i) what that environment has to offer (ii) how the person systematizes his learning strategy.

Enriching Learning Environment

(a) Rise in parental education. Educational level of a child's parent has a profound effect on child's life values and behaviour including his appetite for learning. Further informal learning is strengthened by easy availability of books, magazines and newspapers in and around homes of the learners. Circulation of daily newspaper develops awareness level of an individual about important events in the country. Since 1965 Radio Television and film have served a lot more of the world's information, education and entertainment needs. Intercontinental communication satellite has become capable of bringing major events—Olympic meet, coronation, men landing on the moon—instantaneously into the homes in the far corners of the earth. This incredible technological development has enormous implication for the informal learning environment.

Informative and instructive broadcasts enable vast numbers of children and adults to learn important and interesting things about the world that they could never otherwise learn in schools.

(b) Acquiring skill of independent study is an important aspect of informal education.

In view of the changing nature of the environment every adult has to systematize his informal education strategy to keep on accumulating knowledge on the basis of his daily experiences through interaction with people, reading books, using mass media, listening to expert lectures, attending conferences, participating in community events, cultural show etc. To enable him to extract usable knowledge out of the variety of experiences of his daily life he needs the help of external mechanism which allows him to search information systematically, keep a record of the information gathered from various sources through maintenance of personal files, retrieve this information to facilitate creative thinking for solving problems and communicating to his target group.

This involves a home based or office based information system that is specifically designed for storing, retrieving and disseminating information. Systematic design of information systems to facilitate informal education is the need of the day and deserves specific attention of electronic engineers, computer scientists and others concerned with the design of such systems.

While information system for educated adults could be set up more easily, a different type of information system is needed for the illiterate and semi-literate population living in geographically remote areas. This is of vital importance for increasing their awareness level. Taking information and message to such population through community information centres is essential. Here too television and other video and computer based information systems can play an important role.

Electronic Aids for Educational Planners and Administrators : In order that the educational action in schools and colleges, and in homes and offices takes place effectively within the total framework of State and National policies, the policy-makers and the administrators at the national, state and district levels should have and adequate, scientifically organised base for monitoring and evaluating all programmes. The present system of collecting data and storing in files is inefficient. A strong information base is necessary for manpower forecasting, for organising consolidation of the existing educational facilities (physical resources, human resources, financial resources) and for mounting programmes of educational reform.

As in industry, business or commerce, educational decisions are also required to be taken through group discussions. Teleconferencing and video conferencing may make this possible. A democratic way of functioning requires quick dissemination of information so that all concerned can contribute meaningfully to the decision making process. Reprography has therefore become an indepensible supporting service for educational institutions, policy-makers and administrators. A typical reprography section today is equipped with photocopying machines, electronic scanners, transparency making machines, etc., But a more integrated design of reprographic-units is needed which may need the services of electronic specialists.

Suitable secretarial assistance enable policy-maker/administrator to function more efficiently. Gadgets like electronic typewriters, word-processors, efficient inter-communication system, dictaphones, computers are now available. But scientific designs of incorporating such electronic systems for improving secretarial assistance have yet to evolve at a meaningful level.

Importance of Message Design : In the educational context, especially in the design of teaching-learning systems, the effectiveness of electronic media depends much on the way the message is designed. The message format must take into consideration the way a learner perceives a stimulus, retrieves from his memory the relevant set of knowledge and experiences, organises his thinking for devising a course of action for responding to the stimulus, and actually executes the action and gets feedback. Apart from retrieving information from the memory a data base system could be used to aid the learner's memory. The process of planning a course of action by choosing among the alternatives needs a mechanism for presenting and experimenting with alternatives. A computer based information system helps the learner to try alternative ways of organising the knowledge structure and developing a new integrated set of ideas and procedures. Combining, the knowledge of electronic system design with the knowledge of educational technologists whose main task is to design a massage from the point of view of student is therefore essential. British Open University is a fine example of such collaborative effort.

Characteristics of Media

Various categories of media and their characteristics are discussed in this section. The range includes both the conventional and the electronic media.

Human Models : Strictly speaking this is not an educational medium in the conventional sense of the term. Human models are people, held -in esteem by the society in general, for their virtues, qualities, attitudes and attributes which may be learnt more effectively by emulation than through other means. Human models play an important part in developing character and values in a learner.

Print Medium : Amongst the conventional media print is most popular and also the most important. The invention of printing press revolutionised the process of propagation of knowledge. Printed material can be broadly classified as below :

Text Material : Information is encoded primarily through alphanumeric symbols with or without graphic illustration. Printed text material can be sub-classified again under general headings such as fiction, text book, hand book, journal, encyclopaedia, dictionary, monograph, manual etc. Each of these serves a different purpose. A fiction many aim at developing attitudes and values, a dictionary on the other hand is a knowledge based information resource for one or more specific languages.

Pictorial and Graphic : Prints of multi-tone complex photographic colour images to simple outline drawings are used to provide iconic experiences as a part of the education process. Graphics such as pie-charts, bar-charts and curves representing relationships between variables are used to encode information in a symbolic form. The decoding of information coded in iconic form is simple as the similarity between the original and the coded version is apparent. Even an illiterate person can understand the message coded in the form of a picture. Decoding of symbolic representation is more difficult. The ability to read and interpret information are minimum requirements before printed texts and graphics become useful.

Some of the special characteristics of the pictorial and graphic information are :

- They extend the range of stimuli greatly in normal class room teaching and simultaneously allow economy of verbal communication.
- They facilitate concept and principle learning. Where it is difficult to provide suitable enactive experience for skill learning pictures can be used for partial compensation.
- They provide contiguity, generalisation and discrimination.
- Verable prompts are necessary to channelise thinking.

The print medium is well established. Since a large variety of information is available in printed form and browsing is possible, the choice of information resource to suit the diverse ranges and levels of individual needs in relatively simple. In printed form, information is transportable and decoding is restricted primarily by the individuals' capabilities. The time, the place the speed, the content and the level of learning can all be decided by the learner. The medium is highly suitable for a learner managed system of education. Printed text is often unable to describe events, places, processes in the same spatial and temporal details as is possible through the dynamic visual imagery of the motion film medium. This disadvantage can, however, be looked upon as an advantage in certain situations. While a motion film leaves little to viewer's imagination, printed text encourages the development of this particular mental faculty.

One of the major draw-backs of the print medium is the problem of dissemination. The cost and difficulty of information dissemination, beyond a point, increase with the increase in the number of readers and the physical distances to be covered for delivery. The speed of dissemination is low compared to most electronic media.

Considerable intervention of a teacher is essential in the initial stages to develop reading and self study skills in the students.

Still Projection : Slides, transparencies and film strips can be classified under the common category of still projections. Text, graphic and pictorial information can be presented through the still projection media. The major advantage of the projected media is their capability to share the same information to a large number of students simultaneously. A teacher can draw the attention of a large class to any part of the information at any time. The teacher is able to control the speed of presentation. Multi layer or multi-projection system coupled with suitable verbal; prompting can be used to teach highly complex subjects very efficiently. Much more material can be presented in a controlled way than would be possible without the help of the projected media.

All still projection media suffer from a common problem— the quantum of information that can be presented in a single frame is generally very limited. Management of the media both software and hardware is not particularly convenient. These are primarily teacher controlled media and not very suitable for individual student use.

Models : Models in selected cases are extremely useful as a medium of instruction. Situations which demand the representation of an object in more than simple two dimensional views, can benefit by the use of models. Working models can approximate reality closely and be used to supplement abstract ideas and symbolic representations at the appropriate stage of learning. As a medium of instruction, models have the disadvantages of being some what expensive, suitable for individual student or small groups only, difficult to store and retrieve. Additionally, the learner is required to go to the location where models are kept, thus making them unsuitable for mass education or distance teaching.

Audio

Recorded Sound : Sound is recognised as one of the major vehicle of learning. The ability to record sound and reproduce it at a different place, at a different time, any number of time, at a desired speed, in any desired sequence or mix of different sounds increases the effectiveness of the medium greatly. Audio tapes and cassettes, audio discs (gramophone records) greatly enhance the teaching/learning process. Audio recordings allow vastly large number of people to benefit from a lecture or talk which could be attended by only a very limited number of students. Sounds which can not be generated in a convenient place and time can be recreated through the medium of recorded audio. It is suitable for providing symbolic experiences. Audio is also ideal for teaching subjects which require learning of intonation, articulation, modulation of sound.

Broadcast Radio and Two-way Radio : The ability to transmit 'live' or recorded sound through radio broadcasting results in the additional advantages of increasing the "reach" of the audio medium enormously in a cheap, convenient and quick way. Broadcast radio allows a large number of people to listen to one of many programmes transmitted over a large area. Usually it is a one way process. The listener can not normally interact with the programme source and has to listen passively. Radio broadcast forces the learners to adjust their time to the schedule of broadcast.

In two-way radio the listener(s) and the speaker(s) can interact with each other. Two-way radio link is established using point-to-point communication techniques. Sometimes an alternative method is used for two way communication. In this second method, the programme is broadcast over a wide area in the normal way. The listener can phone the radio station to interact while the programme is "ON AIR". If the question is considered relevant and useful for other listeners the telephonic conversation itself is broadcast for the benefit of others. The last technique is also known as "Radio phone-in" service.

Whether transmitted via telephone, radio link or simply recorded on tapes, cassettes or discs, the audio medium has one significant problem when used on its own. The attention span of the average listener is rather short when the ears and the eyes receive stimuli from different sources. Students capable of fully utilising the various audio-only media need to be highly motivated. The effectiveness of the media is thus reduced to a certain extent. Inspite of this the value of the recorded audio media, particularly the broadcast radio, in a high populous country, with its population spread over large and scattered zones such as India, in spreading education, is quite high.

Motion Picture

Cine Film : Cine film has three formats, namely 35 mm ; 16 mm and the super 8 format. The advantages are obvious. Motion film combined with recorded sound can often create the illusion of reality, capturing the attention of the viewers in a way, not possible through any of the media discussed so far. It can reproduce events and sequences of events which may be infrequent or inaccessible ; speeded up or slow motion films allow changes in time scale to reveal patterns of events not possible to be experienced from normal observations. The technique of animation bring 'alive' visual images which in real life would either be invisible or stationary.

Film as a medium allows viewing of systematically arranged, well-planned expositions, on complex theoretical and field practices and processes, repeatedly at the convenience of the viewers.

As an educational medium cine film is somewhat expensive.

It is difficult and time consuming to make, and requires projection equipment which is neither very cheap nor easy to maintain. The ability of a good motion picture to hold the viewer's attention for a prolonged period of time, also leads the viewer to considerable passivity. Many limes the passivity leads to an unquestioning acceptance of the presenter's point of view an attitude which is in contradiction to the purpose of education.

Video Film

Video tapes combine all the advantages of motion films with a substantial reduction in cost and time of production. The ease of shooting, editing, copying and playback coupled with cheaper recording/playback equipment has resulted in a rapid rise in the popularity of video as an educational medium. Video can be used for mass communication as well as for individualisation of instruction with equal ease.

A video film can be recorded on video tapes, video-cassettes or on video discs. Because of its great flexibility, a large number of educational courses in various subjects have been developed in many countries of the world on videotape. The popularity of such video courses is so high in some of the more industrialised nations that, a set of complete courseware on tape can now be hired at a fraction of total price for which these would otherwise have been sold. For students who are not able to attend regular classes the video-taped instructions have proved to be of great use.

The drawbacks of the video media need also to be noted. Unless utilised on truly mass scale, the cost of video instruction can be even higher than that of the conventional class room based instruction. Academically, the greatest disadvantage lies in the passivity of the instructional environment based on video learning. Taped video film presents information to the learner in a serial fashion. Although the learner is able to control the speed and order of presentation to a limited extent true 'interaction' between the learner and the media does not take place.

Video Disc : Video disc as a technology is new in comparison to the video tape. A video disc can store complex visual images on a small plastic disc similar to a gramophone record. There are a number of different technologies and formats in this field. The simplest one allows a user to play a pre-recorded video disc on a video player in the same way one plays a long-playing record on a turn-table. Instead of reproducing only the sound, a video disc reproduces the pre-recorded picture on a TV receiver/monitor in addition to the sound. The end effect in this case is no different from that of a video player playing a pre-recorded video tape. More sophisticated versions of video disc players are available, which have built in micro-computers to control, speed, sequence and time of presentation of visual images and the corresponding sound recorded on the disc. The control can be pre-programmed through the controlling microcomputer or can be effected as the student proceeds with the learning process. Typically, on a 30 cm double sided video disc more than 100,000 pictures can be stored, any of when can be accessed within a few seconds.

Broadly speaking, the video disc as a medium of education opens up the possibility of presenting the learner with an electronic audio-visual medium which can store a large amount of visual information along with its audio counterpart, in a highly compact form with quick and easy retrieval, at a cost which is likely to be much cheaper than the other existing media—if the media is exploited to its full potential on a large enough scale. A special feature of this system is its rapid random access capability. Since each picture in a video disc is given a separate code number, the job of preparing a comprehensive catalogue of pictures with brief content description, scheduling of pictures in any desired sequence or speed can be implemented relatively easily under computer control.

The potential of the electronic media such as video disc in revolutionising storage and retrieval of information can be realised when one examines the tentative specifications of the optical Digital Data Disc which is variation of the optical video Disc (Analogue). Typically a single 30 cm digital data disc can store information equivalent to the content of 8000 books, each with 250 closely printed pages. If the medium is commercially fully utilised, the cost of a 30 cm digital data disc is not likely to be more than a very tiny fraction of the total cost of the original material.

Broadcast Television : Television is acknowledged to be one of the most powerful mass communication media. With the falling cost of TV receivers and increasing TV coverage of the country, a significant percentage of the total population is likely to have access to TV viewing in the near future. Given this 'reach' and speed of dissemination, broadcast television can increase the cost effectiveness of the video programmes very greatly.

Unlike some of the more conventional teaching aids (such as the overhead projectors, the film projectors etc.) a television receiver serves the multiple purpose of entertainment, news source as well as education. This high utility factor implies that many homes and community centres which already have TV receivers will be able to utilise these sets for receiving educational programmes without any additional cost as and when such services are introduced.

In a country like India, having a large population with diverse social, cultural and economic backgrounds dispersed over wide areas from sparsely populated hilly terrains to densely populated large metropolies broadcast television offers an excellent opportunity for advancement of education. It's ability to bring excellent teachers, noted personalities and top quality specialists directly to very large number of students allows considerable enlargement of the scope of distance education system to cover all types of education (primary, secondary, vocational, technical, medical and general higher education). It is possible to design excellent coursewares by involving the best teachers, produce highly imaginative software by utilising the services of the best producers and ensure high technical quality through the use of sophisticated equipment, and yet keep the cost of lesson per student low because of the large number of students involved.

The positive aspects of broadcast television as a media for education can be summarised as below:

(i) Lectures, demonstrations, group discussions by highly competent and skilled teachers and specialists can be brought to the students whether in formal centres of learning such as schools, colleges, universities or at homes or community viewing centres, thus partially offsetting the problem of shortage of good teachers.

(ii) A great many teaching/learning situation can benefit considerably through , well organised field trips to expose the learner to real life situations. However, lack of financial, material and organisational resources as well as time, do not allow in majority of the cases, any field trip of significance. This gap can be closed to a large extent by showing motion pictures of relevant places, people, processes, events, facilities etc., on television. It can enrich the learning experience considerably and raise the quality of education.

(iii) If sufficient amount of educational programmes can be generated and telecast for a variety of courses in a well planned manner with sufficient repetition of the courses and with suitable supplementary support by the way of contact programmes and additional instructional materials, a substantial qualitative and quantitative improvement can be brought about in the education system. The additional increase resources which need to be mobilised for this purpose are likely to be much less than would be required to achieve similar results within the same period of time through conventional system.

(iv) A well designed distance education system based on television as the primary medium with other necessary supports can combine the advantages of mass media with some of those of individualised learning system. A student having access to video recording can repeat any lesson any number of time and in any place convenient to him/her.

Closed Circuit Television (CCTV) : Large and relatively affluent institutions imparting highly specialised/technical/medical training, which, in addition to lecture needs to demonstrate complex sequence of activities, develop skills in their students or modify behaviour pattern through training, can use CCTV very effectively. A complex surgical operation can be viewed by a large number of trainee surgeons through a CCTV system in the classroom while the operation is in progress elsewhere. Teacher training which involves behaviour modification can become very effective when the trainee teacher is allowed to view video recording of his/her practice teaching along with corrective suggestions. A trainee craftsman can watch each movement of a master craftsman repeatedly and closely through a CCTV system allowing him/ her to reduce actual practice time. Demonstration of laboratory experiments can be made more effective to large groups of students if the teacher uses closed circuit television as a medium.

Since CCTV requires one or more TV cameras, lights etc., in addition to the picture monitors/receivers (and optionally VCRs) the cost of the system is higher. The skill in handling and maintaining such equipment, the additional space requirement all add upto higher resource requirements.

Computers : With rapid advances in micro-electronics, computers are becoming smaller, lighter, cheaper, more powerful and consequently more popular. The changes and the trend have been dramatic and are likely to continue, if not, become more pronounced. The range of available software has also increased rapidly in recent years. A time has now come to seriously evaluate the potential uses of computers in our educational system.

The application areas can be divided into three categories :

— Computer as an Aid to Teaching.

— Computer Assisted Instruction.

— Computer Managed Instruction.

Computer as an aid to Teaching Lecture :

Computers can be utilised effectively for large group teaching. In the class-room it can be used to solve numerical problems, to display graphics/pictorial information, to provide simulation examples and to retrieve relevant information resource from any central media library/common database. To allow a computer to be used as a common class-room tool for use by teachers, who may or may not be familiar with computers, it is necessary to design suitable user interfaces as well as appropriate software. Some examples of the types of software which may be required are :

— general purpose interactive graphics/mathematical/ simulation softwares.

— specific, purpose oriented data bases and simulations.

Tutorial : Computers can be used to assist in and supplement conventional tutorial as well as drill and practice work. The burden of routine work on the teacher can be considerably lightened allowing more time for creative activity. By providing feedback such as performance profile of groups of students, a computer can help a teacher in identifying areas of weakness and take corrective measures.

Laboratory : It is possible to envisage a time, in not too distant a future, when computers can be used effectively to supplement the teachers' efforts in providing students with the desired laboratory experiences. The problems associated with inadequate teacher to student ratio, inadequate facilities in the laboratories and similar others can be partially taken care of, by careful use of computers. Because of inadequacies of space, equipment and other physical facilities, students are often required to perform experiments, much before they have had any exposure to the relevant theory. Similarly, often it becomes very difficult for a teacher to provide guidance to different groups of students within the limited time of the laboratory period. It may be possible to utilise computers in teaching background theories necessary for various experiments, explaining experimental procedures, evaluating student's performances and keeping record of performance data. The range and the scope of experiments can be extended considerably through simulation techniques. In addition to helping the teacher in managing laboratory work efficiently, computers may be used in the laboratory as data logging devices as well as measurement and control tools.

Computer Assisted Instruction General Concepts : It is an integrated system comprising of Computer hardware, software and courseware aimed at providing interactive, individualised or group learning. The system provides an effective and bi-directional student-computer communication for presenting textual and graphic information, analysing the student responses and assessing the needs of the students in an adaptive manner.

The CAI system may wholly or partially have the following features :

(i) provide an interface which permits bi-directional natural interaction between the computer and the student.

(ii) be flexible enough to incorporate new teaching strategies.

(iii) provide flexibility in the manner in which the courseware is used by teacher or student.

(iv) provide interactive environment where student is active and charts his own path through the information base.

(v) offer the flexibility of shifting the control in the teaching-learning process, between the system and the student as the situation demands.

(vi) provide facility of continuous monitoring of student path and performance for analysis at a later stage.

(vii) be simple enough for the teacher to modify the courseware and for the student to operate.

Modes of Instruction : CAI includes various modes or styles of instructions as stated below. However, an instructional system necessarily uses combination of these styles for effective acquisition of knowledge and development of mental abilities.

Drill and Practice Mode : Drill exercises are aimed at quick recall to aid memorisation while practice exercises are associated with processes such as learning algorithms or combining concepts to solve problems or improving manipulative skills. In this mode, problems are presented to the student and based on pre-determined response and if required, the computer provides step by step assistance in solving the problems. Thus, a student is trained to respond quickly thereby aiding in the assimilation of basic concepts and memorisation of information.

Tutorial Mode : The aim of this mode is to impart knowledge by providing information. It consists of presentation of a sequence of textual information, followed by question—answer sequence, response analysis and feedback.

The path of instruction is determined either by performance based decision rules as in programmed instruction type dialogue or by adaptive decision rules allowing the student to be less machine dependent. When the dialogue is genuinely bi-directional, it takes the form of Socratic mode. Tutorial mode is ideal for concept teaching. This can be achieved by providing carefully chosen mixture of examples and counter examples and directing questions so that the attributes of a concept are identified by the student on his own.

The Socratic mode, ideally simulates the class-room environment on an individualised basis.

Simulation Mode : Computers are ideally suited for this mode of instruction because of their ability to compute at high speed, ability to store vast amount of data and their interactive graphic capability. Simulation is more a method of making a student interact with the simulated system than a method of teaching. Many of the knowledge structures in engineering and science are quantified as sets of equation or data bases which specify parameters and relationships between them. These mathematical relationships or models are used in the instructional programmes, and the courseware allows the student to vary the values of input parameters and observe the variations in the output. Through this process the student attempts to understand the knowledge structures and relationships between the variables.

Gaming is a particular variant of simulation, and is highly motivating. Gaming differs from simulation in so much as it emphasises on competition and unique successful solution while simulation concentrates on exploration of relationships.

The Adaptive Instructional Systems : These instructional systems are intelligent enough to assess the student performance for a given learning task and prescribe a suitable instructional course. It is in a way an enhanced form of Socratic dialogue mode of teaching. Such systems are generally intelligent enough to probe and generate alternative hypothesis and solutions and to question and provide reasons for the decisions taken by either the system or the student.

Learning-Teaching Tools : This is strictly not a mode of instruction. A set of 'Working Tool', usually a set of programmes is provided to the student which help him to solve complex problems in a wide variety of subjects. Such packages provide new ways of learning conventional subjects. Natural mathematical languages, graphic interfaces, data base packages, word processor and LOGO are some examples of this category of tools.

Computer Managed Instruction : The effort of developing CAI systems for individual instruction and many other innovative instructional plans like Kellers plan have put the teacher in the position of a resource manager. The management of a dynamic individualised instruction system is a trouble some task. Processing of educational data, providing timely and adequate instructional guidance to individual students proves unmanageable without technological aid in an educational set-up which is large and or complex. The use of computer to support management functions associated with individualization of instruction was perceived for these reasons and was called computer Managed instruction or CMI.

Implemented CMI systems, however, have different scopes within broad definition given above. CMI systems provide information to all concerned-students, teachers or administrators. Some systems support single course and single instruction while others support several courses, large number of students and many teachers. CMI systems can be implemented to cater to any level of instruction, from those of armed forces to post graduate university level. The evolution of such diverse systems, make the job of defining CMI a difficult task.

A comprehensive CMI system is likely to have the following features :

- store questions.
- generate test papers.
- administer tests.
- evaluate scripts.
- store student records.
- provide general statistical and other data.
- report relevant information.
- diagnose the student deficiencies.
- provide guidance to study plan.
- allocate and optimize resources.
- offer computer based courses.
- generate student profiles.
- monitor student progress.
- prepare time tables/study schedules.

The CMI mode assumes great importance independent learning systems and non-formal education systems.

Miscellaneous Electronic Media

Videotex and Teletext System : Videotex or viewdata, as generic terms, apply to interactive systems for transmitting text or graphics stored in a computer database, via telephone network, for display on a television screen or other relatively inexpensive terminals. Unlike other video systems, here the textual information is of primary significance, and graphics play a complementary or, in some cases, decorative role. While animation is possible, videotex information typically consists of simple graphics dealing with specific topics. Videotex systems are simpler to use and cheaper catering to large number of users. When compared with complexity and cost of accessing information from large computer centres on time sharing basis.

The concept of Teletext is similar to that of Videotex. However, the information is transmitted as a part of the broadcast TV service in a digitally coded form, instead of through the public telephone network used for videotex transmission. The viewer needs a modified TV receiver or a separate teletext decoder to display the Teletext information on the TV screen. The information may be seen in place of normal programme or super-imposed on the normal programme as desired by the viewer. The ability to deliver digitally coded information through standard broadcast TV channel opens up new possibilities of delivering computer software to remote locations in the future. At present the Teletext information is sent as indexed and individually accessible pages of text/graphics which are updated at frequent and regular intervals.

The user of the videotex system has the freedom to choose any of the information stored in the central computer at any time, in any sequence and at any desired speed. Teletext user can choose between the pages of information which are being transmitted. The freedom is limited in terms of content, sequence, speed and timing.

Tele-Conferencing System : Tele-conferencing can be used for audio only, for video and audio as well as computer data. The interaction takes place between geographically separate groups of people through verbal exchange of opinions and ideas in the case of audio teleconferencing and through additional visual contact in the case of video tele-conferencing. Computer tele-conferencing allows a number of users to exchange information with each other using telematics, i.e. a combination of computer and communication technology. Each of these tele-conferencing systems can play their due part in supporting a modern education system. It is possible to visualise a time when a group of international experts can address several class-rooms in several countries using interactive video conferencing system through geosynchronous communication sattelites.

Slow-Scan Television : Communication engineers have long been aware that the information content of a scene with no movement (still picture is much lower in comparison with the scene which has a lot of movement. Since the bandwidth and hence the cost of transmission of information is directly proportional to the rate of information flow (amount of information/unit time), great saving in cost and complexity of transmission systems can be made if instead of using the standard broadcast televisions scanning rate, slow scan is employed for pictures with little or no movement. A careful analysis of majority of the common teaching-learning situations shows that most images used for teaching (including graphics, textual information, numeric data) are of the still-frame type. Even when movement is involved, as in animated visuals, the movement is relatively slow. Because of a drastic reduction in cost and complexity, it is perfectly feasible to use even ordinary domestic telephone lines to transmit/receive still pictures at slow rate. In addition to the above, various data compression techniques such as DPCM, delta modulation, transform coding etc., can be used to reduce the bit-rate (if digital transmission is used) to a very low figure. Such techniques hold great future promise for education application.

Tele-Lecture System : A tele-lecture system connects a number of specially equipped classrooms in the same city or in different cities through the public telecommunication network as in audio tele-conferencing. A teaching can address a large number of class-rooms scattered over a wide area from his/her own institution/home/ office by connecting to the tele-lecture network. Students from any of the tele-lecture class can choose to interact with the teacher at any time through microphones provided on their desks. It is possible to conceive of a situation where the major institutions of learning in the country are provided with say, one tele-lecture class-room each ; and all connected to a common tele-lecture network, to allow top specialists to address a large number of students together. The possibility of availing the services of renowned experts from outside, by a large number of institutions simultaneously makes this concept an attractive one, provided the tele-communication network is able to support such systems.

Tele-writing and tele-write-vision : The Tele-writing medium transmits two components : The voice of an instructor and his handwriting. The tele-written image appears on a screen. Originally known as tele-autograph the tele-writing has been used as a substitute for instructional television satisfactorily in teaching courses where the visual element generally consists mainly of chalk board writing. A basic course in physics or mathematics is an example in point. When a large number of schools are scattered over great distances, tele-writing can be economically more viable than instructional television. In many technologically advanced countries tele-writing is used on a regional basis to share the instructional resources of high schools in the presentation of subjects, such as physics, for which good teachers are not easily available. When tele-writing is combined with local visual materials, the combination is referred to as tele-write vision. Tele-write vision makes possible the inclusion of still pictures and nearly all other types of graphic materials along with the transmitted elements of sound, writing and drawing. Furthermore, in the case of tele-writing and television, it is very easy to provide through installation of microphones in the classroom and tele lines between classrooms and teacher, audio-feedback from the students.

Integrated Video-computer system : The Video media is highly suitable for showing complex, multi-tone dynamic colour images. Video films on tape or cassettes offer a cheap way of providing instructions when used, for large number of students, particularly in broadcast situations. One of the drawbacks of the video is its inability to interact with the learner in a meaningful way. Taped video films present the recorded instructions to the learner in the sequence and manner in which the original recordings are made. The students do not have much active role to play.

The use of computers in conjunction with video can result in a system where the advantage of each media counteracts the disadvantage of the other.

An integrated video-computer based system can be used very effectively for the qualitative and quantitative improvement of the education system. The computer can take care of textual and complex dynamic graphics requirement, provide opportunities for interaction by the students, while the video can take care of situations requiring the use of still pictures (video disc) and motion pictures (video tape and video disc). In an integrated system the computer can additionally help in producing and editing of video programmes, in controlling the time and sequence of presentation of video programmes, in cataloguing and in retrieval of video based information. A computer controlled interactive video disc is one such example. When this integrated video computer system is supported by modern communication technology, further interesting possibilities open up.

System of Dial Access

This is a system in which a centrally located Resource Centre stores various types of Information Resources (audio and video cassettes, type slides, sequences, transparencies, cine film strips, text books, charts, graphs, etc.). All Information Resources (IR) are given individual code numbers and catalogued for quick retrieval through computerised accessing techniques. Intending users send 'requisition' by dialling the relevant code from remote locations. The requested information are transmitted from the central resource library to the user either directly or through intermediate network of regional centres. The transmission channel may be landlines or wireless. Communication satellites, computer data network, telephone lines can be used as and when required. The dial access system sometimes referred to as DIARS has been tried, although on a limited scale, for connecting various schools and libraries in Beverly Hills Unified Schools District (USA) to a central resource library. With advancement of information and communication technology more comprehensive DIARS may become economically feasible.

Economic Considerations : At this stage, it might be useful to speak something about the economic aspects of various media. In calculating the cost of educational system one divides the cost into (a), Capital cost consisting of buildings, transmitters, receivers, projectors, books etc. In the capital cost, it is necessary to deduct the portion for depreciation and add interest or 'social discount' that represents an estimated cost of investment in necessary capital equipment rather than in something else like bonds in industry, (b) Recurring cost i.e. salaries, electricity, maintenance, rental, consumables and other goods and services on an annual basis.

Economists also ask two other questions (a) how much it will cost to expand the system (b) how much the total cost will be if, after a few years, it is decided to abandon the system and change to something else. For this, the cost is divided into 'fixed' and 'variable' cost. For example in radio or television system, programming and transmission costs are about the same regardless of the number of students until the coverage area reaches a size where a single station is not sufficient. On the other hand, reception cost depends upon the number of classrooms and number of students. The simplest equation for the cost of an instructional media system is TC (N)=F+VN

Where TC=Total cost of the system N=Number of students F=Fixed cost V=Variable cost per student.

An educational planner wants to know the variable cost per student. An educational planner also tries to evaluate (a) Cost-effectiveness of the system (b) Cost-benefit of the system.

In computing cost-effectiveness one considers not only the cost of alternative systems but also whether one system will come closer than another to accomplish the specified goal. In other words one weighs output against input, and compares that factor for different possible systems. Cost effectiveness analysis is designed to determine the 'best buy' in terms of immediate gains (such as enrolment or results of test), but education is designed also to serve long range social and economic needs. Cost benefit analysis estimates the input or an educational system against its output into these long range goals. The cost of not introducing electronic media for educational reform in terms of long range social and economic benefits is explained towards the end of this section.

General Learning Corporation of USA conducted a study for calculating the cost of different media systems under different conditions. For the purpose of analysis, it assumed that annual production of 1000 hrs of instructional material would be required of the system and this would have to be increased to 1600 hrs. When very large region and over 10,00,000 students were to be served. Cost of providing necessary capital equipment, producing and delivering the amount of instruction through each of the media system were estimated for five different situations. The student population size for each of the situation is shown below :

Local	:	Serving about 15000
City	:	1,50,000
Metropolitan	:	6,00,000
State	:	10,00,000
Region	:	1,00,00,000

The study indicated that the cost of different media tend to cluster in two broad bands, corresponding to what we call Big Media (TV & sound film) and little media (radio and audio tapes) and that, Big Media will cost about between 3 to 15 times as much as little media depending upon the size of the coverage. Economics of scale is therefore very important. The following table gives the comparison of media cost per student per year :

Media	***Student Population***		
	15,000	150,000	600,000
	$ per student per year		
ITV	$ 40.00	$ 10.00	$ 9.00
Film	$ 52.00	$ 50.00	$ 52.00
Radio	$ 9.00	$ 3.00	$ 2.00
Dial Access (one speaker per class-room)	$ 8.00	4.00	$ 3.50

It may be noticed that the cost per student for ITV and radio rapidly decreases as the audience increases while that of film remains the same regardless of the coverage.

There are a number of ways of delivering ITV programme — TV broadcasts, Satellite TV, CCTV, Open Circuit TV (VHF), and video tape. The production cost of all these will be the same, but the difference in cost will show up in distribution. A comparison of the distribution cost shows that satellite and broadcast television are suitable only for large coverage. VTR is costly even for local use. But in view of cheap availability of video cassettes, the scope may change in near future. Radio is the cheapest i.e. $ 2.00 for local area and $ 1.00 for large areas. Close circuit television is competitive with VHF in cost of delivery at the city level i.e. 1,50,000 students, while for larger areas, open circuit television has a cost advantage. Recurring cost of various type of TV programmes mentioned above also varies from $ 4/student to $ 8/per student.

Comparing the total cost (production, delivery and receiving cost) ITV programmes can cost $ 10,000 per student once the coverage extends 1,50,000. Radio starts out as the cheapest with 1/3 to 1/4 the cost of ITV and it is the only little media which can be used to cover large areas

However, instructional television can be used economically even when the number of students is not very large. For example, CCTV can be economically used for a system which enrolled 350 students or more. GLC, USA has given some recommendations regarding the reasonableness of using a variety of media from financial considerations . The table is reproduced below :

Medium			*Area*		
	Local	*City*	*Metro*	*State*	*Region*
Broadcast	No	No	No	T?	T?
Satellite TV	No	No	No	No	T?
Open Circuit TV (VHF)	P?	P?	Yes	T?	T?
Closed Circuit TV	P?	P?	Yes	T?	T?
VTR	P?	P?	Yes	Yes	Yes
Film	P?	P?	P?	P?	P?
Radio	P?	Yes	Yes	Yes	Yes
Language Lab	Yes	Yes	No	No	No

Classroom Dial access Yes Yes Yes No No Legend : Yes Reasonable to use medium situation. No Unreasonable, T ? Questionable, meaning that in this situation the user must seriously P ? Consider the technical or production problems involved.

From this table it would appear that smaller media are reasonable in cost for smaller areas. Of all these media radio is economically viable in all situations, but in 'local' situation the user must consider the production problem. Television comes at a reasonable cost to serve a large metropolitan area. For smaller areas production problems limit the usability of television. Similarly, at much larger level the economic viability is compromised by the technological consideration of having to set up a network of additional stations.

Computer Assisted Instruction Cost : Computer assisted instruction is classified as Big Media. In recent years the unit cost of CAI has decreased dramatically as would be evident from the figures given below :

$ 5.85 per student hour for a college course in Physics during the period 1965-69.

$ 3.73 per student hour for elementary mathematics and English courses in period 1968-71.

$ 1.06 to $ 2.18 per student hour projected for a medium size computer distributing to the few satellite centres in 1975.

$ 0.34 per student hour, projected for a large computer system with wide distribution to satellite learning centres in the period 1972-75.

Inspite of the lowering of the cost, the CAI cots are still higher than ITV cost for large areas.

It is interesting to note the following table which gives "ball park" estimates of the cost of different instructional media per hour per user. The wide variation between high and low boundaries of the estimates is due in part to the uncertainty of available figure and in part to the differences in quality and in scale of use. While it is possible to argue in view of this spread in the estimates that it is possible to use almost any medium in relatively inexpensive way by fitting media into situations, it is clear that conventional approaches—class lecture, group discussion, printed instruction—are far costlier than electronic media.

Media	*Estimated cost per user hour in $*
Class lecture	0.15— 3.00
Small discussion group	0.5 — 15.00
Books and journals	0.05—10.00
Printed programmed instructlon	2.00—25.00
Instructional radio	0.01— 1.00
Dial access audio tape recording	0.01— 2.00
Broadcast TV (live)	0.02—10.00
Closed circuit ITV (live)	0.03— 3.00
Broadcast ITV (taped)	0.01— 5.00
Close circuit ITV (Taped)	0.03— 3.00
Dial Access ITV (Tapes)	0.50— 5.00
Other standard audio visual aid	0.05— 8.00

In short, economic analysis suggests that system built around broadcast media in particular can be used with favourable results to extend and expand learning opportunities. Field evidence from the British Open University, Australian Tele-correspondence school system German Tele-college, Kenya radio-correspondence schools for teachers etc., indicate that such projects not only furnish high level of instruction but they also save money over doing the same task with the usual methods and facilities.

Economic analyses stated above provide a basis to hope that a variety of media, especially electronic media, would be used in future in this country for effecting a major educational reform.

We have discussed at some length the magnitude of the task ahead in spreading educational facilities to all areas and all sections of population, improving quality of instruction and providing continuing education to meet the consequences of knowledge explosion. Not only is the task gigantic in magnitude, it also has to be completed as soon as possible. Not undertaking this task seriously and within a reasonable time frame, will cost the nation heavily in terms of the following :

(i) Heavy drop-out rates and 'loss' of investment.

(ii) Insufficient manpower of indifferent quality leading to slower social and economic development.

(iii) General lowering of productivity.

(iv) The country will not have mature, educated citizen so important for proper functioning of the democracy.

(v) All this will lead unemployment demoralisation, lawlessness, forcing the government to spend money on unproductive efforts like law and order machinery and social welfare schemes.

It is necessary to introduce technology to supplement the efforts of the conventional system of education and where necessary, even to replace it. The wide spread use of media in general and electronic media in particular in an imperative of the future educational effort.

Experiences : Past and Present : Past Experience : As stated earlier, new media can be employed to reach large number of learners as well as to attain individualised self-learning. The country has already attempted various experiments to reach large number of rural/urban children and adults through radio and satellite transmission on television (1975-76). The country now plans to utilise its own satellite INSAT IB to reach the vast rural population as well as mofussil colleges and universities of the country. Utilization of technology for education cannot be, however, a casual input into the already existing framework of the educational system. In a country as diverse as India in terms of languages, culture and religion, establishing broadcast and other types of communication network possess several problems of planning, research, equipment, manpower, software generation as well as management so that appropriate action are taken at regional, state and institute level.

Following are some of the organisations in India which are already doing substantial work in educational technology including electronics media.

(a) *Department of Teaching Aids of NCERT :* This was

established to promote production, training and utilisation of teaching aids at school level through production, teacher preparation and generation of skilled manpower for producing low-cost aids. Experience of DTA, shows that the planning at the national level needs to be supported by planning at the regional or state level in order to promote its spread over the entire country.

(b) *Doordarshan :* Doordarshan established 'tele clubs' in 1965. At present educational programmes for schools are being telecast by Delhi, Mumbai, Srinagar and Chennai Centres.

(c) *Central Institute for Educational Technology (CIET) of NCERT :* This was established in the early seventies and with the aid of UNDP, it set out to reach large number of teachers and students with the help of television, radio and film media. Here again, the efforts of CIET in training for production does not get multiplied adequately at regional and state levels and the execution of projects at these levels it is tied up with the pace of implementing the schedule in terms of equipment, building and training of manpower.

(d) *Space Application Centre (SAC) Ahmadabad :* This was established to produce science programmes for SITE. This Centre has been able consistently to produce programmes for Kheda District with the help of community involvement. It has trained people from user agencies like National Dairy Development Board State Institute of Education, Ahmadabad ; for software production etc.

(e) *Centre for Development of Instructional Technology (CENDIT) :* This is a non-profit society established in 1972 with the aim to work with the Govt. and actual users to improve education, including extension at all levels, through research, development and application in equipment, instructional material and system, and teacher preparation aspects.

In addition, there are several other organisations which produce audio, video and film materials in their own areas of education and training, compilation of software and research. They are: Indian Institute of Mass-Communication, New Delhi ; Directorate General of Technical Training Institute, Kanpur ; Advanced level Telecommunication Training Centre, Ghaziabad, of Post & Telegraph Department ; Agricultural Communication Centre, Pantnagar; and Central Institute of English and Foreign Languages, Hyderabad.

From the experiences of these organisations, barring some exceptions, it is clear that most of the earlier effort has not gained momentum due to lack of total system design and comprehensive planning covering all elements required for its development and growth. Equipment have always been the starting point of many educational technology organizations but without enough emphasis on software development. Software production requires a strong input of understanding the educational processes (which is unaffected by the glamour of media) as well as an interdisciplinary approach. A comprehensive and integrated training programme is needed for software production, hardware operation and maintenance, training, and research and management of media in general. Furthermore training persons to prepare software is meaningful only if they can go back and find facilities for production in their organisations. People who provide training, if not also engaged in research and production, could become outdated as far as the art and technology of communicating ideas are concerned.

Integration of school, college and university education with broadcasting requires enormous coordination among agencies and facilities which is not easy to sustain over long periods. Formal structures for bringing about such coordination may have to be set up.

Financing would have to be provided not from year to year but ensured for the long period needed for building infrastructure, preparation of software, promoting research, teacher preparation and so on. Clearly investing only in infrastructure without planned financing of production, maintenance, distribution, training and research etc. will lead to poor quality and quantity of software and under-utilization of hardware.

(f) *Class Project :* This project has been piloted jointly by the Departments of Electronic, and Education, Government of

India, to introduce computer literacy and studies in secondary schools. As the computers are being introduced for the first time in schools the short term objectives of the project are to provide exposure and hands—on experience, familiarize school students in general with the potential of micro computers and their applications in various situations including in the educational environment. Financial and other assistance have been provided in the first instance to 750 schools and this is proposed to be extended to another 500 schools in 1986-87. The project is conceived as a total package—from providing and establishing computer facilities in the schools to provision of software, maintenance arrangement and a substantial effort with the help of resource centres distributed throughout the country, for training of teachers separately, research into the pedagogical aspects, a programme for selection, adaptation and generation of software, and monitoring and evaluation, support the CLASS programme.

(g) *University Grants Commission Scheme of Introducing Mass Media and Educational Technology:* UGC has established Four media centres for introducing educational technology in education; (1) Educational Resource Media Centre, Gujarat (2) Institution of Communication Studies, University of Pune (3) Institute of Mass communication Jamia Millia, New Delhi ; (4) Educational Media Resource Centre, University of Roorkee. The first three are fairly well established and operational and the fourth one at Roorkee is getting established.

(h) *Technical Teacher's Training Institute at Chandigarh, Channai, Bhopal and Kolkata :* These are resource centres for the overall improvement of technician education system. Starting from the efforts to introduce well designed print-material and transparencies, slides, film-strips, 16 mm films, etc., some of the TTTIs have moved into producing video films both for broadcasting as well as supplying video cassette recording to polytechnics for class-room instruction.

Strategies for Future

On the basis of the past experiences of those countries which have successfully implemented the use of educational technology and also the Indian experience described earlier in this section, it is possible to identify important strategies for the country to adopt educational technologies including electronic media on any meaningful scale. The strategies are : (a) organising research for detailed understanding of the nature of each educational technology tool and its contextual relevance, integrating these tools with the teacher and the educational process, testing the effectiveness of the integrated approach to teaching and learning ; (b) organising selective dissemination of information for developing attitudes among teachers and administrators for experimenting and adoption of educational innovations ; (c) Planned development of educational software (d) Planned approach to installation and maintenance of hardware (e) Establishing organizational structure for policy-making. Administration, R & D and educational action at the national, regional, state, district and institutional level, (f) Manpower development for use of Educational Technology in education. Each of these strategies is explained below.

Research in Educational Technology : It is necessary to initiate research work in educational technology to identify better methods of teaching and learning through the use of newer technologies in particular the electronic media. The nature of research would be basic, applied and action research since all are necessary for successful educational reform. It is important to examine all aspects of the technology-pedagogical, economic, technical and production the practicability of use in a given socio-economic-technological context.

Dissemination of Information : Organised collection of information and experiences and systematic dissemination to various target groups is a necessary condition for creating an understanding of the potential of each media, informed support to efforts for changes and innovations, and creating motivation, interest and commitment. Knowledge of successful innovations introduced in one institution stimulates the interest in others to introduce new methods and media in their own organization. This clearing house function has a great multiplier effect.

Approach to Software

The basic elements to be kept in view are :

- — assessment of quantum and nature of software required at college, school and non-formal levels
- — trained manpower
- — subject expertise
- — facilities for production
- — facilities for testing in user environment
- — facilities for publication and distribution
- — facilities for utilization
- — information on hardware and software

Approach to Hardware : Approach to hardware should be the total system design from the view point of educational objectives. Choice of media ranging from broadcast television to posters depends primarily upon the learner, the educational content and the intended coverage of student population. What for whom, by whom, with what educational objectives, with what means and with what organizational frame work is the broad sequence which should determine the MEANS or the media and its range of equipment. In case electronic media is chosen, especially in the case TV and Radio, its compatibility with broadcasting network, needs to be ascertained.

Approach to Organizational Structure

(a) *Management Function :* For introducing media in general and electronic media in particular, it is necessary to make nationwide effort to plan and execute scheme in such a way that educational institutes will get all necessary inputs—financial, physical and informational to introduce educational technology. For this a comprehensive organizational network will have to be designed with following management functions in view :

(i) Policy making

(ii) Coordination and Administration

(iii) R/D monitoring and evaluation

(iv) Resource institutions for implementation

All these functions will have to be carried out at national, regional, state, district and institutional levels.

A possible matrix inter-relating management function and the different levels of functioning is given in the attached table.

(b) *Network for Implementation of Educational Technology :* The organisational structure should link software generation, its production and distribution within each sector of education—elementary, secondary, higher education, technical education, etc. There should be a network connecting (i) audio-visual centres in individual institutions for orienting faculty towards educational media and promoting its use in instruction (ii) Educational media centre at selected institutions for production of finished educational material and learning packages, and distribution them to institutional audio-visual centres (iii) National Centres for Educational Media which will act as information clearing house for audio-visual material, check up quality of educational material, produce those educational programmes which will have nation wide use, act as a focal point for planning national network of INSAT, broadcast television etc. A suitable cell/ directorate/bureau as secretariat for Educational media should also be developed to plan for the growth and development of educational media at the national level.

Manpower Training : Manpower development in education technology is a relatively new and unchartered area. Manpower is needed for training teachers in educational design, for developing software, for installation, use and maintenance of hardware, and for media-management.

(a) *Training of Teachers for Instructional Design :* Demand for multi-media packages including those provided by electronic media will increase only when teachers are motivated to learn how to integrate content, learners, entry behaviour, and media in their teaching. This requires equipping teachers with basic concepts of educational sciences and educational and training them in production and use of media on scientific lines. Both initial and in-service training programmes will have to be designed.

(b) *Manpower for Software :* Software development is a team work of subject matter expert, educational technologist, script writers, production experts, editors and media-evaluators to name some. In the first instance a well designed faculty development programmes is needed to orient them to educational technology and reorganising presentation of the content to suit learner's needs. Secondly, there should be a band of script writers, producers and other specialists necessary to produce software in sufficient quantity and range. Programmes for generating such man-power would have to be mounted.

(c) *Manpower for Hardware :* Especially in the case of big media like television, computer and radio, many professional people are required in the category of systems engineers, TV technicians, operators, cameramen, etc. This also needs long-range planning and cooperation of institutes like Doordarshan. FTII, Pune, SAC, Ahmadabad for their training.

(d) *Manpower for Media Management :* The medium, be it television, radio, computer, or any other, calls for substantial management inputs. These inputs are needed in the context of development of support material, human relations and organisation of various elements such as research, production, duplication, distribution and evaluation. Good manager will not only be as able general administrator but will also need sufficient understanding of the nature of media and its processes. The strategy could be to select appropriate persons with potential who then receive training in various aspects in organizations mentioned elsewhere.

These are in brief the broad lines of future action in order to introduce electronic media at the national, regional and state levels.

Summary : At this stage it would be pertinent to quote from the new National Policy on Education 1986, which has just been approved by the parliament.

"Modern Communication technologies have the potential to, by pass several stages and sequences in the process of development encountered in early decades : Both the constraints of time and distance at once become manageable. In order to avoid structural dualism, modern educational technology must reach out to the most distant area and the most deprived section of the beneficiaries simultaneously with the areas of comparative affluence and ready availability." "Educational technology will be employed in the spread of useful information, the training and retraining of teachers, to improve quality, sharpen awareness of art and culture, inculcate abiding values, etc., both in the formal and non-format sectors. Maximum use will be made of the available infrastructure. In villages without electricity, batteries or solar packs will be used to run the programme" "The generation of relevant and culturally compatible educational programmes will form an important component of educational technology, and all available resources in the country will be utilised for this purpose."

The policy is clear and specific about the role and tasks of media and educational technologies. The time for action is now. The authors feel that the country will have to gear itself to introducing electronic media in a substantial way, if the entire country is to be provided with adequate elementary and secondary education facilities, if vocational education has to reach out to the out of school population, if wastage due to drop-out is to be reduced, and if each student has to be taught according; to individual needs and at his/her own pace.

10

AUDIO VISUAL MEDIA

Audio and Visual Media have been used since the dawn of human civilization in conveying thoughts and messages from person to person and from one group to another. With the advent of scientific and technical aids like the photographic camera, slide projector, sound recording and reproduction, T.V., closed circuit T.V., and, above all, the coming in of electronics for control and monitoring of the active disjointed audio and visual methodology, the newer perceptions of the expanding horizons of education have been fully integrated with Audio-Visual philosophy and principles.

The audio-visual aids are being increasingly used in education, business, publicity, entertainment and to solve a large extent in mass communication. The T.V. system encompass a vast area of such equipment as the sound motion picture systems, slide projectors, epidoscope/T.V. system, videotape recorder and audio-tape recorders etc.

The advent of electronic aid have totally changed the concepts and methodology of various aspects of educational technology. T.V. automatic synchronised tape slide system and Radio are the components of the electronic media for education. All the three are being extensively used in developed countries, while in our own country things are just getting introduced in the entire education system.

This paper presented the various options of the electronic media cited above and makes a comparison of the various alternatives. The experience gained in this area from various experiments conducted at CEERI Pilani is presented to give an idea of the difficulties and advantages involved in the new media.

Synchronised System of Tape Slide

The system consists of the hardware parts and the software in the shape of slides and corresponding recorded description and music correcting to these slides. The hardware basically consists of stereo tape recorded, electronic dissolve unit, Kodak type slide projector electronic coder and decoder microphone record player and mixer preamplifier.

For programming a theme, story message or lesson etc., is choosen and still 35mm slides are made and the actual message inclusive of music is recorded on tape and link up of the software and the hardware through the coder and decoder unit.

Description : In this system command signals in the form of short bursts of sinusoidal waves are recorded on the one track of stereo tape recorder.

During play back these signals are decoded and these actuates a pair of slide projector through a dissolve unit. On receiving the signal one projector fades out and other fades in.

Advantages : Synchronised tape slide system proves to be the most adaptable and suitable system. It can be used in the best way as it offers a practical solution for every method of communication information without undue effort and at reasonable cost. The main advantages of tape slide system can be summarised as the favourable relation between technical equipment the amount of work put into teaching and the results achieved, plus outstanding image quality. One very important aspect with regards to teaching is that the slide system is simple to operate and most teachers are sufficiently familiar with it.

Disadvantages : The main disadvantages of tape slide system is that it is not possible to show animation work and motion pictures. Another thing is this that it is time consuming system.

Multi Slide Projection System : The multivision system is a more complex system for changing slide in upto 15 projectors in synchronism with speech or music. It consists of coder and decoder unit.

Coder : A coder unit having a specific logic combination of four frequencies appears at this output terminal. These combinations of logic signal selects which projector to operate predetermined sequence. These signals are to be recorded on one channel of stereo tape recorder.

Decoder : The reproduced signal from the tape recorder are decoded with the help of filters and logic circuits. A digital demultiplexer with four input and 16 output terminals is used to separate out the 15 channel signals and finally given to 15 separate projectors.

Advantages : There might be several reasons for using more than one media in a single presentation. Some of the following possibilities may suggest applications to help decide whether a multimedia multi image presentation is justified.

(i) To hold an overview or "Lony Shot" on one screen while showing a series of detailed close ups on another screen, such as stages of laboratory procedure.

(ii) To allow side by side comparison of two or more images, such as works of art "Before and After" schematic drawing compared with the actual object.

(iii) For "Visual Pragraphing" holding a title or classification heading on one screen while adding sub heading or a series of examples elsewhere.

The system is flexible in so far as the control signals in the channels can be used for switching off or on the studio lights, for controlling curtains, screen and any other special effects. The advantage of periodic updating of the slides and translation into a number of languages are the same as in single slide projection system.

Disadvantage : Due to multi-projection more hardware is involved hence their mobility is restricted, because of number of projectors, large screen etc.

Audio Cassette : This has been the earliest electronic teaching aid after the Audio cassettee recorder was invented. It is extensively used in lectures and in distance education.

Video Tape Recording : Video tape and film are the two major television programme sources. Most of the programmes you see on television have been pre-recorded on one or the other.

Although film is produced by its traditional film techniques and simply played back on television, video tape constitutes a major production element of television itself. Indeed, video tape has influenced television production technique to a great extent.

Description : The basic system consists a television camera that converts what it sees into a video signal, a microphone that converts what it 'hears' into an audio signal and a television that 'sees' and loudspeaker that reconverts the two signals into picture and sound.

T.V. Camera : All T.V. Camera have three main parts; (i) the lense (ii) the camera itself with the camera pick up tube, which converts an optical image into on electrical signal and (iii) the view finder which reconverts the signal into visible images.

Audio : Audio, the sound portion of a television show is necessary to give us specific information and to help the mood of a scene. Audio production elements include (i) Microphone (ii) recorder (iii) Amplifiers.

VTR's : Most shows are pre-recorded on Video tape, with Video tape, we can :

(i) Assemble a coherent show from recorded programme segments.

(ii) Record entire shows for later replay.

(iii) Duplicate programmes.

(iv) Preserve programmes for later references.

There is a vast variety of video tape recorders, which differ basically in the size and portability, tape width, recording process and quality.

Editing : Past production editing means the assembly of video taped program segment in a specific order. With electronic editing and an editing control unit we can select certain video taped material from one video tape recorder and transfer it to another in a specific order without having to cut the video tape physically.

Work at CEERI : At CEERI on Audio Visual system different equipment were developed. They were coder, decoder for single and multislide projection. Electronic dissolve unit to give continuity between two slides. Now the part of the equipment is being commercially produced by CEL, Sahibabad, U.P.

Summative Analysis : Modern education technology has lot of choice now from various developments in the Audio and Video field and it is gratifying to note that our country is also planning to use modern electronic aids for education.

Alternatives in Audio Visual Aids

The task of providing new schools, training new teachers and motivating children to complete their studies satisfactorily is going to be a formidable one in our country. On its success will depend the well-being of our country in the 21st century.

A practical problem facing our educators is of inducing young men and women to take up teaching as a career. With the opening up of new lucrative avenues for jobs and newer and better opportunities in commerce and industry, it is difficult to persuade young people with good academic record to come forward to teach in schools. Finding good teachers to work in rural areas is even more difficult. On the other hand it is an ironical fact that most of India's intellectuals and great leaders have received their initial education in the village schools. They will continue to come from such backgrounds even in the years to come.

Teaching is a process of communication. Its success depends on how well the teacher manages to hold the attention and interest of his students in their studies. The student's mind is an active one and tends to wander if the lessons are not interesting enough. The teaching materials available to a teacher from an average school have remained static over the years. These have consisted of chalk, blackboard, text books, ill-equipped libraries and in some cases, very elementary science laboratory facilities.

One advantage of the chalk-and-blackboard-approach is that, particularly, for smaller classes, education becomes personalised and an intimate equation of relationship grows between the teacher and the taught. This is an advantage and we all remember our good teachers who inspired us in our schools and colleges. However, the burden on the teachers is increasing day by day as, among other constraints they have to cope with larger sized class-rooms. Knowledge is also increasing at a rapid rate and the teachers neither find any time nor do they have the incentive to keep themselves up-to-date. Hence, new methods of learning are as much applicable to them as to their pupils.

Recent Trends

Every one is agreed that the time is appropriate to harness modern technology to assist both the teacher and the taught. A judicious use of modern information technology will help to bridge the educational gaps in a developing country like ours. The need to use electronic and audio-visual aids at all levels of sophistication, and at ali levels of teaching, has been realised by our educationists and also by planners in education. These aids can reduce the burden on the teachers and open up new avenues of learning for the students. The importance of electronic aids has been discussed on many occasions and Government continues to give assurances on the availability of resources for all levels of education.

New Teaching Aids : The common teaching aids used in schools till recently consisted of simple coloured charts, a few models, an epidiascope, a radio, and perhaps a 16-mm film projector. Among the newer techniques available to the teachers are the use of colour-slides, synchronised tape-slide projection systems, television, video tapes, video playback systems, computer-based learning systems, such as Computer Aided Instruction (CAI), and so on. All educational institutions, whether in rural area, or in the urban areas, are aware of the advantages of these aids.

A school Headmaster would tell us today that it is a question of resources. Will the government or the school management buy a TV or a computer and dump it on the school or will they give schools the money to invest on aids according to their priorities? This point can be debated at length but it is well-known that if anything is thrust upon from outside, there is an inbuilt hesitation in using it. If the teachers have decided to have some particular aids and these are procured then they will willingly use them. If resources in the form of money are made available to the school, then they would have to think how to make the optimum use of the money. It is high time the teachers gave reasonable thought to their requirements. It is also high time teachers gave a thought to preparing software to convey ideas.

The choice of systems to be used in an educational institution depends on factors such as (1) convenience of use by many teachers, (2) initial costs, (3) availability of software on a continuous basis, and (4) ease of maintaining the equipment. Let us now examine these different aids and systems from convenience, costs and availability of software points of view.

(a) The earlier known aids such as coloured charts, maps, models, etc., are available in the market even today. The slightly more advanced versions of models are available from organisations specialising in the educational aids. These are relatively cheap and as such durable.

(b) Indigenous 16 mm film projectors are available at Rs. 7,500/-. Over the past three decades numerous films have been prepared and these are available from film libraries on rental bases. However, the cost of preparing a 16 mm film is high and becomes economical only if a large number of prints are produced, otherwise the cost factor is prohibitive.

(c) Simple slide projectors are available from Rs. 600/- upwards. The semi-automatic projectors, which operate with trays, cost around Rs. 4,000/-. The more sophisticated Kodak Carusol Projectors, which are imported, cost about Rs. 18,000/- each. These projectors can be used in class-rooms to project colour slides and this methodology is particularly advantageous in teaching subjects as Botany, Zoology, Geography, etc. These slides can be prepared by the teacher himself if he has a camera. The teacher needs to get himself involved in preparing software. Slides are also procurable from various agencies.

(d) A more advanced version is a tape-slide presentation. This may appear too simplistic in these days of Video technology. However, the software is easy to prepare by the teacher himself. A tape with a lecture recorded on it is played back to the class. The teacher changes the slides manually in synchronism with his lecture. The software consists of a packet of slides and a pre-recorded tape. The teacher operates the slide project and the cassette tape recorder. Such canned lectures can also be prepared by a central agency and made available to schools and colleges. The techniques has an advantage since the tapes can be recorded in different languages. Also new slides can be substituted for old, thereby updating the programme. This makes the system versatile. Moreover, the student can borrow recordings of the tapes and hear them at home for purposes of revising.

The cost of a pre-recorded tape will be around Rs. 50/- and the coloured slides may cost between Rs. 6 to 8 each. Hence, a canned lecture consisting of 25 slides and a prerecorded tape should cost about Rs. 250/-. A cassette tape recorder costs about Rs. 1500/- these days. Is a PA system is required in the class room, then an amplifier and a loudspeaker together are available today from Rs. 3,000/- to Rs. 5,000/-.

A fully automatic synchronised slide projection system consists of a pair of projectors, an electronic control-cum-dissolve unit and a stereo cassette tape recorder. The current cost of such a system with imported projectors but indigenous electronics would cost Rs. 60,000/-. The software now consists of a cassette tape and two sets of slides for the two projectors.

(e) The "VHS ½' tape format" has become popular for domestic entertainment as well as for educational purposes. A VHS playback system is available at about Rs. 18,000/- in the market today. A colour television set costs between Rs. 8,000/-and Rs. 10,000/. This technique of presentation and instruction is a convenient one, provided one has access to a library of video tapes. Specialised lectures to students from school to advanced instruction levels, particularly in technical subjects, can be prepared and made available. The operation of VHS tape recorders and television sets does not require any specialised skill.

The experiment with which the UGC is already engaged on Channel II is well known. Many specialised lectures can be recorded on the VHS format and made available to colleges, i.e. they need to wait for an actual broadcast but can watch the programme in the class rooms or even at home.

Projection TV helps a larger number of students to watch the programmes conveniently. However, the current cost of such systems is excessive (about Rs. 1,00,000) and these are not so freely available in our country.

(f) Computers are relatively newcomers to India in the field of education. It was with the advent of cheap microchips, the encouragement provided by the Department of Electronics and the keen competition among the computer manufacture and vendors that the prices of the table top micro-computers or the PCs started coming down and more organisations can now afford them. This has led to increased usage of computers in all walks of life including scientific calculations and electronic data processing. A computer system for educational applications consists of a CPU with RAMS, floppy drives, keyboard and a video Display Unit. Such systems are available for Rs. 60,000 or even less, depending on the actual configuration. For example, a conventional home television could be used in place of the VDU, thereby reducing the initial investment. This is commonly done in home computer systems.

Educational programmes such as CAL and CAI (Computer Aided Learning and Instruction) are available on floppy discs and the student can interact with the computer through the key-board. Excellent educational programmes have already been evolved particularly in the UK, to teach students at all levels. These programmes may have to be adapted for the Indian educational environment. This topic is under serious consideration at the Department of Electronics and they have already launched a pilot project.

A general comment one can make is that only one student can handle a computer terminal at a time. Hence, a large number of such terminals are needed to educate a class and to provide them with "hands on" experience. It will resemble a laboratory with the teacher having to give some attention to each student at the computer terminal. On the other hand, the 16 mm films, video tapes and synchronised slide projection systems help to inform or educate an entire class at the same time. These considerations have to be kept in mind while deciding on the options.

Software Preparation

Preparation of software is of utmost importance and hence requires experience and ideas. Educational material has to be properly researched and the appropriate visuals conceived and prepared before the programme is prepared. Programmes can be experimented in a few schools to see how effective they are before finalisation. The programmes are subsequently duplicated and distributed.

Experience has shown that establishing a regular studio with facilities for preparing video programmes is expensive and involves a capital outlay of Rs. 60 lakhs or more. This is by way of basic electronic equipment, floor space, lighting, etc. An advantage of this technique is that the tapes are ready for playback immediately unlike in the case of photographic cine films which need to be processed using chemicals. Another advantage is that one can use the same magnetic tape over and over again.

The programme is first prepared on the emetic format but after finalisation can be converted to 1/2" VHS for distribution to schools. The basic cost of such tapes is about Rs. 200/- but after recording (3 or 4 programmes per tape) its value goes up to say Rs. 1,000-. These tapes can be played back any number of times and so benefit a very large number of students. Educational tapes are also available from other countries on outright purchase basis or exchange through international agencies.

Simple 35 mm coloured slides can be taken with cameras which cost about Rs. 3,000/-. An original slide costs about Rs. 10- each (which includes wastage during photography). Duplicated slides are available at Rs. 6/- each. An audio cassette costs Rs. 30/- and after recording a lecture its value may go up to Rs. 50/- or 70/. An advantage of the tape slide presentation is that software can be prepared in the school itself. The teacher can improvise with just a microphone and a tape recorder. Such programmes can add local flavour to a presentation by recording in the regional dialect. The viewers are able to recognise the local views in the slides and understand the dialect of the narration and this is known to have a tremendous impact.

For preparing synchronised slide presentation on a professional basis the capital investment on a recording studio and photography facilities is about Rs. 3 lakhs. This is much less compared to that for video recording. As already mentioned the software consists of sets of slide and a cassette tape. These are economical to duplicate and easy to transport.

Computer programmes require software experts to work in close co-operation with educationists. For this purpose they need a large computer system preferably with graphics facility. The programmes will be made available on audio cassettes or floppy discs which are easy to transport. Care has to be taken to ensure that dust does not settle on to the floppy discs during transit.

Maintenance and Upkeep

Electronic equipment including computers, synchronisers, tape recorders, video playback systems, etc., and instruments such as cameras, slide projectors, etc., all need to be handled with care. Although these are labelled as 'robust' and 'foot-proof, yet these equipments need care and maintenance at periodic intervals. Dust, heat, humidity and fluctuating electric voltages cause malfunctioning of the equipment. Computers and allied equipment are recommended to be operated in air-conditioned environment. Experts needed to repair and maintain such equipment are expensive and so also are the spare parts they recommended. In fact if a circuit fault occurs then one has to replace an entire card which is expensive.

An infrastructure has to be built up to look after these equipment. A few teachers can of course be trained to ensure preventive and maintenance and to replace parts such as fuses, bulbs, etc. and to look after the software. An alternative is to introduce redundancy by way of additional equipment but this is an expensive procedure as almost all units will have to be duplicated. Basic spares have to be kept in stock.

The VCR have a tendency to deteriorate with humidity, dust and dirty tapes. Replacing the magnetic heads is a skilled assignment as they are made of ferities and are very fragile. On the other hand looking after the slide projectors, audio cassette players, public address systems, film projector, etc., are all within the scope and capabilities of trained teachers.

Summative Analysis : Educationists have no option but introduce audio visual aids and electronic system including computers in educational institutions in the near future. They are convinced that such aids have an important role to play in the education of our children in the decades to come. It is necessary to use them for (a) better and effective communication with the students, (b) to illustrate topics of interest, (c) to hold their interest while important concepts are being conveyed and (d) to reduce the burden on the over worked teachers.

Most educational institutions would like to equip themselves with all the aids. However, they may not be able to do at one go on account of financial constraints. Their choice one depend on (a) resources and (b) the availability of software in reasonable quantities. Finally, there is the overriding factor of evolving an infrastructure to keep the equipment in good working condition so that they are always available. If this exercise in introducing aids is going to receive government patronage on an extensive scale then it would be worthwhile to redesign many of these aids and to make them robust since students will also be handling them.

In conclusion it is suggested that

1. The teachers should be encouraged to decide on the aids they would like to use in their teaching. Our job should be to make the teaching community aware of the various educational aids available and their advantages.
2. The engineers should design or redesign the aids so that they are robust and the industry could ensure that the pricing is reasonable.
3. A range of educational aids should be available to the schools (it is just one system that will solve all the problems of the teachers).
4. The teachers mast be involved in the preparation of the software, They have vast experience in the learning problems which are quite often regional and local in nature. Any attempt to thrust on them something made and devised by outsiders will prove counter productive.

Role of Computer Graphics

The role of Television in education is well established. Digital Electronics brought sophistication and more flexibility into T.V. Studio Operations/techniques and also paved the way for greater automation. The development and use of computer graphics in TV systems has added another dimension to the functional sophistication of the T.V. systems. It not only greatly enhances artistic presentation of a T.V. programme but also provides a flexibility and effectiveness not easily possible with the present equipment like vision mixer and special effects generator.

The computer graphics is capable of generating both text and graphs, windows, screen-spliting, variety of colours, overlays, zoom and pan, rotation, scrolling and above all animation effects so important for live and natural displays which carry the information to the viewer in an order of totality not possible without this medium in a class room.

The role of computer graphics especially in colour for education will discuss all the above aspects as well try to show the increased versatility this sophisticated equipment will incorporate into an Educational T.V. Studio setup.

The Introduction : Rapid expansion (dimension and variety) of knowledge primarily due to research and development in practically every field of human activity and the need to educate more and more people have created a big demand for teachers who can undertake effective teaching both at undergraduate and post graduate levels. In order to cope with this situation, the T.V. as a medium of education came handy and provides a real support in alleviating the shortage of teachers. The medium's efficiency and effectiveness is well established now, as a consequence of its use over several decades. The medium has been gaining more and more flexibility, sophistication and versatility with passage of time as also because of technical developments aimed at improving the operational and qualitative features of the system. The developments in digital electronics and computers have directly benefitted this medium in many ways.

The development of computer graphics and its use in the Television medium has opened up tremendous possibilities for more realistic presentation of teaching material so that it becomes not only more effective but also more attractive. It allows us to create more realistic effects, generate schematics, circuit-diagrams, write figures of various types just through the application of software without the need for artists to spend a considerable time in generating graphic images before the whole lesson is televised.

The "online editing" available with computer graphics is a very powerful and timesaving feature which every producer loves to have before a final recording is created. Further it is possible to selectivity update the recorded images without destroying or adversely affecting the rest of the recording material at a later date. Also the computer generated image can be 'selectively animated' instead of the whole frame-to-frame technique which is also possible. This is a very powerful and important feature of computer graphics. The zooming and panning characteristics of a computer graphics system are also very important for educational applications.

Education Programme : Characteristics

1. The text should be so written and constructed in such a way that it successfully conveys the ideas, concepts or information for which it is designed or at least it should initiate the process of understanding concepts, ideas or information if the same cannot be covered in one lesson.
2. Ambiguities, repetitions and contradictions in various statements of the text should be eliminated by use of proper words and establishment of a proper sequence of the ideas to be communicated. Sometimes it will be essential to illustrate by examples.
3. The ideas, concepts or information must be cleverly and clearly supported by diagrams with animation wherever it may be essential to do so. This substantially helps the student in understanding many ideas/concepts through the visual models simulating the actual working models.
4. Certain features or portions of the lesson should be capable of being 'zoomed', 'panned' or 'rotated' to focus the attention of students on some important features of a process, model, machine, plants, animals, etc. for better clarification and understanding.
5. The technique adopted should be capable of providing separation of various informations or concepts either by ways of various colours or use of varying character sizes, *Colour is the best way to produce separation.* Moreover it also provides coding mechanism which can be most

advantageously used in preparation of lessons for education.

6. It should be easily possible to take out good number of copies of the lessons without appreciable deterioration in the quality of the programme. This advantage is 100% available with computer graphics terminals.

Use of Computer Graphics

Computer graphics terminal processes the graphical information input to it by a microcomputer board or a host computer and displays it on a monitor in the form of geometric shapes and characters making up a text which describes important points or parameters of an industrial process, design and engineering problems and their solutions as well as ideas, concepts and information in the case of educational programme. Basically a graphics terminal consists of a micro-computer, a graphics, board and a T.V. monitor. In the case of colour graphics, the latter two items will be designed to handle and process colour information.

The Micro-computer prepares the graphics data for the graphics board in a form which the latter can understand and process further for display on a T.V. Monitor. The graphics board breaks up the data supplied by the microcomputer into bits of information and stores it in the image memory of frame buffer. It continuously refreshes the frame buffer to avoid flicker in the displayed pictures. Before the graphics data is supplied to the Monitor it is converted into an analogue signal so that the viewer can interpret the image properly.

Features of a Typical Computer Graphics Terminal : Dual processor architecture, true Zoom and pan, pixel replication Zoom and pan, preview capabilities, upto 16.7 million colours palette, display resolution 768x512, 2 thru 8 Planes, text and graphics independently controlled, Addressable map 1536 x 1024, displayable characters 80 X 32, (5 X 7 or 7 X 9 size), colour selection, blink, blank, reverse video, smooth scrolling, windowing, clipping, rotation, view ports, layering, Animation.

Hardware Design Styles

Conies	Circles, ellipses, arcs
Lines	Dashed, Dotted, Solid
Text	96 ASCII Characters,
	Overlay or background erase
Area fill	Solid or pattern

If we carefully study the features and hardware design styles of a graphics terminal it is easy to conclude as follows :

1. It is possible to produce and record a complete lesson on a graphics terminal without using T.V. Cameras, distribution amplifier, mixer, switcher and other T.V. studio facilities and produce such effects in these lessons which are not possible with a conventional vision mixer. Even a normal T.V. studio building is not required—a tremendous cost saving.
2. Once a good graphics terminal is available with its essential peripherals it is not necessary to have T.V. graphics facility with a number of artists working to create the graphics essential to be incorporated into the lessons prepared for educational needs.
3. It is possible to use an incredibly large number of different colours (256 at a time) out of a total colours of 16.7 million which is not possible with any other present video sources in use in T.V. Studios. This will be very expensive affair with normal T.V. Graphics facility now in use. This capability of a graphics terminal provides you with a highly potent tool to code and separate very effectively and attractively varieties of informations in a given page without extra expenditure.
4. Any part of the page can be selected for emphasis on important details through zoom, pan, rotation, clipping view-porting, windowing which are the basic tools for animation. This is very important for biological and engineering subjects teaching.
5. Phenomena like waves, ebbs and tides, storms, accidents, planetary objects and their motions, earthquakes, etc.,

can be displayed only by writing appropriate software for them without even actually having the photograph of these phenomena.

6. It is also possible to add the sound reproduction facility to the monitor to complete the vision and sound facility required in any educational programme.
7. Three dimensional graphics is also possible which will serve very useful purpose in teaching of models of various m/cs, buildings, architectures, animals, plants, geology, botany etc.
8. Practically, it is possible to draw 'any figure, diagram or drawing with the inbuilt capabilities of the graphics terminals to support the text of the lesson.
9. Layering and area filling are very important characteristics of a graphics system which enable us to display simultaneously several layers of a drawing for study and explanation. This is not possible with conventional T.V. Studio equipment and techniques.
10. The programme produced and recorded on discs can be edited, updated and modified if so required any time on the same m/c. This is very important especially for scientific and technological lessons and helps to avoid creating a completely new record of the lesson and their copies.
11. It is also possible to write-project the recorded lessons by incorporating secret codes in the beginning of each lesson, so that no body is able to destroy or spoil the lessons even accidentally without knowing the secret protective code. This is also possible to achieve mechanically by closing a tab on the disc.
12. The overall operating cost of a graphics system-based-education facility will be much less than for a normal T.V. Studio set up where the number of equipment required along with the T.V. Studio building make a substantially higher contribution to the cost of a programme. Further the cost of the copies of lessons on a video tape will be much higher than on a floppy disc. Also the quality of copies of the video tape will deteriorate after 3-4 copies. This is not the case with the floppy disc copies—a great and very attractive advantage.

13. Also the library space required for storing a given number of discs is extremely small compared to that required for video tapes. This further reduces the cost involved in space required for computer graphics based techniques for education.
14. A number of such graphics terminals can be interconnected for exchange of programmes so that it is possible to independently produce simultaneously several different programmes in different departments of a university or an institution and increase productivity. This is a significant advantage in a large country like India.
15. When the terminal is part of a T.V. Studio set up it substantially increases the capability of the studio in terms of the special effects, graphics, text and recording of programmes. It reduces dependence of the TV studio production team on T.V. graphics to be produced by artists. Even the paraphernalia required for production of Educational programme is reduced.

The work on the development of high resolution Colour Graphics terminal has already been undertaken at CEERI Pilani. The design is primarily a general purpose type but it can be adapted for specific application by certain modifications as per the requirements of the particular application. Therefore it is quite safe to assume that this colour graphics terminal will also be applicable to educational applications where the country is seriously involved in restructuring the whole education system for betterment of the country.

Summative Analysis : From above it is obvious that computer graphics will find extensive use in near future for production of Educational programmes with reduced cost and reduced dependence on special staff. With time this medium is becoming more and more sophisticated and useful. The medium, apart from providing excellent copies, on floppy discs for distribution to educational institutions, is also capable of providing printed copies. Also the medium is capable of being networked in a big setup for exchange of programmes as well as simultaneous production of some programmes at several places as well as independent programme production of various types.

BIBLIOGRAPHY

Andrew W. Halping : *Administrative Theory in Education*, The MacMillan Company, New York, 1967.

Aparna Basu : *The Growth of Education and Political Development in India 1898-1920*, Oxford University Press, Delhi, 1970.

Apter Michael, J. : *Educational Technology*, MacMillan, London, 1968.

—— : *The New Technology of Education*, Macmillan, London, 1968.

Ashby, Eric : *Instructional Technology in Higher Education*, McGraw Hill Book Company, New York, 1972.

—— : *Introduction to Educational Technology*, Sterling Publishers, New Delhi, 1981.

Awasthy, G.C : *Broadcasting in India*, Allied Publishers, Bombay, 1965.

Beck, Carlton : *Philosophical Foundations of Guidance*, Englewood Cliffs, New Jersey, 1964.

Beiggs L.S. : *Instruction Media*, Fitteburgh American Institute for Research, 1966.

Bernard, Berelson : *Human Behaviour*, MacMillan, London, 2001.

Bhatia, S.C. : *Education and Socio-Cultural Disadvantage*, Xerxes Publications, Delhi, 1982.

Bloom, B. S. : *Taxonomy of Educational Objectives*, David Mckay, New York, 1973.

—— : *Human Characteristics and School Learning*, Harper, New York, 1976.

Bloom, Benjamin : *Taxonomy of Educational Objectives: The Classification of Educational Goals,* Mackay, New York, 1956.

Brown, J.W. Lewis R.S. and F.F. Harclebroad : *Instruction Materials and Methods,* McGraw Book Co., New York, 1964.

Brown, James : *Instruction: Materials and Methods,* McGraw Hill Book Co., New York, 1964.

Chatterjee, R.K. : *Mass Communication,* National Book Trust, India, 1988.

Chauhan S.S. : *A Textbook of Programmed Instruction,* New Delhi, 1982.

Clifford, Morgan : *A Brief Introduction to Psychology,* Oxford, New York, 1996.

Cream. David : *Explaining Teaching Machines and Programmes,* Featon, San Fracisco, 1961.

Cronbach, L.I. : *Essentials of Psychological Testing,* Horper, New York, 1970.

Dale, Edgare : *Audio Visual Method in Teaching,* Dryden Rinehart and Winston, New York, 1969.

Das, R.C. : *Educational Technology,* Sterling Publishers, New Delhi, 1998.

Dash B.N. and G.M. Tripathy : *Essentials of General Psychology,* MacMillan, London, 1999.

David Cram : *Explaining Teaching Machines and Programming,* Fearon, San Francisco, 1961.

De Ceccoo, J. : *The Psychology of Learning and Instruction,* Prentice Hall, New Jersey, 1968.

Denis, Lawton : *Education and Social Justice,* Sage Publications, London, 1977.

Dewey, John : *Democracy and Education,* MacMillan, New York, 1963.

Dharni, P. Sinha : *Descriptive-cum-Critical Study of Education System in Andhra Pradesh,* Administrative Staff College of India, Hyderabad, 1976.

Dhinnie, Dinald Mc and Dutt Sunitee : *The Art of Radio*, Faber & Faber, London, 1961.

Dieu, Zeide, H. : *Educational Technology & Development of Education,* UNESCO, 1990.

Don Adams : *Education and Modernisation in Asia,* Addison Wesley Publishing Company, London, 1970.

Dosajh, N.L. : *Advanced Educational Psychology,* Oxford, New York, 2000.

Due, R.C. : *Teaching Techniques ASC Newsletter,* Utkal University, Bhubaneswar, 1990.

Dutt, Sunitee : *Learning Process,* NCERT, New Delhi, 1960.

Dutta, Ruddra : *"Distance Education in AD 2000",* Journal of Educational Planning and Administration, NIEPA, New Delhi.

Ebel, Robert L. : *Encyclopaedia of Educational Research : Educational Communications Media,* The MacMillan Co., London, 1969.

Faure, Edgar : *Learning to be,* UNESCO, Paris, 1972.

Fletcher, F.M. and Riddle, W. : "*The Guidance Movement in India*", Personnel and Guidance Journal, 1962.

Gagne, R.M. : *Conditions of Learning,* Holf & Rinehart & Winston, New York, 1965.

—— : *The Conditions of Learning,* New York, Holt Binsort and Winston, 1965.

Gardner, Lindzey, Hall and Thompson : *Psychology,* Royal Pub., London, 1998.

Gaur, J.S. and Saraswat, R.K. : *Occupational Literature: An Annotated Biblography,* NCERT, New Delhi, 1978.

Goel, D.R. : *A Study of School Broadcasts in India,* Baroda University, Baroda, 1982.

Goel, S.C., *Education and Economic Growth in India,* The MacMillan Company, Delhi, 1975.

Goodman, Loster : *Educational Radio,* NCERT, Delhi, 1977.

Gunnar, Myrdal : *Asian Drama : An Inquiry into the Poverty of Nations,* Abridged, Allen Lane, London, 1972.

Haban, Charles, F. : *Movies that Teach*, New York, Dryden Press, 1945.

Hancock, A.: *Planning for Educational Mass Media,* Longman, London, 1977.

Haragopal, G. : *Administrative Leadership and Rural Development in India,* Light & Life Publishers, New Delhi, 1980.

Husen, Torsten, : *International Encyclopaedia,* Pergamon Press, Oxford, 1989.

Iqbal Narain, K.C. Pande and Mohan Lal Sarma : *Panchayati Raj and Educational Administration,* Aalakli Publishers, Jaipur, 1976.

James, S. Kinder : *Audio-Visual Materials Television,* American Book Co., New York, 1959.

John W., Hanson and Cole S. Brem Beck : *Education and the Development of Nations,* Holt, Rinehart and Winston, New York, 1966.

Joshi, R.N.: *Education—Elsewhere and Here,* Bharatiya Vidya Bhavan, Bombay, 1979.

Kaul, B.N. & Others : *Studies in Distance Education*, Association of Indian Universities, IGNOU, New Delhi, 1988.

Kinder, James S. : *Audio-Visual Materials and Techniques,* American Book Co., New York, 1960.

Kishore Gandhi : *Issues and Choices in Higher Education: A Sociological Analysis,* B.R. Publishing Corporation, Delhi, 1977.

Kochhar, S.K. : *Methods & Techniques of Teaching,* Sterling Publishers, New Delhi, 1978.

Kothari, O.S. : *Indian Education Commission*, Sage Publication, New Delhi, 1966.

Koul, B.N. : *Studies in Distance Education,* IGNOU, New Delhi, 1988.

Kulkarni, S.S. : *Introduction to Educational Technology*, Oxford Publishing Company, New Delhi, 1990.

—— : *Teaching Learning Process: A Systems Analysis*, UNESCO Regional Office for Education in Asia, Bangkok, 1975.

Kulkarni, S.S. : *Introduction to Educational Technology,* IAET, New Delhi, 1986.

Louis Malassis : *The Rural World : Education and Development,* Croom Helm, London, 1976.

Lowman, J. *Mastering Techniques of Teaching,* Prentice Hall India, New Delhi, 1987.

Mangal, S.K & Uma Mangal : *Audio-Visual Education,* Arya Book Depot, New Delhi, 1999.

Matheson, Alastair : *The Communication Materials and Methods.* McGraw Hill Book Company, New Delhi, 1964.

Mayer, T. : *Preparing Objectives for Programmed Instruction,* Palo Atlo, California Fearon, 1962.

Mc Farland H.S.N. : *Psychological Theory and Educational Practice,* Blackwell, London, 2000.

McLuhan : *Understanding Media,* Routludge, London, 1964.

McWhinnie, Donald : *The Art of Radio,* Faber & Faber, London, 1961.

Menon, Narayan : *The Communication Revolution,* National Book Trust, India, New Delhi, 1976.

Mody, Bella : *"Lesson from the Indian Satellite Experiment,"* British Council, London, 1978.

Mohanty J. : *Educational Technology and Communication Media,* Nalanda, Cuttack, 1980.

—— : *Current Trends in Higher Education,* Deep & Deep Publications, New Delhi, 1985.

—— : *Dynamics of Higher Education in India,* Deep & Deep Publications, New Delhi ,1988.

—— : *Educational Broadcasting: Radio & Television in Education,* Sterling Publishers, New Delhi, 1984.

—— : *Educational Guidance, Measurement & Statistics,* Takshashila, 1996.

—— : *Educational Technology,* Deep & Deep Publications, New Delhi, 1991.

—— : *Indian Education in the Emerging Society,* Sterling Publishers, New Delhi, 1982.

——: *Studies in Distance Education*, Deep & Deep Publications, New Delhi, 1992

—— : *Studies in Educational Broadcasting*, Vol-I & II, Deep & Deep Publications, New Delhi, 1995.

——: *The Book Through Ages*, J. Mohapatra & Company, Cuttack, 1973.

Mukherji, S.N. : *Administration of Education in India*, Acharya Book Depot, Baroda, 1962.

Mukhopadhyay, M. : *Educational Technology Year Book*, 1988, AIAET, New Delhi, 1989.

Munn, Normal, L.: *The Fundamental of Human Adjustment*, Houghton Miffin Co., Boston, 1956.

Narayan Rao S. : *Educational Psychology*, Atlantic Pub., New Delhi, 2001.

Niblett, W.R. : *Essential Education*, University of London, London,1955.

Ogburn W.F. & Nimkoff M.E. : *A Handbook of Sociology*, Kegan Paul, London 1947.

Oldhan, J.N. : *Village Education in India : The Report of Commission of Enquiry*, Oxford University Press, London, 1922.

Ottaway A.K.C. : *Education and Society*, Routldqe and Kegan Paul, London, 1962.

Prem Kripal : *A Decade of Education in India*, Indian Book Company, Delhi, 1968.

Raghunath Safaya : *Innovations and Latest Trends in Education*, The Associated Publishers, Ambala Cantt., 1976.

Rahman, S.A. : *Study in Educational Television*, Orissa, 1972.

Raju, V.B.: *Commentaries on the Constitution of India*, Eastern Book Company, Lucknow, 1973.

Rauntrea, D. : *Educational Technology in Curriculum*, Harper & Row Publishers, London, 1974.

Rewntreu, Desk : *Educational Technology in Curriculum Development*, Harper and Row Publishers, London, 1984.

Roeber, E. C., Smith, G. E. and Erickson, E.E. : *Organisation and Administration of Guidance Services,* McGraw Hill, New York, 1955.

Rudolph & Rudolph : *Education and Politics in India Studies in Organisation, Society and Policy,* Harvard University Press, Cambridge, 1972.

Saini, S.K. : *Development of Education in India : Socio-Economic and Political Perspective,* Cosmo Publications, New Delhi, 1980.

Sampath, K. : *Introduction to Educational Technology,* Sterling, New Delhi, 1981.

Sateswari Saxena : *Education Planning in India : A Study in Approach and Methodology,* Sterling Publishers, New Delhi, 1974.

Schramm, Wilbur : *Big Media, Little Media,* Agency for International Development, 1974.

—— : *New Media: Memo to Educational Planners* UNESCO, 1967.

—— : *Programmes Instruction : Today and Tomorrow,* The Funds of Advancement of Education, New York, 1962.

—— : *The Process and Effects of Mass Communication,* University of Illinois, Urbane, 1990.

Sharma A.R. : *Educational Technology,* Vinod Pustak Bhandar, Agra, 1985.

Sharma, G.D. & Ahmed, S.R : *Methodologies of Teaching in Colleges,* Sterling Publishers, New Delhi, 1988.

Sharma, G.D. : *Dynamics of Higher Education in India,* Deep & Deep Publishers, New Delhi, 1993.

Shrimali, K.L. : *A Search for Values in Indian Education,* Vikas Publishers, Delhi, 1974.

Shukla, P.D. : *Towards the New Pattern of Education in India,* Sterling Publishers, New Delhi, 1976.

Singla M.M. : *The Constitution of India-Studies in Perspective,* The World Press, Calcutta, 1975.

Smith, H M. and Eckerson, L.O. : *Guidance Services in Elementary Schools,* Government Printing Press, Washington, 1966.

Sundaram, P.S. and A.B. Shah : *Education or Catastrophe?,* Vikas Publishing House, New Delhi, 1976.

Thomas, F. Station : *Dynamics of Adjustment,* MacMillan Co., New York, 1953.

Towntree Berek : *Educational Technology in Curriculum Development,* Harper and Row publishers, London, 1972.

Vedanayagam : *Teaching Technology for College Teachers,* Sterling Publishers, New Delhi, 1989.

Vernon, P.E. : *Intelligence and Cultural Environment,* Methuen, London, 1969.